W9-BUY-311

# ACTION INTO NATURE

Frank M. Covey, Jr.
Loyola Lectures
in Political Analysis

*Richard Shelly Hartigan*
GENERAL EDITOR

# Action into Nature

*An Essay on the Meaning of Technology*

BARRY COOPER

University of Notre Dame Press

Notre Dame London

*Library of Congress Cataloging-in-Publication Data*

Cooper, Barry, 1943–
    Action into nature : an essay on the meaning of technol-
ogy / Barry Cooper.
        p.    cm.—(Loyola lectures in political analysis)
    Includes index.
    ISBN 0-268-00629-6
    1. Technology—Philosophy.    I. Title.    II. Series.
    T14.C577    1991
    601—dc20                                        90-50975
                                                         CIP

*Because we've been to Europe,*
*It's safe now.*
*This one is for Denise.*

[Hippodamus] also wanted to pass a law concerning those who discover something useful for the polis, that they might obtain honour . . . [but] to pass a law that they obtain honour is not safe, though it sounds appealing: it would encourage blackmail (sykophantia) and, perhaps even a change of regime.

Aristotle *Politics*

Boni quippe ad hoc utuntur mundo, ut fruantur Deo; mali autem contra, ut fruantur mundo, uti volunt Deo; qui tamen eum vel esse vel res humanas curare iam credunt. Sunt enim multo deteriores, qui ne hoc quidem credunt.

St. Augustine *De civitate Dei*

(The good, of course, use the world that they may enjoy God; the bad, on the contrary, in order to enjoy the world wish to use God; at least those who believe that IIe is and that IIe cares for human things. Those who do not believe even this are much worse off.)

Le science cherche le mouvement perpetuel. Elle l'a trouvé; c'est elle-même.

Victor Hugo, *William Shakespeare*

There can be no prescription, no set of rules, for living within Gaia. For each of our different actions there are only consequences.

J. E. Lovelock, *Gaia*

# Contents

PART I

## The Technological Phenomenon

PART II

## Modern Worldlessness

PART III

## Critical Disorientation

# Series Editor's Preface

*Action into Nature* is the latest volume published in the continuing political philosophy lecture series, begun at Loyola University Chicago in 1968. The series has recently been renamed the "Frank M. Covey, Jr., Loyola Lectures in Political Analysis" in honor of the generous benefactor who has permanently endowed it. Though the name has changed slightly the purpose of the series remains the same—to provide a forum and opportunity for the presentation of contemporary philosophical analysis. With this work Barry Cooper joins a distinguished list of scholars who have lectured in residence at Loyola over the years and whose ideas can be shared with a wider audience through their publication.

Many writers have approached and defined various questions and problems relating to modernity in the latter half of this century. Indeed, the term "crisis of modernity" has become a shorthand phrase of reference to volumes of analysis and criticism. The present volume is not just another in this genre. Instead, mindful of his own caution to "take care that one's analysis does not make matters worse," the author guides his readers through a formidable body of literature with the intention, not of critiquing modern technology, but rather of first understanding the meaning of the phenomenon.

The success that this volume deserves will reflect that of the lecture presentation itself. I speak for everyone at Loyola University Chicago in again thanking Professor Cooper for personally sharing his ideas with us in what was truly a week-long intellectual engagement.

Richard Shelly Hartigan
Director and Editor

# Preface

The establishment of any regime is the creation of a world. From a formless flux of conflicting desire, atrophied traditions, antagonistic interests emerges a precarious order. External enemies threaten the existence of a regime from without, and these must be met with violence or threats of violence. But violence can at best only preserve the existence of a regime and is never its purpose. The purpose of a political order is to shelter human beings from the aforementioned formlessness so that they can discover a kind of meaning to life. Meaning is expressed in stories, prayers, and rites, but also in drama and philosophy. Characteristically, such symbolic representations are concerned with depicting the meaning of the cosmos as a whole, the meaning of its internal order, and the relationships between the particular political regime and the order of the whole.

The details by which the particular regime discovers the meaning of its existence depend on several factors of which these may be taken as typical: the conception of reason and of nature, the place of God in human life, social and economic structure, the ethnic traditions of the society, the origin of its political organization. Despite variations in detail, there seems to be a constant movement beyond particularity as such and toward a general or comprehensive understanding of meaning. Under these circumstances, the externalities by which existence has been sheltered become secondary contingencies, useful but not inherently meaningful. Occasionally, these useful externalities are deliberately rejected. More usually, a compromise between political attitudes and attitudes that transcend politics is obtained, so that an image of perfection and completeness can be evoked to give meaning to existence beyond the preservation of pragmatic order.

These observations seem to be true for any regime. Even in a technological society, once external preservation has been achieved, human beings turn their attention to the question of meaning. The language used to express meaning is primarily formative or evocative, not cognitive. The analytical attitude of political science is accordingly directed more toward discovery of the meaning that has been created than toward what the language has described.

The principal external features of the technological society are well known because they are experienced daily. They include the transformation of natural and human science into technology, industrial production, urbanization, demographic increase, formation of new social groups from the industrial and intellectual proletariat to white-collar administrators, new power units based on population, raw materials and technological expertise, increased affluence in dominant technological societies coupled to the appearance of increased misery elsewhere. The technological society is found preeminently in the New World, a symbolic space whose chief characteristic is that it is devoted to doing away with poverty and oppression. Although it is true that historically the technological society originated in the West, it is also true that, as Herbert Butterfield observed a generation ago, when one speaks of "Westernization" what is meant is not the transportation of Homer, classical philosophy, or the Bible to the East but the diffusion of science and technology. Toynbee likewise distinguished between Hellenic and Western civilizations. It is one of the conceits of Western technological consciousness to seek to appropriate, willy-nilly, as its heritage, the insights and beauty of several antiquities.

This essay is concerned with the meaning of technology. Some attention must be paid to the external aspects, the genesis of the technological society, but the focus is on the alteration in human consciousness of God, nature, the world, and society. Part I deals chiefly with externalities and with certain troublesome questions of method. Part II presents the most easily accessible meaning of the technological society, its worldlessness. Part III constitutes a critical analysis of the evidence described in the preceding sections. Several people have summarized the meaning of technological modernity as constituting a crisis: of the West, of humankind, of Christianity, of capitalism. If this is so, one must take care that one's analysis does not make matters worse. Accordingly, a methodological introduction has been added, and a few prudential conclusions drawn.

The questions raised in this study grew out of an earlier book on the interpretation of Hegel's *Phänomenologie des Geistes*. In that work, which I somewhat prophetically called *The End of History*, I undertook to explicate the soundness of Alexandre Kojève's commentary on Hegel's text. I argued that Kojève's reading of Hegel provides the most satisfactory and comprehensive account of the self-understanding of modernity. I still believe that to be true, even though, as Francis Fukuyama has said, *ad capitum vulgi*, the consequences are sad and boring. This present book may be seen as drawing out a few of the implications of the earlier discussion. On the more positive side, readers will soon enough discover that I owe substantial intellectual debts to the major political philosophers of this century, Eric Voegelin, Leo Strauss, and Hannah Arendt. I have also relied extensively on the work of Hans Jonas and George Grant. It is my opinion that anyone who thinks very much about technology and the modern world will incur such debts sooner or later.

Several institutions have assisted me in writing this book. The Calgary Institute for the Humanities at The University of Calgary awarded me a Fellowship for 1986–87, during which time I was able to make a good start on writing the present study. I am especially grateful to the Institute for Research on Public Policy, which funded what must have seemed to them a very peculiar project. Earlier phases of the research were assisted by grants from the Social Sciences and Humanities Research Council of Canada (SSHRCC). During 1987–88 I was granted a sabbatical fellowship from The University of Calgary, aided by the SSHRCC, and for that, too, I am grateful. And, of course, to Loyola University of Chicago a special acknowledgment is due. Under the auspices of the Frank M. Covey, Jr., Lectures in Political Analysis, that institution provided hospitality, an audience, and an honorarium for some of the analysis developed here. No scholar could ask for more.

Several people have helped along the way: Abe Rotstein, the late George Grant, Leah Bradshaw, Zdravko Planinc, John Kerr, Tom Darby, Peter Emberly, Margaret Osler, Rainer Knopff. Judi Powell has had the unenviable task of typing countless revisions, her toil having been lessened only somewhat by technology. Not for the last time, Denise, Meghan, and Brendan have put up with a lot. To you all: thank you.

Barry Cooper
Calgary

# Introduction:
# Technology and Consciousness

The method employed by political philosophy is not complex. It consists, more or less, in reading texts, thinking about them, drawing connections, and writing. When asked to describe his method, Leo Strauss, one of the few political philosophers of this century to whom one returns for guidance, sometimes called it "content analysis." His was a method of careful reading. Political philosophers use many literary genres: the textual exegesis, the treatise, the tract, the meditation, the essay. Occasionally some still employ the dialogue. This book is an essay. It takes the form, as Dr. Leavis used to remark, "This is so, isn't it?" accompanied by the implicit response "Yes, but . . . ," in which that *but* indicates civilized disagreement and qualification.

Methodology, the account of method, is not itself method. It is a discourse about method, about the way one puts a discourse together. One of the ways to account for the significance of technology is to account for its genesis. Borrowing from Foucault and Nietzsche, the methodology might be described as genealogy. Foucault's category power-knowledge accords well with Bacon's aphorism "Knowledge is power." Moreover it is well connected to other Baconian aphorisms: one puts nature to the test, a euphemism for torture, in order to secure the relief of man's estate, and so on. Genealogy as methodology has a certain intellectual appeal or at least an appeal to certain intellectuals. It is both obscure and up-to-date, for example.

Foucault himself once remarked that Merleau-Ponty and Hyppolite were his intellectual masters. Merleau-Ponty was a phenomenologist; Hyppolite translated Hegel's *Phenomenology* and wrote a commentary on it. Merleau-Ponty argued that Hegel's

1

phenomenology was not so different from Husserl's. One could make a case that Foucault's genealogical studies might accurately be described as instances of historical phenomenology, a term used by Merleau-Ponty. The first point to be made, therefore, is that the methodology used here is phenomenological. The term *phenomenology* is not, however, unambiguous. To be clear, even at the beginning, one must specify more closely what phenomenology is. That is, one must raise the question, which has many times been answered, What is phenomenology? This question was raised and answered well enough by Merleau-Ponty in the preface to his great book, *The Phenomenology of Perception.*[1] One could do worse than recall his remarks.

He began by observing that in 1945 it was strange to ask "What is phenomenology?" half a century after Husserl began publishing. He then provided several shorthand answers: it is the study of essences but it puts essences back into existence; it is a transcendental philosophy inasmuch as it puts in abeyance our naive or commonsense understanding, but it begins with the commonsense world already there and aims at establishing a direct contact with that world and accounting for that contact; it is a "rigorous science," but it also offers an account of the world as it is lived. In general, phenomenology tried to give a direct description of experience without taking account of its psychological origin or of any other causal (or "scientific") account such as might be offered by sociologists and other social scientists. Such a description is personal without being subjective either in the sense of being arbitrary or in the sense of being distinct from objective. It is participatory, a "style" of thinking, which means that one is directed not to the object or text itself but to the actual experience of thinking phenomenologically. As Merleau-Ponty said, "Phenomenology is accessible only through a phenomenological method." This methodological insight, which is also a phenomenological insight, accounts for the fact that many phenomenological thinkers prefer to talk of themes rather than, for example, of methods.

To illustrate a few themes will, perhaps, indicate what Merleau-Ponty meant by doing phenomenology for ourselves. Literally, phenomenology means giving an account of appearance. That is, it is a way of describing and not of analyzing or of explaining. In Ricoeur's words, it begins as a hermeneutic of trust and participation, not as a hermeneutic of suspicion.[2] Or, as Michael Polanyi said, we begin by "indwelling" the phenomena.[3] A return to the "things themselves" (as Husserl taught) means a return to the experience of a world that precedes such knowledge of it as is found in scientific accounts. If we are aware of what a prairie is because we have hunted gophers or geese, for example, we do not need to rely on geography or plant science to tell us of isotherms and ground cover. The world appears there, by way of our actions and "projects," and our account of appearance is experienced as recognition rather than cognitive analysis and still less a construction of consciousness. As Merleau-Ponty said, "The world is nothing but world-as-meaning." Accordingly, to the extent that human beings are in the world, which is a very large extent, we are enmeshed with meaning.

Merleau-Ponty's understanding of phenomenology entailed several revisions or amplifications of key Husserlian terms: *intentionality, essence, rationality,* and so on. The details of his changes and their legitimacy for Husserl's "strict science" have been controversial. But these controversies can be incorporated within the range of Leavis's "Yes, but . . . "

Consider the matter of bracketing, the famous Husserlian *epoché.* The purpose of this intellectual maneuver was to suspend the judgment, prejudice, or commitment that had been shaped by concepts or intellectual constructions; to suspend what Husserl called the natural attitude. The natural attitude is what is familiar, habitual, traditional. Accordingly, it changes according to circumstance. For us, in our circumstances and as regards technology, it means suspending the conceptual supervision of our presumption that the being of nature is material, that it is matter and motion, as Descartes and Hobbes said. Or as Husserl understood in his *Crisis* lectures, it means analyzing the assumptions that have undergirded the mathematization of nature.[4] It means undertaking the effort to describe what presents itself to experience, but without a prior commitment to the transparency of theoretical concepts. Husserl's phenomenological program was established initially in the first volume of *Ideas,* published before World War I; it was adhered to as recently as Heidegger's famous "Question Concerning Technology" of 1954. It is appropriate, perhaps, that such a technique was developed during this century, but it is also true that there is nothing new about it today. A generation ago Merleau-Ponty said that encountering phenomenology meant finding what one had been waiting for, namely a recovery of the experience of wonder at the reality of meaning. And wonder, we have learned from antiquity, is where philosophy begins.

However that may be, a phenomenology of technology does not simply mean bracketing conceptual prejudices and "ideas" of nature, humankind, history, fabrication, and so forth. One also must imaginatively bracket artifacts insofar as they have come to mediate the world to human beings and human beings to the world, and insofar as what mediates also hides. In addition to a conceptual bracketing, then, a practical bracketing is called for. Not only do we usually think of nature as matter and motion, such thoughts are sustained by daily experience. One walks on asphalt, not earth; one obtains beef wrapped in plastic, not on the hoof; rice as Rice Crispies, not as the reward for toil in steamy paddies. That is, one must suspend imaginatively ideas of artifacts and also the world of artifacts. It is relatively easy to perform the conceptual bracketing and gain some understanding of what premodern nature means. To say, for example, that the Heavens declare the glory of God and the firmament sheweth His handiwork (Ps. 19:1) is not unintelligible on a summer evening in southern Alberta. But bracketing the world of artifacts sounds like a call to nostalgia, the self-indulgence of wishing for a simpler, truer, purer world.

From Hegel's phenomenology, if not from common sense, one has learned to distrust such nostalgia and romanticism. It is a sentiment that owes its sweetness to the continued existence of the unreformed world rejected. Its appeal is akin to that which seduces enlightened socialist intellectuals to criticize imaginatively out of existence the productive capitalist economy that sustains them materially. Common sense asks, Who wants to trust health to seventh-century medical arts? Who would visit a dentist who refused to use novacaine? Who wants to trust the safety of the country to fourteenth-century arms? Such questions point to a more fundamental one: Who *can* do such things? That is, the achievement of a technological society is neither an accident nor a necessity but the actualization of a possibility. If, nevertheless, the technological society hides its own origins, if it appears as autonomous, as fate, then one may be led to wonder at what has been hidden, or at what has been forgotten or neglected.

Examples often persuade where argument merely convicts. Where distinctions are basic, examples are indispensable, and so we will consider one. Much earlier in this century, Jakob von Uexkuell sought to describe how the world appeared to animals. To do so he proposed "A Stroll through the World of Animals and Men."[5] The purpose of this thought experiment was to introduce humans imaginatively but meaningfully into the world as constituted by particular animal perceptions. For each animal, according to von Uexkuell, there existed a phenomenal world within which the animal lived as subject. His first example was the tick, or rather, its mature life.

After issuing from an egg the tick attacks larger animals such as lizards, generates additional legs and sex organs, sheds its skin several times, and mates. It then begins its search for mammals. The tick can neither see nor taste and its senses of smell and touch are rudimentary. Three things are meaningful: light, which draws the female to the top of a bush; the smell of sweat, which announces the proximity of a mammal on which she can fall; and heat, which tells her that she has landed on the right target, namely one filled with blood, with which she pumps herself full. She then falls to the ground, lays her eggs, and dies. To such a creature, the sky is not blue and no birds sing; there is no difference between human and bear nor bear and skunk; blood is sampled only once, so it must be the right flavor. Or rather, experiments have shown that the tick will engorge itself with any fluid found on the other side of a warm membrane that stinks of butyric acid. Experiments have also shown that a tick can wait up to eighteen years without food for her first and last drink of blood. In short, a description of the world of a wood tick indicates that it lacks the imaginative distance to have a worldview. Rather, it is one.

A half-century later Erazim Kohak made a similar imaginative thought experiment about one of his neighbors, a porcupine. "A porcupine is a *life*, the reality of lived subject experience." Porcupine existence, like human existence, "though subsuming within itself the atemporal, inorganic dimension, is not reducible to it."[6] If, nevertheless, a reductive account is given, the result,

phenomenologically speaking, is comic. A cat stalking a mouse or
a bird (whether to eat or merely to play with it, that is, to batter
it to death, is secondary) can be accounted for in the scientific
language of cybernetics. The sensory cue, "Bird!" would, by this
account, trigger a nerve stimulus resulting in behavioral adapta-
tions according to known sensorimotor feedback mechanisms in
response to various homeostatic gradients. By this style of reckoning a mailbox is a system-input buffer device. The limits of
comedy are reached when, for example, human beings become
human resources.

The contrast in style between the description of the world of a
tick or of porcupine existence and the cybernetic account of a cat
indicates a traditional distinction that is often signified as being
between understanding and knowledge. Corresponding to this
distinction is another, between substance and phenomenon. It is
clear that stationary mailboxes, falling ticks, grazing porcupines,
stalking cats, and praying humans can be known in terms of an
immanent, self-confirming, self-sufficient, cybernetic, conceptual, scientific theory. What is missing from such theory is the
full amplitude of substantive meaning. "Humans," said Kohak,
"can sell a home, but they can buy only a house."[7] The meaning
of a home is not something added to the material object called
house but is a fundamental trait of its worldly reality. Real estate
agents, however, have a knowledge of houses and of the housing
market.

*

The world of a tick or of a porcupine is not that of a human
being. Human beings can appear in the world of a tick or of a
porcupine in certain characteristic ways: as the source of butyric
acid and blood, as a threat. Human beings, however, can imaginatively understand the meaning of the world of a tick or a porcupine. In conventional language, they can do so because they
are conscious in a way that animals are not. Whatever else human
consciousness is, it is something more than the consciousness of
ticks and porcupines. This is why Hegel, for example, used the
term *sentiment-of-self* to describe the self-awareness of animals
and intended thereby a distinction to be drawn between that kind
of self-awareness and the self-awareness of humans, which he
called *self-consciousness*.[8] At the same time, both human and
nonhuman animals are subject to the same physical forces as in-

animate things: a tick, a porcupine, a human, and a stone will all fall to the ground. In general one may say that human consciousness is rooted in or based on animal, vegetative, and inorganic being. Whatever weight is accorded such metaphors, it is clear that they indicate that human consciousness is not a process going on in the world alongside other physical or biological processes without contact with them save as objects of scientific or quasi-scientific cognition and knowledge.

It was the burden of Merleau-Ponty's early work to indicate the inadequacies of the scientific *partes extra partes* model of the world and to describe the ways that human consciousness is based or rooted in these other processes. In the paraphrase just given of the preface to *The Phenomenology of Perception*, it was stated that phenomenology is a philosophy of transcendence because it questions the commonsense lived experience of being-in-the-world. Phenomenology can transcend lived experience because it understands human consciousness as containing the capacity to transcend the givenness of that experienced by reflecting on it. It is this capacity of transcendence that allows humans to understand the meaning of the world of the tick, whereas humans can appear only within the tick's world in the ways already indicated. There is more to transcendence than the capacity of human consciousness to understand the world of the tick. Nevertheless, the insight regarding this human capacity is an important achievement.

About the same time that Merleau-Ponty was working out his arguments regarding perception and perceptual consciousness, Eric Voegelin was independently formulating an account of consciousness. Both began with the phenomenological reflections of Husserl, but as Voegelin remarked: "Phenomenological philosophizing such as Husserl's is oriented in principle on the model of the experience of objects in the external world," whereas "classical philosophizing about political order is oriented also in principle on the model of noetic experience of transcendent-divine being."[9] Voegelin was concerned with the problems of political order and so with the relevant noetic experiences; Merleau-Ponty was not.[10] The difference between Merleau-Ponty and Voegelin with respect to the question of noetic experience is central to a proper understanding of the present methodological questions. The difference may be illustrated aphoristically. Whereas

Merleau-Ponty announced that the world is nothing but world-as-meaning, Voegelin said, "All expressions of knowledge are this-worldly, . . . but not all knowledge is knowledge of this-worldly being."[11] Knowledge of world-transcendent being can be expressed only by analogy with this-worldly being. Prior to the expression of knowledge, however, is the experience of it in the soul of the thinker.

Deformations of consciousness, such as the *partes extra partes* notions that Merleau-Ponty criticized (or, indeed, his own Marxism), can be measured by comparison with the proper formation of consciousness, identified by the Greek philosophers by the term *nous* (reason). Socrates, Plato, and Aristotle were engaged in acts of resistance to the deformations and disorder of consciousness and society that they experienced around them. "From this act there emerged the Nous as the cognitively luminous force that inspired the philosophers to resist and, at the same time, enabled them to recognize the phenomena of disorder in the light of a humanity ordered by the Nous."[12] Reason in the noetic sense or noetic reason was discovered as a diagnostic instrument, as the animating source of existential order, and as the criterion of order.

The methodological issue between Merleau-Ponty and Voegelin concerns the limits to phenomenology in its Husserlian form, even as that form had been modified by Merleau-Ponty. Helmut Wagner has undertaken an analysis of the larger philosophical problem as it appeared through a long exchange of letters between Voegelin and Alfred Schutz.[13] The common starting point was Husserl's phenomenology of consciousness in general, and the *Crisis* lectures in particular. Schutz developed from that starting point his own theory of social order on the basis of his theory of relevance. The decisive point between these two life-long friends found the following expression: For Schutz:

> Whether it is Socrates dying a martyr's death because he is accused of *asebeia* or Christ dying because he did not respect the Koranic character of Torah, whether it is heretics being put to death in the earliest days of the Church because they did not respect the dogma of the councils or traitors to the doctrine of dialectical materialism suffering their deserved punishment—in every case the same thing is happening. Power creates its Koran and creates its taboos. The heretics always perish in this conflict.

In one of your earlier writings [*Rasse und Staat* (1933)] you have
very successfully worked out the concept of the counter-idea. Every idea, once it comes to power (or, in your language, every idea
as soon as it has arrived at existential representation under a symbol), needs its counter-symbols. Generally speaking, I ask myself
whether every symbolic system in your sense is not at the same
time a negative symbol system, whether every theology does not
at the same time presuppose a negative theology. And hence
whether there may not—and must not—be a dialectic tension between the two poles, positive and negative, of the symbol systems
and the theologies and whether it is not perhaps here that the
eidos of history is to be sought, as Hegel in a sense tried to do.[14]

To this argument Voegelin replied:

I do not think we can stop at this general observation, precisely
because this situation—position versus counter-position—is found
everywhere. For historically as well as in speaking of the truth of
the human order of the soul, everything ultimately depends on
what one's point concretely entails. So, methodologically speaking,
the generalization is carried too far if it makes the problems of the
concrete historical position disappear. Formally Socrates is in conflict with Athens; you can set up either side as the position and
then call the other side the counter-position. But this, it seems to
me, leads to historical relativism. A case like this calls for a decision: Socrates is right, Athens is wrong. (Or the modern liberals'
decision: democracy is right, Socrates was a Fascist.) This is the
parting of the ways.[15]

It would seem that truth, according to Schutz, amounts to a kind
of neutrality with respect to the truth claims of others. Here we
have a first instance of the Husserlian *epoche*. This epoche, in
turn, sustains a "transcendental" attitude with respect to those
truth claims—or, more properly, to those opinions. The valida-
tion of this transcendental philosophy comes with the apprehension of the *eidos* of history as dialectical tension. Voegelin, in
contrast, did not seek to hover above truth-claims in a transcendental attitude but to respond to the claim of truth—concretely:
Socrates is right; Athens is wrong. The philosopher, according to
Voegelin, does not move back and forth, neutral between competing opinions. Nor, according to Merleau-Ponty, was that the

task of the philosopher. Merleau-Ponty, however, was a Marxist and Voegelin considered Marx an intellectual swindler.[16] Formally, therefore, the question concerning Socrates and Schutz could be expanded to include Marx and Merleau-Ponty. That is, the issues between them are formally equivalent.

Here a host of questions centered on one major issue arise: by what authority does the philosopher decide that Athens is wrong and Socrates right? Voegelin had already indicated, in principle, the answer: the concrete (rather than formal) situation of Socrates under accusation for impiety, as dramatically encountered by the equally concrete individuals, Schutz and Voegelin. That dramatic encounter is an event whose reality is attested by the consciousness of the individuals involved. To the objection that this attestation is just another opinion, Voegelin developed his own theory of consciousness and indicated thereby the limits of Husserlian phenomenology.

Perhaps the easiest access to Voegelin's account is by way of his critical remarks regarding Husserl.[17] Voegelin began by praising Husserl's essay "as the most significant epistemological performance of our time." He immediately added that, although epistemology is important, "it does not exhaust the realm of the philosophical; it is neither a self-sufficient theme of philosophy nor the basis for all other philosophical problems." It is, in fact, a prolegomenon to philosophy. In support of this observation Voegelin developed four related arguments.

First, Husserl's image of history was inadequate. There were for him only two periods of interest, Greek antiquity when the rational entelechy of human beings was established, and its refounding by Descartes, which was defective in certain respects that were clarified by Kant and finally cleared up by Husserl himself. What was omitted through silence was the two thousand years between Greek antiquity and Descartes; what was omitted through dismissive quotation marks was Indian and Chinese "philosophy." Human being is for Husserl preeminently Western and rational.

Second, Voegelin pointed out what is obvious: this doctrinal assumption was an essential presupposition to Husserl's speculation, not an inadvertence. Phenomenology was, for Husserl, the final foundation of philosophy that, as final, fully revealed the historical end of philosophy that had only partially or inadequately been revealed by the self-understanding of Husserl's predecessors. Like Hegel's science of wisdom, Husserl's final foundation cannot be contradicted by historical arguments that indicate, for instance, that a philosopher interpreted by Husserl intended something quite different than accorded him by Husserl on the basis of Husserl's final foundational knowledge. Like Heidegger, Husserl did not seek to understand a thinker on the thinker's own terms, which Strauss has tirelessly insisted is the first task of political philosophy, but rather sought to understand the thinker "creatively."

Third, the systematic relationship between the history of philosophy and Husserl's transcendental philosophy of final foundation was inadequately clarified though adequately expressed in the formula that Husserlian philosophers were "functionaries of mankind."[18] For the formula to make sense, "mankind" would have to be understood as an intramundane collectivity of which individuals were instances or particles. What is primary is not the humanity of the individual nor human dignity, but a kind of world soul or world spirit, which Husserl called mankind, and of which he is the functionary. One finds similar speculative contractions in Hegel and Marx; indeed, Husserl's tendency to categorize the Chinese and Indians as "mere empirical anthropological types" recalls equivalent categorizations of "man" as specific finite historical instances: the proletariat emergent from the industrial revolution, for example.

Voegelin's fourth critical point concerned Husserl's distortion of Descartes's epoche. According to Voegelin, however, the Cartesian meditative complex was far richer than the reduction of the world understood as an epistemological theme. The proper context for understanding Descartes was that of an Augustinian meditation, the purpose of which was to turn the soul toward God. Husserl never undertook the originary Cartesian meditation but appropriated the derivative literary results for his own epistemological purposes. As a result, "In order to found his own position, he has taken the way out in the immanence of a historical problematic, and with the greatest care blocked himself off from the philosophic problem of transcendence—the decisive problem of philosophy."[19]

The decisive focus of Voegelin's criticism of Husserl was the latter's philosophy of history. The exclusion of Chinese and Indian experience as marginal curiosities, the silence regarding two millennia of Western experience, the pretense at claiming a final founding of philosophy in light of a telos that such a pretense brings to light—in short, the entire elaborate defense against what for Voegelin were the real problems of philosophy—had the dubious result of enabling Husserl to mutilate Descartes's *Meditations*. Moreover, the defense mechanism, the imaginary construction of a historical telos, namely Western rationality; of a historical carrier of that telos, "mankind"; and of a historical process of clarification of the relationship between the two that culminates with the creation of a sectarian community of phenomenological functionaries ensures that mere empirical evidence from the merely anthropological types will leave the entire apocalyptic enterprise unshaken. It could hardly be otherwise. Apprehension of the rational entelechy of humankind by its functionaries constitutes equally the apprehension of the eidos of history. In order for this event to occur, functionaries must be capable of observing history as an external object rather than as a participant. The conventional way of doing so is to account for the end of history in light of which the retrospective functionaries can cast their glance backward and bring its eidos to light, usually by an account of the process by which their own final account was formulated.[20] And that final account invariably does violence to one or another aspect of reality for the simple reason that there is no eidos to history, that history has not ended, and so on.

The next stage in analysis would seek to determine why Husserl consigned the humanity of the Chinese and Indians to the margins, or how the entelechy of humanity entertained itself between the time of the Greeks and the new foundation of Descartes. One is reminded here of a similar operation by Hegel that transformed Mohammed into a representative of the Germanic spirit, since that was so obviously where the System required him to fit. We must forego an exploration of these curiosities, however, and return to the concrete example of Voegelin's encounter with Husserl.

Having analyzed Husserl's restrictive vision of human existence, "something had to be done. I had to get out of that 'apodictic horizon' as fast as possible."[21] The exit was clearly marked: if Husserl's initial distortion entailed the exclusion of historical reality—China, India, and the Western Middle Ages—any alternative would begin by restoring it. Such a restoration would not entail the attempt at substituting history for philosophy. Husserl's philosophical achievement was incontestable, at least as regards the intramundane intentionality of consciousness. "The historical dimension at issue was not a piece of 'past history' but the permanent presence of the process of reality in which man participates with his conscious existence."[22] Just as human consciousness participates in inanimate and animal nature, which is the basis or root referred to earlier that enables humans to understand the world of the wood tick or porcupine, so too does it participate in history, understood as the permanent presence of the process of reality.

Voegelin did not deny that reality could be understood as an object of thought intended by a subject of cognition but that this understanding was derivative of a primordial participatory experience of which human beings are conscious. "Man's conscious existence," Voegelin said, "is an event within reality, and man's consciousness is quite conscious of being constituted by the reality of which it is conscious. The intentionality [of consciousness in Husserl's sense] is a substructure within the comprehensive consciousness of a reality that becomes luminous for its truth in the consciousness of man."[23] To return to the question of Socrates and Athens, it seems clear that the basis for a right decision lies in the concrete experience of reality by concrete human beings who are able to articulate their sense of participation in reality by means of intelligible language symbols. Plato's philosophy was the literary precipitate of the experience of reality made present to the consciousness of Voegelin by his reading the Platonic text and to which he responded with a specific decision.

This understanding of the verification of the truth of consciousness indicates that truth does not inhere simply in a text nor simply in one's experience of it but in the process or procedure by which the truth of a text becomes "luminous" in the tension between the experience of a consciousness that responds to the symbols, the literary form of which was, for example, a Platonic dialogue. The task of the philosopher sensitive not only to Husserlian problems of the intramundane constitution of consciousness but also to the historical dimension of the presence of the process of reality in which human beings consciously participate is "to penetrate every historical-spiritual position to its resting point, i.e., to where it is deeply rooted in the experiences of transcendence of the thinker in question. Only when the history of spirit is undertaken with this methodological aim can it attain its philosophical aim, which is to understand spirit in its historicity or, in other words, to understand the historical forms of spirit as variations on the theme of experiences of transcendence." The primary task of genuine historical reflection is therefore to penetrate the spiritual-historical form of other thinkers, including their experience of transcendence, "and by such penetration to train and clarify one's own formation of the experience of transcendence."[24] This means that a philosopher must be guided by the "self-testimonies" (*Selbstzeugnisse*) of the thinker in order to understand the truth that the thinker expressed.

The element of "personal knowledge," to use a term of Michael Polanyi, indicates the concrete character of the conscious response of the individual. To use commonsensical language, "The only true knowledge is living and firsthand knowledge, and such knowledge has no actual existence unless it is known by someone."[25] In Voegelin's case, he found in the restrictive horizon of Husserlian phenomenology something similar to the restrictions of consciousness in the mass political movements of the day. "But if that was true, I had observed the restriction, and recognized it as such, with the criteria of the observation coming from a consciousness with a larger horizon, which in this case happened to be my own."[26] One may generalize Voegelin's observation: any critical analysis will be undertaken by concrete individuals who, with respect to any particular restrictive horizon, will necessarily be more comprehensive.

Let us summarize the main elements in Voegelin's account of the structure of consciousness. First and most importantly, there is no absolute starting point from which a "theory of consciousness" could be developed because philosophizing about consciousness is itself an event in the consciousness of the philosopher. As Anibal Bueno remarked, "The only possible starting-point for a thinker is his own concrete consciousness, i.e., all the pre-reflective experiences that have led him to ask questions about the nature of consciousness and the reality of which it is a part."[27] It follows from the prereflective experience of participation in reality that the differentiation of the modes of participation, from inanimate material to animate nature, to the specific modes of human existence, is also an event in the process of reality. Looking at the question from the perspective opened up through an analysis of Husserlian phenomenology, one would say. Although it is indubitably true that the intentionality of consciousness in finite experience transcends itself into the world, this is only one mode of transcendence. Consciousness also transcends itself into the lived body, into the community, history and the divine ground of being. These modes of transcendence are simply coeval with consciousness and so are prior to systematic reflection. Likewise, the systematic reflections of the philosopher are particular biographical events but also events in the history of his particular community, of mankind and of the cosmos. Reflection does not make consciousness an object; rather, reflection "is an orientation within the sphere of consciousness by which [the thinker] can push to the limit of consciousness but never cross those limits."[28]

Voegelin's account is by no means idiosyncratic. For at least two generations phenomenological philosophers have made equivalent arguments, at least as regards the interrelationship of matter, life, and consciousness.[29] Considered simply as organism, the phenomenon of life in the world looks neither as an idea nor as a mechanism but as an act or motion that appears both spontaneous and teleological. Neither spontaneity nor teleology can be explained by causes without first having been transformed into an element of a causal system, which is to say having been destroyed as spontaneous and teleological. In order to understand even the "simplicities" of metabolism, for example, one must introduce nonreductive terms such as *form* to indicate the persistence of the organism by means of the alteration in its material being. Once an organism becomes (its) material being, it is dead and no longer an organism. So long as it endures, it is the achievement of itself as a distinct form. Its distinctiveness is the measure of its independence from its own material contents. The achievement of the organism is, so to speak, one degree of freedom. With it, with the act that constitutes the organism, are introduced heterogeneity and identity. This act amounts to a challenge to homogeneity or to the forces of entropy and sameness. With challenge comes risk. This dialectic holds for the entire hierarchy of life, from plain organic being to self-conscious, reflective human being. The world of von Uexkuell's tick or Kohak's porcupine is intelligibly connected to the world of Husserlian phenomenology.

Matter, we may say, is self-sufficient. Plants are distinguished, in several senses, by their direct physical and chemical commerce with the world, a meaningful configuration opened up by the initial biological act. If there is world, there is also a kind of interiority even to plants. Without sensitivity or "feeling" (Whitehead) there can be no activity. By the same token, even plants must have (however faint) a temporal immanence; not every acorn becomes an oak. There is no implication in such description that acorns are disappointed if they are eaten by pigs, but only that the significance of "acorn" includes an internal direction that is expressed as it becomes an oak or not. That is, life, even the lowest form of life, is not determined by what is external and antecedent. It expresses itself by what it becomes, which, to repeat, is that life is a spontaneous and teleological act or motion.

If so much be granted, the rest comes easily. Animals may be distinguished from plants by the mutually implied attributes of motility, perception, and emotion, which together express a greater freedom and a more perilous necessity. By comparison with plant life, which is in direct contact with its nourishing environment, animals first must acquire and internalize their material (and organic) nourishment before it is metabolized. The increased complexity of animal mediation of the cosmos to the organism raises animals above plants in the hierarchy of beings. This means as well that animals have farther to fall; animal life is richer than plant life, but less secure. Moreover, it strives to preserve itself not merely as organic or metabolizing but as motile, perceiving, and feeling. As one moves up the hierarchy the edges of freedom and necessity both become sharper. The animal moves, which is the appearance of freedom greater than that of the plant, but it must, which is the appearance of greater necessity. The gain lies not in the one or the other but in the combination of the two.

In this context, human being may be distinguished from animal being, as animal being was distinguished from plant being, by means of the increased complexity of its forms and mediations. In particular, perception is accentuated in humans. The excitement of action, the pleasures and pains, successes and failures, that are in animals more or less equitably distributed among the attributes of motility, emotion, and perception are in humans concentrated and transformed. Specifically, sight can be internalized and extended as ideative perception or insight.[30] Humans, that is, can mediate the relation of sense and object of sense with abstract and mentally manipulable images. Initially this new capacity hardly interferes with animal emotion and motility, and it never overcomes them fully. They are, however, transformed, especially when mediated themselves as mental or imaginative entities; the awakened imaginative capacity perceives the world without the world's being present. It is here that phenomenologists speak of the reflexivity of consciousness, by which is meant the ability of consciousness to take itself as an imaginative object and relate itself to the world as other.

Our imaginative capacity is able to detach meaning from the occasion of its appearance and to retain it as memory. The image is therefore not found in the object but through it. The difference between animal perception and vegetative encounter with the environment was expressed by the relative detachment of perception; there is here a second-order detachment and appearance appears as appearance, and thereby in contrast with something else that is invested with the index of reality or truth. Several implications may be drawn from this specifically human capacity. The most important, considering the present topic, is that human being does not exist in "metaphysical isolation" (Jonas) from animal, vegetative, and physical being.

This same capacity is what enables us to conceive of human being in such isolation. Being detached from the sensed presence of a thing and thereby from the stubborn factuality of its existence, an image can be freely altered. Perceived forms can be imaginatively transformed and reproduced externally as perceptual objects that may be communicated as stories, rituals, or other "works." These may be intended as the truth or meaning of the original perceived form, but then again they may not. And in any event, there is nothing to ensure that they will be perceived in tune with the original animating intention. The capacity of imagination, cut loose from the relative immediacy of perception, is free to rework perceptions in order to express or symbolize truth, but also to integrate the imaginative capacity and the meanings it expresses to desire or will. In this way humans can endow their actions with significance that may be contested by alternative interpretations.

As with the increased complexity and precariousness of animal over vegetative being, so too the concern for truth or reality expresses the gain in the amplitude of human over animal experience. Corresponding to the increased complexity of mediation is an increased capacity to intervene in the environment. We said earlier that matter was self-sufficient and by the same token did nothing. The interventions of life are disturbances of that self-sufficiency, paid for in the coin of risk and eventually by death. The degree to which life intervenes in matter is directly related to the degree to which it mediates being to itself. At the apex again is human being, the "natural alien."[31] As a result of the imaginative capacities of humans, we are capable of "alienating," that is, mediating imaginatively, nature to consciousness. The precariousness of human being here appears, precisely, in our ability to understand ourselves in the "metaphysical isolation" against which this discussion has been directed. Technological consciousness may be specified as the mode of imagination that permits limitless scope and depth of intervention in nature.

Technological consciousness, metaphysical isolation, and alienation are comparatively recent deformations of consciousness. These deformations can appear as deformations, however, only in light of more comprehensive diagnostic criteria such as can be established by noetic reason. For example, Aristotle's characterization of human being as the *zoon noun echon* or *zoon noetikon*, the living being who has *nous*, expressed the personal order of the soul, much as the term *zoon politikon* expressed the order of human existence in politics. Such terms have become verbal definitions of "human nature," though they began as a summary conclusion to analyses of reality experienced. To the Aristotelean pair Voegelin has proposed adding the term *zoon historikon* to describe the dimension of existence that is historical.[32] All three characterizations constitute adequate but partial summaries of human being.

In addition to the noetic, political, and historical experiences, those associated with the body rather than the soul must be added. Jonas has already indicated the importance of embodiment. Material, vegetative, and animal realities are all expressed through the human organism. Moreover, the psyche is not simply rational: human beings experience as real the passions and desires that move them away from order. And finally, human existence is aware of itself as not containing its own meaning within itself. This experience is expressed in terms of anxiety regarding the precariousness of life between birth and death, truth and untruth, good and evil. As a zoon noetikon, human being is preeminently a questioner of the whence and whither of life, a searcher for the ground and sense of existence.

The conclusion to be drawn is that the full amplitude of human experience extends from the cosmic ground of being, symbolized by Anaximander as the *apeiron*, the boundless, through material, vegetative and animal nature to the passions; to reason; and to the divine beyond. The boundless is the source or foundation from which generated things emerge and back to which they perish; the beyond was symbolized by Plato as formative force of all things (*Philebus*, 30b–c).

Such reflections place Husserl's attempt to refound Western rationality in their proper light. His attempt must be understood as an apocalyptic fantasy, whatever the insights it contains regarding the structures of intramundane consciousness in which the objective and "scientific" order of the world is constituted. As a historical event, the significance of Husserlian phenomenology is that it expresses a symptom of crisis. About the nature of the crisis Husserl was clear. "The exclusiveness with which the total world-view of modern man, in the second half of the nineteenth century, let itself be determined by the positive sciences and be blinded by the prosperity they produced, meant an indifferent turning-away from the questions that are decisive for a genuine humanity."[33] The condition for that prosperity, as Husserl made clear later in the book, was the Galilean mathematization and technicization of the world.

*

One of Hegel's evocative images was that of the owl of Minerva. It flies at dusk, when the activities of the day end; likewise philosophy accounts for the facts after the fact, by putting them into a meaningful story. The storytelling, in Hegel's work as in Plato's *Republic*, goes on at night. Hegel's image may indicate what has been forgotten or neglected. In the technological society dusk has been reduced in fact and has in principle been eliminated. Electric lights extend the harshness of daylight far into the night. Leaving aside for a moment the implication that technology is deeply hostile to philosophy, let us ask what it means to say that electric lights have, in principle, triumphed over darkness.

To begin with, electric lights flood our rooms with illumination, unlike lanterns or even gas lights. Imaginatively we can conceive of encroaching completely on the darkness, with reflectors suitably positioned in space, for example. Even if we have not yet done so, what we have done is flood the night, but the darkness has merely retreated. In retreating, it has become alien and a source of fear. Moreover, by pushing back the darkness with technology, it is certain we will never understand it. If we push it back completely we still will not understand it. It is true, of course, that we are creatures of light and believe that electric lights are good. It is not without reason that we associate darkness with evil. But by the same token, it is not clear that dispelling the darkness would be good. Among other things, the beautiful visibility of the darkness of a moonlit night would be gone.[34] Or to put it another way: we are also creatures of darkness, of dreams, and of recovery that is aided by storytelling. After all, even in Plato's story, the philosophers, who would prefer to live their lives outside the cave, must go down. By understanding such a "phenomenology for ourselves," as Merleau-Ponty taught, and imaginatively bracketing artifacts as well as our conceptual prejudices, we may create a critical distance that allows the technological society to appear to us as it is.

The difference between scientific and technical knowing and phenomenological description of meaning requires us to return from a concern with obtaining objective or technical knowledge to immediate and commonsense experience. In this fashion we can understand technological knowing as a form or kind of knowing, and not as knowing simply; ceasing to believe in the knowing evident to technology, that is, we may understand the meaning or significance of technical knowing. In this way the limitations of technical consciousness may appear. The intellectual and practical act involved amounts to a Husserlian epoche, with the understanding that the purpose is not merely to make visible the intentional ties of consciousness to the world, but to bring to attention the full amplitude of human experience in light of which technological consciousness may appear as it is.

Although it is possible to make appropriate distinctions among theory, science, and technology, it is more important to recognize what these things have in common.[35] As a first approximation one may say that science, technological knowing, or theory exists when the scientist, technician, or theorist declares his or her independence from philosophy. In the words of Leo Strauss, the latter term is understood to mean the "quest for wisdom, . . . for universal knowledge, for knowledge of the whole."[36] The quest for knowledge of "the whole" is the quest for knowledge of "all things," which is to say "for knowledge of God, the world, and man—or rather [the] quest for knowledge of the natures of all things: the natures in their totality are 'the whole.' " Elsewhere Strauss has written, "The whole is the totality of the parts. To understand the whole then means to understand all the parts of the whole or the articulation of the whole." Accordingly, the being of "things" is of a different kind than the being of the whole. " 'To be' means therefore 'to be a part,' " so that the being of the whole must be "beyond" the being of the things that it comprises.[37] Now, a great deal may be said by way of interpretation of Strauss's observations. Is there, for instance, a distinction between knowledge of the whole and understanding of the whole? These enticing epistemological explorations must, however, be foregone in order to emphasize the major point: philosophy is a quest, a *zetema*, as Plato called it (*Republic*, 368c).

Moreover, every quest is accompanied by desire, the desire that the quest end and that whatever one is looking for be found. Whether one reflects on the significance of the quest or of the desire that motivates it, similar paradoxes are encountered. To use Strauss's terminology, in the quest of philosophy the end, the thing the philosopher is looking for, is wisdom, knowledge, or understanding of the natures of all things. If the end of philosophy is gained, the philosopher stops searching because he or she no longer desires to be wise. More precisely, such a being would have no desire to raise questions or, indeed, to speak at all. But, as Aristotle observed, silence marks beasts as well as gods. Thus, in order not to be mistaken for a beast such a being would have a desire to speak; by speaking the beast would indicate that he or she was neither a beast not a god but a human being, and so not wise.

These paradoxes—and others can as easily be spun out—indicate the participatory mode of being that characterizes human experience of reality. Reality is experienced, that is, insofar as human beings participate in it. The participation, however, is not a kind of option that human beings may exercise or not. Rather,

the metaphor of participation is intended to evoke an awareness
of mystery or an anxiety about the meaning and purpose of human life. At the core of philosophical experience, therefore, exists
a kind of ignorance. The philosopher "professed to know this
only, that he nothing knew" (Milton), which nevertheless means
that he knows something. Of the large number of things that are
implied by this formulation only two will be mentioned: first, that
there remains something unknowable at the heart of human existence; but second, that it is possible to distinguish what remains
essentially unknowable, the "mystery of being," as Voegelin has
called it, from what is knowable. The task of differentiating the
two has already begun with assent to the argument that consciousness transcends into the body, the world, the community,
history, and the divine ground of being. It does so, moreover,
prior to any systematic philosophizing. Accordingly, philosophy
sets out from these experiences in its attempt to provide a noetically formed articulation of them. It begins on that quest by at-
tending to opinions or to common sense. Phenomenology, even
in its Husserlian form, is helpful insofar as it directs our attention
to the meaning of what appears in the world.

By claiming that technological knowing cuts itself off from philosophy and so from our commonsensical participation in reality
or the whole, we imply three additional things about technical
knowing. First, as Husserl showed in his study of Galileo, there
is an anticipation by technical knowing of apprehending an exact
nature or an intentional constitution of such a nature. In principle, all appearances can legitimately be reduced to geometrical
entities.[38] Second, by attempting to geometricize nature, the
technician must find the necessary means to do so; this is accomplished by the procedure of abstraction that constitutes the true,
mathematical world behind the complex of appearances. Third,
technical knowing must forget that this true, mathematical world
was constructed or abstracted, that it is hypothetical. It does so
by proceeding to *act* on the assumption that nature is geometric,
which effectively disguises its original intentionality, that it anticipated what it subsequently claimed to find.[39] Phenomenological
attention to meaning, to substance, to essence, in this context,
implies the task of rediscovering the prescientific or pretechnological world.[40]

The contrast between technical knowing of a geometricized
nature and phenomenological description of meaning, to say

nothing of philosophical desire, wonder, and participation of consciousness in reality, raises at the same time the question of continuity. Granted there is a difference between technical knowing and philosophy and that the former exists only by a kind of forgetting of its own origins, it does not follow that, to use the language of political philosophy, the technological society is a novel regime. The discontinuity between pretechnological and technological modes and orders or forms of life is not absolute because technical activity is coeval with human existence. One may say that the technological society is unprecedented if one means thereby that it cannot properly be understood by reference to precedents, which is to say that it cannot be reduced, causally, to precedent. We begin, therefore, by emphasizing discontinuity. An account of the technological regime follows in chapter 3.

PART ONE

# The Technological Phenomenon

# 1
# Novelty

The novelty of technology may be indicated in several ways. Our daily lives are performed within an encompassing technological milieu. We are awakened by a clock-radio, not the sun or a rooster; we drive to factories or large-scale complex bureaucracies along superhighways or are transported by specialized trains; we take care of our needs in supermarkets and medical centers; we operate our homes on energy produced miles away. We know that our society has done and can do things that heretofore have only been imagined. "In our time," wrote Winner, "*techne* has at last become *politeia*."[1] It is more difficult to know what these novelties signify.

Comparison of our current self-interpretation with the self-interpretation of human beings at other times or in other places is always a useful way to gain a perspective on our own capacities and on the conditions of our existence. In *Antigone*, for example, the chorus celebrates humans' assertiveness and their cleverness in building homes for themselves within the creative/destructive and necessitous rhythms of the cosmos (lines 335–70). Ingenuity allowed humanity to resist and interrupt necessity so as to become civil, but the lasting and passing of nature continued. Sophocles' reflections on the human capacity to build were accompanied by wonder and awe at humans' audacity at having done so. Most audacious of all was man the nomothete, the founder of cities, because cities would last, if not "forever," at least for many generations. The lasting of cities and the stability of their laws were accordingly understood by analogy with cosmic regularities. To use Voegelin's term, the city is a cosmion, a little

27

cosmos illuminated with meaning.[2] The laws of the city provided
stability in the midst of generation and change to the extent they
reflected justice, the measure of the cosmic rhythms. Within the
laws of the city as within its walls existed the web of human relationships that constituted the substance of ethics and politics.
Outside the space of appearance afforded by the laws and outside
the accountable present time, matters were left to chance or fortune. Human action occurred within the context of unquestioned
authorship and immediately visible ethical and political significance.

All this has changed. The *Antigone* chorus contains a different
meaning for us. It is no longer sufficient to honor the laws of the
land; "The gods' sworn right" has for several generations been
incapable of measuring and even less of checking or limiting human action (lines 368–69). The old prescriptions of Aristotelean
ethics, moderation, magnanimity, liberality, and so on, are still
"valid" for our immediate relations with others, "but this sphere
is overshadowed by a growing realism of collective action where
doer, deed, and effect are no longer the same as they were in the
proximate sphere."[3] Justice as the measure of cosmic rhythms no
longer makes sense for us and not because of experiential atrophy
or the eclipse of "pagan" opinions by revealed truths. Far more
important than the complex relationship of Athens and Jerusalem
or of philosophy and the Bible has been the recent and everyday
experience of the vulnerability of the cosmos or of "nature" to
human activity. After the damage has been done, we recognize
without effort that Sophocles' confidence in the invulnerability of
nature was an assumption.

The enhanced capacity for action, the "wondrous power" (line
335) of human beings, has extended political and ethical responsibility beyond the walls and the laws of the city into what heretofore was left to chance or force. For the first time, technology
has created a kind of unity on the planet expressed equally by the
appearance of such diverse phenomena as commercial ecumenism, fear of atomic warfare, or space flights. Speculations on
the topic "world history," familiar since Hegel's day, are no longer
intellectual conceits but constitute today "an actual and pressing
reality."[4] These historical novelties have found expression in doctrines of human rights, of animal rights, and of sequoia rights.
That we are perplexed by such doctrines also indicates their nov-

elty and thereby the discontinuity between the technological society and its predecessors.

The term *technology* dates from the early seventeenth century.
It retained its literal meaning derived from the Greek, namely a
*logos* concerning *techne*, for nearly three centuries. *Techne* was
the Greek equivalent to the Latin *ars*, from which derives the
English word *art*. An art or a *techne* was a making, a *poeisis* or
production. A production is a leading forth; a technical production is one that requires for its actualization the intervention of
human beings. Such productions are usually *technemata*, works
of the hands or handiworks. For the Greeks nomothetics was
also a kind of art; it was the highest or "royal" art because it
governed or directed all the other arts and because it aimed at
producing the highest human thing, justice. In addition, however, the arts were a kind of knowing: a true artist (a true technician) could give a logos, an account, of his or her art. We know
from Plato's dialogues that many who claimed to practice the nomothetic arts were in fact defective technicians because they
were unable to give an account of justice, which was the point of
practicing the art. Alternatively one may say that the political art
was a quasi art because it was guided by prudence rather than by
a vision, the way a carpenter's art would be guided by the vision
of a table.

By the same token, practical knowledge, to use Aristotle's
term, the knowledge of leading forth that is made evident in coherent discourse, was only one kind of knowledge. In addition,
there was theoretical knowledge. The Greek for knowledge,
*episteme*, was translated by the Romans as *scientia*, from which
derived the English *science*. Aristotle's language is often confusing to contemporaries, especially regarding the meaning of the
term *political science*. The distinction between what might be
designated the practical and the theoretical sciences rests on
a distinction between two modes of being. Art, the practical or
the technical, was concerned chiefly with the mode of being that
just as easily might not be, with accidental being. This included the
production of tables and of laws and of horses. Theory, we may
say, was concerned chiefly with the mode of being that necessarily was what it was. This included topics such as geometry, numbers, and astronomy. There were exceptions and ambiguous
biguous usages, of course, and these were not simply grammatical

mistakes by otherwise careful users of the Greek language. The ambiguities reflected the ambiguity of being and its modes. Leo Strauss, who read as carefully as anyone, indicated this by observing that no one had yet given a complete and adequate account of Plato's teaching concerning the Ideas. This ambiguity was expressed dramatically in the dialogues as well when one recalls that the defective lawgiving technicians appeared defective in light of their inability to account for justice, which, according to Plato at least, was not itself produced but rather was an "idea," the mode of being of which was not produced.

Despite these ambiguities about which classicists, philosophers, and political philosophers have disputed at length, the intention of the language regarding the modes of being was not ambiguous: it was intended to convey a firm distinction between the arts and the sciences and ground it on a distinction in reality between the modes of being as necessary or essential and accidental or existential. Sometimes the distinction was formulated as between eternal and generated being or *ousia* and *genesis*, or again, between substance and phenomena.

The modern English word *technology* does not mean discourse concerning art. Moreover, the distinction between modes of being that sustained the separation of art and science in antiquity is no longer made. What is of interest to us is not to determine whether or in what respect the antique account is true (a notion nearly unintelligible to contemporary political philosophy) but to account for what has changed in the meaning of the word. For the ancients, logos grasped or aimed at grasping the purpose or form of a thing; it did not direct the actual process of production, though it might account for it afterward. Modern technology, in contrast, proposes to furnish a logos of production, a "rationalization of the process of production, independent of, it not actually divorced from, any particular conception of *eidos* or form."[5] This is new.

One way of dealing with the question is to speak only of technique. In his magisterial study of 1954, Jacques Ellul gave an account of *La technique,* but it was translated (quite properly) under the title *The Technological Society.* As George Grant has observed on this point, the European use of the term *technique* maintains "verbal purity" but at the cost of obscuring "modern reality."[6] The term *technology* in modern English implies the copenetration of art and science. A glance inside any laboratory confirms that interdependence: new inventions make possible new knowledge, proof for the truth of which is furnished by new inventions. As one of the great physicists of this century, Viktor von Weizsaecker, said, "The thinking of our science proves itself only in action, in the successful experiment." This is new.

The new relationship between human being and the cosmos undreamed by Sophocles and the new relationship between knowing and making issue in a new kind of questioning, which may be called technological questioning. The novelty of technological questioning may be indicated with reference to the premodern separation of knowing and making.

Notwithstanding the ambiguities, it seems clear that for classical political philosophy there existed a hierarchy of arts. The art of the bridlemaker was subordinate to the art of the horseman; the art of the horseman to the art of the cavalry officer; the art of war to the art of politics. At the apex, as is indicated in the *Republic,* the philosopher was also king, which we may interpret to mean that the hierarchy of arts, which established the royal art of politics at the top, was justified by science, *episteme.* This indicates again the paradoxes of philosophy already encountered, but, in spite of those paradoxes at the apex, there existed for Plato clear limits to the several arts. The claim to establish and maintain those limits was based on the knowledge or at least the vision of the good. Good in its lower as well as its highest meaning meant what something was fitted for. A good bridle was one that was fitted for riding a horse; justice was what human beings were fitted for. This is not to deny that there was great dispute about what concretely justice or happiness or a good life was. That dispute was the anthropological substance of classical philosophy.

The basis for the difference between ancient techne and modern technology lies in the difference between ancient and modern conceptions of material being or in their distinctive metaphysics of nature or of matter. If matter is given form in production, it is regulated by the prior (or "essential") being of form (or "idea"). Only one thing is produced by the exercise of an art a techne. However, if nature or material being is formless, then technology can produce anything. That is, if nature is also "energy," then you can "apply" external energy to it and make all things, which is the achievement, or rather, the process, of technological productivity. When the structure or thingness of things is as changeable as things themselves, then it is as if there were no form, idea, or *eidos* to guide production.[7] Trying to account coherently for what this ontology signifies, but having to rely on philosophical language handed over from antiquity, has led to new questions and sometimes to very perplexing answers.

In classical terms, the novelty of technological questioning arises from an absence of vision of the good or of justice or of truth given to us by noetic science or by philosophy. One of the reasons is that our science, unlike the science of antiquity, which in a shorthand way we have identified as philosophy, is copenetrated with art. If truth is to some extent produced, how could it possibly set limits to other productive arts? The common observation, that we do not know what should be made, expresses the problem clearly. What imparts a sense of urgency to questioning in this new technological mode is the vastness of our wondrous power of making. The combination of a vast capacity to act with a lack of wisdom regarding the purposes of action is also an index of the novelty of technology as a regime.

According to Heidegger, the novelty of technology appears in yet another way. His questioning concerning technology aimed at thinking through the meaning of technology.[8] Enframing, *das Gestell*, which we may translate into commonsense English as the summoning of nature as object to give us her reasons for being, is the meaning of technology. Because it is we who do the summoning, we exist within the meaning of technology and help constitute it by our actions. As a result, human beings, too, become understood as being at-hand to be used, or as what Heidegger called "standing reserve." On our own terms, however, we who live as technological humanity call ourselves masters of the universe. Heidegger said this self-understanding of modern technological humanity is both the final delusion and the uttermost danger.

*

Hannah Arendt once observed that events, not ideas, change the world. More precisely, events are changes within the world that alter our consciousness of the world. Three paradigmatic events may be said to have expressed the formative character of the modern age: the discovery of America, the Protestant Reformation, and the invention of the telescope. None was itself modern; no hidden undercurrents exploded suddenly into the light and none of the participants insisted on the special novelty of the event.

Prior to the age of the great voyages of exploration, the horizon was open and without limit, forbidding and dangerous but also tempting. Today the world is a sphere, its surface known by human beings as they know the lines in the palms of their hands. It is a platitude to observe that none of the significant parts of a human life, not even a day, is required to reach any point on earth. The transformation of the earth into the globe was accompanied and accomplished by human survey. One can survey, literally look over from above, only by placing a distance between the surveyor and what is nearby. This is simply a requirement of perspective: the greater distance between humans and their earthly or worldly surroundings, the more will they be able to survey and measure and the less will worldly, earth-bound space be left to them. Any decrease in terrestrial distance can come only with an increase in alienation from humans' immediate surroundings. Aircraft, satellites, and spacecraft have removed human surveying capacity to the unbounded range of space itself in a kind of universal recapitulation of the pre-Columbian world.

Seeking to recover what they took to be an original Christian "otherworldliness," the reformers substituted "innerworldly asceticism" (Weber). The two experiences had in common only a verbal expression of alienation from this world. From the perspective of the residual church, the Reformation signified only their incapacity to repress heresy. From the perspective of the world, the Protestant ethic and the spirit of capitalism meant expropriation. Property, whether communal, private, freehold, or usufruct, indicated a share of a common world and therefore was the most elementary political requirement for human worldliness. Expropriation and alienation from the world were accordingly interrelated. The immediate consequences of Henry VIII's expropriation of the monasteries in Britain were perhaps less important than that his action constituted an attack on authority and tradition, both of which had provided a degree of stability to politics. More important was the subsequent expropriation of the peasantry, who were thereby deprived of the protection of family and of property, which prior to the modern age had sheltered the life process and the activity of labor from the world. Herded into the new manufacturing towns, they literally lived hand to mouth. Their lives were taken up with care for their daily bread in exchange for which they labored. The wealth gained through expropriation was turned into capital by being transformed and made productive by these same expropriated persons, peasants-turned-laborers. This expropriation, all observers from Karl Marx to Peter Laslett agree, was a major constituent of "the world we have lost."[9]

The novelty of the industrial revolution considered from the perspective of the world was found not in its cruelty and misery; Marx's "primitive capitalist accumulation" was in many respects less horrible than what Preobrazhensky, the Soviet economist (murdered by Stalin in 1937), called primitive socialist accumulation. The novelty was that the expropriation did not stabilize in a new distribution of wealth and new property. Rather, wealth was returned to the process of expropriation-and-accumulation to generate even more. Expropriation was not limited to the church and peasantry but was extended, in principle, to all levels of society. The reason for this self-augmentation was that expropriation was not undertaken to satisfy wants or desires but to create further capital. Unlike other societies, which have undertaken expropriation as a means to gain wealth (consider the actions of any number of non-Western governments in expropriating foreign firms), Western societies did not stagnate as a result, also in contrast with many so-called third world expropriations. Instead, in the West, the process of capital accumulation spread throughout society, initiating a steady increase in wealth. This "life process of society" (Marx) remained bound to the initial conditions of world-alienation. It makes no difference, in this regard, whether one labors for one's daily bread or a weekly, monthly, or annual wage. The process can continue, moreover, so long as no institutions, no worldly things at all, are permitted to interfere with it. "Wealth accumulation," Arendt said, "is possible only if the world and the very worldliness of man are sacrificed."[10] Recovery of the public world is not achieved by getting rich.

A second phase of expropriation occurred when society rather than the peasant family and its property were subjected to the cycle of expropriation-and-accumulation. In place of family solidarity was class solidarity; in place of family property was the territory of the nation-state. The age of world wars following the age of imperialist expansion marked the end of the comity of nations and signaled the disintegration of the European system of nation-states. The culmination of the process in our own day is found in the actual creation of a contemporaneous global society, a "humankind" whose representatives can meet in less time than it took to gather representatives of a single nation a generation ago. Just as the national territory and social class replaced the family and its property, so "humankind" and the earth or "the planet," as the earth is now fashionably called, have replaced national society and national territory. But nothing in this detracts from the continuing process of world alienation. Just as societies cannot own property, citizens cannot be citizens of the world. On the contrary, a general condition of worldlessness, apparently the necessary condition for the continuation of the process of expropriation-and-accumulation, also is the necessary condition for the formation of not only worldless but selfless mass men and women, the willing participants in the ideological mass movements of our times.

It is a commonplace to observe that the sixteenth-century "scientific revolution" was intelligibly connected to the establishment of the technological society. It is more difficult to understand how the intellectual developments of that era constitute a step toward contemporary world-alienation. The great theoretical simplication that expressed the new phenomenalism was the Copernican heleocentric cosmology, a topic to which we return later. But the event that paradigmatically began the modern age of scientific cosmology was Galileo's act of looking at the sky with the aid of a telescope. Human eyes cannot see that the irregular colors of the moon's surface are craters and mountains, nor can they see the rings of Saturn or the phases of Venus. With Galileo's telescope all these things, plus innumerable invisible stars in the Milky Way, were rendered visible. The first implication to be drawn was that nature did not reveal itself to the human senses directly, that our senses were therefore untrustworthy means to perceive the universe, that everyday experience was a constant source of error and delusion. Truth, apparently, was what our instruments served up to our senses. Our senses, in other words, could be adjusted or modified by instruments to apprehend what otherwise would have remained unknown and beyond them.

Perceptual truth, however, *is* apparent. The substitution of instrument-mediated perception for the perception of the "naked eye" might better be called the substitution of one perceptual/apparent truth for another. Merleau-Ponty, and before him the Gestalt psychologists, recalled that the moon on the horizon looks huge compared to the moon at the zenith. The same moon when looked at through a tube has the identical size on the horizon and at the zenith. The second moon, the mediated perception, Merleau-Ponty called (with some irony) the moon of "true apparent size." Considered phenomenologically, the mediation of magnifying instruments such as the telescope does not simply serve up truth to our senses. On the contrary, some features are amplified and others are reduced. When we look through a tube at the moon on the horizon, the peripheral features disappear. A fortiori, the same is true with the telescope.

The mediation of instruments amplifies/reduces natural perception. The change is structural insofar as one area of reality is emphasized and another is neglected. Something is gained (amplification) but also something is lost (reduction). However, the two do not balance. As Don Ihde has pointed out, "The amplification tends to stand out, to be dramatic, while the reduction tends to be overlooked, or may be forgotten."[11] We take the "true apparent size" of the instrument-mediated perception to be true because it is more dramatic. With magnification we appear to be closer to the moon than we "really" are. Magnification alters apparent distance so that we perceive microstructures as more real than the middle-sized structures we perceive directly. If we interpose imaginatively our scientific understanding of heliocentrism, that is, a macro- not a microstructure, we can discount the middle-sized structure of perception that sees a sunrise. The technological perfection of the structural change of amplification/reduction is to employ a substitute "eye." The camera has given way to the computer-generated image for which there need be no corresponding human or middle-sized perception at all, as is the case with infrared images of crops, radar images of clouds, and so on.

In order for all of this activity to make sense to us, as it evidently does, we must make a prior commitment to phenomenalism, which I discuss in detail in chapter 3. In the present context, the term refers to the belief and trust that phenomenal reality is simply real. The appeal of phenomenalist truth, its dramatic magnification of certain structures and its virtual eclipse of what is lost to experience, is analogous to the appeal of epistemology. When the term was invented by James Frederick Ferrier, professor of moral philosophy at St. Andrews, he believed his new science necessarily was accompanied by agniology, a science of ignorance. A balance is necessarily lost when the growth of ignorance is overlooked through too great an attention to the growth of knowledge.[12] One thinks as well of Aristophanes' satirization of the scientific study of a gnat's anus (*Clouds*, 156ff.).

Looked at from the point of view of the world rather than from any metaphysical consideration of the difference between substance and phenomena, Galileo's activity was much more important than the speculations of astronomers and philosophers. Its importance derived not from the question of its truth or falsity, which, philosophically, is a nonquestion, but from its status as an action; it was an event, and thus a genuine novelty, with unforeseen consequences such as electronic images of the planet made by satellites orbiting the earth. Ideas and speculations come and go and are never entirely unprecedented. Copernicus's heliocentrism was, in certain respects highly traditional; Galileo proved something to be factually true, not rationally or speculatively reasonable. That action was received as a metaphysical reversal of the first order, despite the initial resistance of authority.

According to the traditional distinction between action and contemplation, truth is ultimately grasped in still, speechless, actionless, noetic seeing, the beholding of what truly is.[13] Contemplation, properly speaking, aimed at the apprehension of substance and meaning; it relied, as Democritus said, on trusting sense experience to reveal phenomenal truths. Galileo's act threw all that into question. He had necessarily cast doubt on the notion of truth as phenomenal revelation because he demonstrated that it was mistaken to trust that things are as they appear. Indeed, the entire meaning of theory changed from that of a reasonably connected series of truths that had been given directly to the senses and that was directed at accounting for the reality of substance, to become a scientific "working hypothesis."

Since things are not as they appear, theory, that is, the modern scientific meaning of theory, changed in accordance with the results it produced. Thus, its validity is determined not on the basis of what it reveals but on whether or not it works. The immediate consequence was to assist in the rehabilitation of curiosity. The telescope was a splendid mediator because, "unlike any experimental intervention in the objects of nature, it could be adapted to the classical ideal of the contemplation of nature."[14] The ultimate consequence was that the events, the course of history, are invoked to prove that doing has priority over reason in matters of truth. Alternatively one may say that the meaning of truth has changed from the noetic apprehension of substance to the production of phenomenal results that accord with the anticipated capacities of instruments to measure continuous variables.

New facts, new experiences of things mediated by instruments, called forth new theories and a new meaning to theory. From the perspective of the world, the most astonishing feature of the new scientific approach was the assumption that the same kind of external force was manifest in the fall of terrestrial bodies and the movement of heavenly ones. This assumption was utterly at variance with anything even remotely similar in antiquity or the Middle Ages.

Modern "classical" physics, by contrast, adopted a standpoint that is imaginatively outside the earth. In order to do this it was necessary to abolish the age-old distinction between earth and sky. All events, terrestrial and celestial alike, were said to be subject to a universally valid law, a law that held beyond the range of human experience (even if aided by strong instruments), a law that antedated the appearance of human beings and would be valid when the earth itself disappeared. Considered from the perspective of the world, modern "postclassical" physics is even more odd. For instance, there is a class of unified theories of elementary particle interaction that seeks to account for all observable natural forces.[15] The significant aspect of these theories concerns the peculiar characteristic of elementary particles: apart from location, they are absolutely identical whether in the same atom or in different ends of the universe. This is why, for example, the "language" used to discuss the early universe is identical with that used to describe elementary particle interaction. Quantum field theory and modern symmetry principles have not meant a return to the speculative relativity of Cardinal Bellar-mine or Copernicus or even of Leibniz. Contemporary physicists and cosmologists, the two designations often being the same, do not deal with hypotheses but rather choose a perspective or standpoint wherever it is convenient for a specific purpose.

During the last few decades human beings have existed not merely in a world determined by science and technology but in one whose truths and know-how are derived from standpoints outside the earth. Such technology is not simply destructive, though that is its most immediately impressive characteristic, but is also enormously creative. Human beings have populated the heavens with new stars, created new elements and forms of life. From the perspective of philosophy or of biblical religion, human acting into nature, especially creative activities regarding life, seem more blasphemous than development of atomic weapons because, by opening the potential of changing the image of hu-mans, it seems as if humans have arrogated to themselves a task heretofore reserved only to God. But the possibility of destroying the earth was also traditionally in God's hands. So the obvious question is, How is this possible?

We are not dealing here with any Nietzschean questions of di-vine murder or of drinking up the sea. Rather, we need only to follow out the implications of Archimedes' quest for a universal standpoint. If that location could be assumed, humans could imaginatively imitate processes that were decisive in the genesis of matter and life but that played no part in maintaining the sta-bility of matter and life on earth. In order to do so all that had to be forgotten was the fact that "the answers of science will always remain replies to questions asked by men; the confusion in the issue of 'objectivity' was to assume that there could be answers without questions and results independent of a question-asking being."[16] The problem, however, is that it is possible to find the Archimedean point in space only with respect to the earth. Once arrived in space a new Archimedean point would be needed, and so on. The continuous quest for the Archimedean point in fact, though not imaginatively, leaves one lost in space; the only way home is to recognize that the search for knowledge of the uni-verse is inherently limited. This conclusion was known from the start. Swift, for example, satirized the abandonment of middle-sized perceptual structures in his story of the Laputian tailors who measured by sextant rather than tape. Behind the comic confusion of the familiar issue of objectivity and subjectivity lay the central experience of modern philosophy, doubt.

\*

Galileo's telescope did more than challenge the reliability of the senses: it proved that the senses could fundamentally err and carried the implication that, unaided, they could never grasp the truth of phenomena. Accordingly, the old remedy, an appeal to the higher authority of noetic reason, was useless. The invention and intervention of an implement that might never have been created, and not an error of sense perception or of reason, had shown that humans had been deceived. What was worse, *ex hypothesi,* if Galileo had not acted, if he had never been born, humans would be deceived yet. Moreover, the deception occurred not because people trusted their senses but because they trusted that reality would reveal itself to them. The implication was obvious: nothing is given but appearance, and that is untrustworthy. Certainly truth and reality were no longer understood as having been given to the senses; only the destructive interference with appearance, the intervention of instruments, could hold out hope for true knowledge. But then again, if only scientific instrument-mediated observation was reliable and appearances were deceptive, how are human beings fitted to reality at all? Or, what amounts to the same thing, if Galileo's telescope was an improvement on unaided sight, what would improved telescopes reveal? New truths? Then Galileo had simply revealed another error by revealing a temporary truth.

Descartes's solution to the perplexities of doubt that came from imaginatively adopting Archimedean point was to move it from an indefinite location outside the earth into human beings themselves. Less metaphorically, Descartes was understood to have argued that, if everything is doubtful, then only doubting is not. Certainty arose from method, from the consistent application of the principle of doubt. The several conclusions Descartes drew came to constitute much of the agenda of modern philosophy. Two of his conclusions are important in the present context. The first resulted in the operationalization of doubt in experimentation. Here the overriding conviction was that, even if humans cannot know what is given and disclosed in the world, at least they can know what they make. The second resulted in the introspective method and was founded on the conviction that, even if I can doubt the whole world, I cannot doubt that I doubt. For Descartes the two were in harmonious accord because the known-made items were mathematical truths that expressed the very structure of the mind. For example, Cartesian geometry, which is not geometry (earth measurement) in the old sense, is a spatial representation of algebra. The terms can be reversed: the mind can overrule the testimony of nature and of the senses in favor of an algebraic representation of space—true space, it is called, this time without irony.

That the accord between truth and method proved temporary is less important than that instruments, from telescopes to linear colliders, were understood as having forced nature to reveal its secrets. Knowledge thus was confined to what could be done, which for Descartes made mathematics the ideal. It alone was pure, consisting solely of the mind's self-made entities. In turn, knowledge could be confirmed only by more doing. As Merleau-Ponty once said, Cartesian consciousness assumed the divine task of creating the world anew each morn.

Despite the fact that Descartes used a medieval form, the meditation, in which to cast his speculations, his thought moved within the modern reversal of contemplation and action. It is less, in fact, a question of reversing the traditional hierarchy than of rejecting contemplation entirely. Descartes was, however, an extremely cautious writer so that the relationships between his intentions (or attempting to understand him as he understood himself) and the received "founder of modern philosophy" is always a matter of considerable interpretative subtlety. In principle, the meditative form serves as an intellectual discipline. By systematic reflection, usually on a passage from Scripture, the mind is instructed, the will is moved, and most important, the soul is opened in prayer. The stages of meditation and the transformations of the soul have received considerable scrutiny and analytical differentiation by mystics and writers on mysticism. One of the purposes of Cartesian doubt was to purge the mind of all consciousness of worldly contents. As the anonymous author of the fourteenth-century *Cloud of Unknowing* put it: it is hard work to stamp out "all remembrance of God's creation, and [to keep] them covered by that cloud of forgetting we spoke of earlier." The "cloud of forgetting" was the author's term for the act of eliminating "the whole created world" from meditative consciousness.[17] The point of undertaking this exercise and "hard work" was to attain the experience of world-transcendent reality. The literary expression of this "hard work" is useful insofar as it enables a reader to recapitulate the experience, because it serves as a guide to the reader's own conscious reenactment of the process.

What was new in the Cartesian hard work was not the formal stages of the process by which consciousness rid itself of all worldly contents but the concrete sentiments that inspired the effort. Traditionally the meditation began from the attitude of the *contemptus mundi*. Precisely because the world is so massively present to consciousness is it necessary to undertake the hard work, the effort, to free the mind from its predisposition to care for the world. The medieval contempt for the world aimed not at producing a psychological state of world-hatred, but at assuring thinkers that the things of the world were irrelevant to their cares, especially to their highest care, which is knowledge of God. Descartes, unlike his medieval predecessors, was in the position of wanting to know the world. At the same time he wished, or more cautiously he probably wished, to remain a Christian thinker. At the very least this would have remained an extremely difficult task. On the one hand, the traditional formulas presupposed the sentiment of "contempt"; on the other, Descartes's meditation has an obvious Christian content. This ambiguity, no doubt, has led to the great controversies regarding the ultimate meaning of his work.

One matter that may be settled with respect to the present concern is that Descartes's desire to know the world (irrespective of his desire to know God) meant that he had to use the results of his own efforts within the cloud of forgetting not in order to ascend higher in the mystical order of experience but to assure himself of the reality of the world. That is, Descartes's epoche of the world led him to his own Archimedean point from which he was able to reconstitute the world he had just meditatively annihilated. In Voegelin's words, "I would therefore formulate as being new in Descartes that the sentiment of contemptus mundi gives way to that of interest in the world, and that from care about knowledge, the experience of [world-] transcendence in the meditation becomes an instrument for being certain about the objectivity of the world."[18] "Interest in the world" is a sentiment that alters the meaning of the effort to attain the attitude appropriate to contemplation.

We may see this in another way as well. The former primacy of contemplation over activity rested on the conviction that no work of human beings could equal in beauty and truth the cosmos whose eternal rhythms were disclosed to mortals only when all movements, including mental ones, had come to rest. But precisely that conviction had been shattered by Galileo and his successors: the only reason modern people know anything at all about the heavens is a consequence of human action. The historical, contingent event of peering through a telescope sufficed to prove to individuals whose disposition led them to take an interest in the world that the notion of eternal truth was sheer fantasy. Henceforth thinking, which had been understood as the means by which the soul was led to contemplate eternal truth, was understood as the handmaid of doing. Consequently, scientific and philosophic truth parted company. Or rather, the truth slipped away and certainty took its place, at least until Kant exposed the fraudulence of the substitution. The new sentiment upheld the conviction that the search for the truth behind mere appearance must in the end reveal only another appearance. At the same time, this unmasking of appearances was endowed with the index of an "advance," though there remained considerable haziness about what one was advancing toward. The conviction remained that the advance must be endless. This was called progress.

*

The following conclusions may be drawn from the foregoing discussions. First, technology is new, but human beings have become familiar with its novelty. That today's novelty is obsolete tomorrow is no longer a cause of widespread anxiety. At the same time, when we try to think what the significance of this familiar novelty might mean, we are forced to recognize the difficulty in employing the old language of philosophy. A commonplace expression of this theme is the observation that we live in revolutionary times. The central agency of revolution is not politics or economics but scientific technology or technological science. The times are revolutionary because the changes are radical, comprehensive, and dramatic. Moreover, they are experienced as a break with the past, as "the world turned upside down," and even as the replacement of worldly stability, tradition, and order with the sheer condition of rapid change. And finally, these changes are understood to be synthetic, not the result of divine intervention, not the result of the growth of polar ice or of solar fire.

Second, therefore, human beings are both agents and patients of the scientific-technological revolution. To be more precise, they are agents first of all with respect to introducing new ways of thinking, and acting and they are patients insofar as they must come to terms with the consequences of those earlier innovations. Technology, said Jonas, "is the metaphysics of science come into the open."[19] The metaphysics was the visible expression of human agency; the results of science have been endured. The first indicates an alteration in the fundamental self-understanding of human beings; the second may imply an alteration in the being of humans. Both are contained in the expression "image of man."

The year 1543 was symbolic: Copernicus and Vesalius both published books that year, the one on the macrocosmic heavens, the other on the microcosmic body; the one speculative and mathematical, the other concrete and empirical. It is the great achievement of scientific technology to have effected a synthesis of these two approaches to nature that at first blush seem opposed. Copernicus's heliocentric model and hypothesis of axial and orbital movement of the earth was an important step on the way from the closed world to the infinite universe, to use the title of Koyré's famous book. The most general consequence drawn from his astronomical speculation was that the universe is made up of a single, homogeneous, and neutral stuff, the changes of which could be expressed in a single set of mathematical laws.

A third conclusion, therefore: of a homogeneous and neutral nature one may say only that it proceeds, not that it achieves. In an older language, nature has no final cause, which is to say, material or efficient causality is blind. Nature is knowable because it is meaningless, a configuration of chance that was nevertheless necessarily the result of causal antecedents. According to this cosmology, nothing was invested in achieving the solar system, which is only a (temporary) homeostatic equilibrium, nor in the existence of life forms or of human being.

Several implications that bear on the initial articulation and subsequent expansion of technological consciousness follow from these conclusions. First, there is no reason to respect nature. Being without purpose or final cause, it sanctions nothing; accordingly, nature permits anything. Because there is no natural order, human beings cannot violate it. Just as there can be no miracles, neither can there be monsters or monstrous acts. Second, the possibility of divine and human action is simultaneously excluded. If nature consists of an ordered sequence of material or efficient causes, action, which is the initiation of novelty, is impossible. Will, and thereby action, must be eliminated or turned into the mere appearance of as yet hidden and blind causal sequences. Third and paradoxically, notwithstanding the metaphysical impossibility or miraculousness of human initiation, human being is nevertheless the only source of will. Having become the object of knowledge, the universe thereby became the object of human will. Knowledge was put at the service of will, which came, metaphysically, from nowhere. Fourth, the exceptional status of human will, namely that it is the source of purpose in an otherwise purposeless universe, has not been interpreted as evidence of the incoherence of the doctrine but as the source of productivity and the grounds for action. Since all things are knowable and without mystery, they can be dissected into parts and reassembled according to patterns devised by human will, the one metaphysical or miraculous exception to blind causality.

These four attributes of technological consciousness were not simply the epiphenomal results of historical events. One may interpret them as expressions of change, but to do so only redirects our attention to the significance of change, which cannot itself be change. Let us say then, in Kantian language, that we are searching for the conditions of possibility of technological consciousness as just described. If it is true that 1543 was symbolic, technological consciousness is a latecomer. To see what was new, consideration must be given to what was old. If one is to avoid merely recounting the history of technology, the assumption must be made that what was old must also be visible by way of a phenomenology of nature. Let me, then, summarize what is novel about technology.

In the beginning was the natural cosmos "full of gods." The constancy of being was expressed by the omnipresence of life, and death was symbolized as the simple transformation of life. In contrast, the modern ontology reverses the order: dead matter is the constant, and life is the exception to be explained. The means lie readily at hand, a reductive interpretative strategy that resolves life into the constituent elements of matter and motion. Vital attributes are transformed into mechanical ones. Here Copernicus and Vesalius join hands. In a universe of homogeneous matter in mathematically described motion, there is no room for life, nor for God. If the constancy of being is now expressed by the omnipresence of death, life is to be explained as a variation of lifelessness. Figuratively speaking, we join Vesalius at the dissecting table; the lived body is explained most perfectly by the corpse. Unfortunately, mechanical explanations of life hold no more intuitive plausibility than do accounts of death as the continuation of life by other means. Hence the attractiveness of dualism, from the ancient Orphic formula, that the *soma* (body) is the *sema* (tomb) of the psyche, to modern Cartesianism. But here too the difference appears: in antiquity the tomb held the psyche; now, as Jonas observed, it is empty.

# 2

# The Technological Society

One of Plato's oft-quoted heuristic tags is that a polis is man written in large letters (*Republic*, 368c–d). In the dramatic dialogue, Socrates explained to his interlocutors that, since justice was what they were looking for, it would be easier to see in the polis than in the individual. Following Voegelin, we may call this formula Plato's anthropological principle.[1] It has two aspects.

Under the first, every social or political order is an expression or a reflection of the predominant types of human beings of which it is composed. In contemporary language, the form of society reflects the predominant forms of consciousness of its membership. To exist as a collectivity capable of historical action, a society or political order is hierarchically organized or "articulated." There must exist a public representative of the society or political order whose "I will" is a binding statement but also one that represents the predominant types of human beings or the predominant forms of consciousness. Because at any one time as well as historically there exist a great variety of kinds of human beings, it is possible to distinguish the order of society or of politics in terms of the representative individual. Plato's example was that Athens was a Sophist writ large (*Republic*, 492b). In ordinary language he was describing the Athenian order by referring his interlocutors to a type of individual, the Sophist, with which they were familiar. Sophists, Plato might have said, are the politically predominant type of individual (Sophistic consciousness was the predominant consciousness) and therefore the appropriate representative of the Athenian polis.

The second aspect of Plato's anthropological principle is apparent from the contrast he made between the sophist and the phi-

47

losopher. In *kallipolis*, which was also the polis of speech, the philosopher would be the politically predominant type of individual and appropriate political representative. The contrast between the two, philosopher and Sophist, was not an empty and abstract catalogue of types but concrete, meaningful, and inevitably polemical. As was apparent from the discussion in the Introduction of the correspondence between Schutz and Voegelin, the philosopher was the true or well-ordered human type, the Sophist the false or disordered type. In Plato's language, the Sophist was the representative of the lie (*Republic*, 382a). In contemporary language, the Sophistic image of the human being distorted the truth of human existence. Adhering to this principle in a general way enables one to raise the following question: What is the form that technological consciousness takes when it is writ large? The term used by Jacques Ellul to describe this form was *technological society*.

*

Since the mid-1930s, Jacques Ellul has wondered whether the Gospel had anything to say in a technological civilization, and if so, what and how. Ellul was not a political philosopher, but he did claim that the Gospel message was founded on principles more comprehensive than those of technology. To the extent that his claim could be made good, it would bring to light the essential features or meaning of technology. His argument began from the assumption that the Christian image of the individual was more adequate to human being than was the technological image of the individual.

It may be useful at the outset to clarify a common misinterpretation of Ellul's work, namely that it has been produced by a pessimist or a fatalist. Both terms express a judgment concerning the apparent disposition of an observer or analyst of the world rather than a judgment concerning the fidelity of his account of the world. Whatever his disposition, it is the account that concerns us. Besides, it is difficult to see how one who professed to believe the Christian good news could be either pessimistic or fatalistic. In this respect, Ellul resumed Augustine's argument in favor of Christian freedom of the spirit and against "pagan" subservience to fate (*De civitate Dei*, 19.4).

Ellul's procedure has been to understand the world as clearly as possible as well as to study the Bible so as to confront the

meaning of the biblical narrative with the meaning of the technological society as it appears through his sociological analysis. The
purpose of this confrontation has been to experience directly or
immediately the irreconcilable contradiction between the Gospel
and the world.[2] Whether one interprets Ellul's theology as tending toward a gnostic dualism or toward a recovery of St. Augustine's two cities is less important than to recognize that the
experience of tension between the technological world and a
more comprehensive whole gives Ellul's writing its internal
strength and persuasive power.

The English translator of *La technique* compared it to Hegel's
*Phenomenology*. Hegel's book was an account of the historical appearance of spirit to its self-conscious fulfillment in the wise individual who was citizen of the universal and homogeneous state.
Ellul's book was a phenomenology not of spirit but of technology.
It may be read as a kind of postscript to Hegel's book insofar as
Hegel merely assumed that the dialectical overcoming of nature
as other was the precondition for the final state, whereas Ellul
has indicated that the process of technological overcoming is itself
the substance and spirit of that state, or rather, of that society.[3]
Even the most unsympathetic reader of Ellul or of this account of
Hegel cannot fail to notice the structural similarity between the
two books. Both began with the lowest or most impoverished appearance, moved dialectically and without reference to causality
to the higher or more comprehensive appearances, and culmi-
nated with an account of the fully developed historical phenomenon. In the example of Hegel, the account showed how the
particularist state divided by the natural or quasi-natural divi-
sions of sex, class, and religion became the atheist, universal, and
homogeneous state. In the example of Ellul, the account showed
how the phenomenon of machine technology developed into the
phenomenon of the technological society. The chief difference
between the two was that nothing in Ellul corresponded to the
development in Hegel of the philosopher into the wise person.
For Hegel, the image of humankind and, indeed, human existence, developed historically as the great contradictions were su-
perseded ever more comprehensively. Ellul's moderation in this
respect was a consequence of his experience that the contradiction between the Gospel and technology could not be dialectically overcome as wisdom. God, for Ellul, remained other, albeit

an Other who draws near. The Christian image of the individual was experienced as truth; the technological image as lie.

However that may be, the present concern is with Ellul's phenomenology of technology, not his theology. "We are," he said, "conditioned by something new: technological civilization."[4] As we argue in part II, being conditioned is distinct from being determined. And in any case, the determining thrust of technology for Ellul had a dialectical significance: it is both a challenge and a summons to act; by responding to the summons in action, one responds to the challenge to become free of the technological determination. That is, freedom exists not beyond the necessitousness of determination but in resistance to it. The practical question concerns the modes of resistance, and for that Ellul's book was a prelude. "How is this [resistance] to be done? I do not yet know. That is why this book is an appeal to the individual's sense of responsibility. The first step in the quest, the first act of freedom, is to become aware of necessity" (*Technological Society*, xxxiii). One becomes aware of necessity by describing its face; by describing, one gains a perspective and it appears as phenomenon not as necessity.

The technological society is not a society of robots, though the machine may be seen as its early entelechy or guiding image. The technological society is mechanical enough to incorporate machines, but spiritual enough to incorporate human beings. Technology mediates human to mechanical being but also machines to humans, and increasingly it mediates humans to one another. The evidence for this assertion is found in our daily life, especially, but not exclusively, in our urban life.

Ellul has described these several mediations in terms of changes in our milieu, where *milieu* indicated the locale from which the means of survival were drawn but also the locale that put one in danger. Accordingly, "a milieu both makes living possible and also *forces change*, obliges us to transform who we are because of problems arising from the milieu itself."[5] Ellul argued that human beings have been conditioned by three successive milieus: nature, society, and technology. The milieu of nature, and of nature only, corresponded approximately to Hegel's "sentiment-of-self" mentioned in chapter 1. The human group existed "in" nature because nature provided sustenance (hunting and gathering, and so on) but also danger (poisons, wild animals, starvation, and the like). Ellul identified this milieu with "prehistory."

Second, humans established societies to defend themselves against nature or to mediate nature to themselves. This "social" or "historical" period apparently began around 5000 B.C. Technologies were instrumental and the great problems were connected to the organization of society. Society allowed human beings to remove themselves from the immediate threats of nature, but in doing so, new difficulties were introduced, chiefly wars, "which are an invention of societies." This milieu corresponded approximately to the historically enacted Hegelian dialectic of master and slave.

The third milieu, technology, replaced society and transformed the achievements and dangers of the "historical" period into secondary problems. In this milieu, "not only are natural data and natural facts utilized by technology, mediated by technology; not only are people alienated from nature by technology; but also social relations are mediated and shaped by technology."[6] With the advent of each milieu the preceding one was transformed and subdued. Natural danger continues to exist in the technological society just as do wars, but such dangers are not seen to be fundamental. In a technological milieu, the fundamental dangers and the fundamental benefits are caused not by nature nor by society but by the technological milieu itself. This observation by Ellul has become a platitude, a stock phrase for nearly all who attempt to reflect on technology. Usually it takes the form: The problems and the promise of our age alike stem from the achievements of technology.

As a historical account of the changes leading to the establishment of the technological society, Ellul's three milieus can roundly be dismissed as theoretically and empirically untenable. This may be indicated by some close analysis. The vagueness of the natural and social, for example, recalls the early modern symbols centering on the "state of nature" developed by Hobbes and Locke. On that occasion the state of nature was introduced in order to sustain the doctrine of a social contract. The notion of a social contract has never been taken as a historical event. At most it amounted to a kind of presupposition for the development of a kind of constitutional doctrine. Moreover, the doctrine indicated that careful analysis of the soundness of the presupposition was not permitted, though judgments about the result, liberal constitutionalism, were welcome. If we play along, the argument takes the following form: Even if the state of nature never existed, and

even if there was never a social contract, it is useful to think
there once were such things because the regime that resulted is a
fine thing. Perhaps it is not actually a fine thing, but it may be
transformed into one with a little effort. Such arguments are designed to defend a civil theology and are not evidence of political
philosophy. By the same token, the regime can be attacked as an
ugly and unjust thing because it is based on a myth or a lie, because it serves the interests of the bourgeoisie, and so forth. This
is conventionally called political debate, and it usually takes place
between liberals, conservatives, and various shades of Marxists.

The inconclusiveness of such controversies is what makes them
such sport for modern intellectuals. If we insist on raising the
question of the validity or truth of the presupposition regarding
the state of nature and the social contract, we should recognize as
well that we are spoiling the fun. As is true so often with modern
disputes, they were adequately treated by political philosophers
in antiquity. Specifically, the question of the truth of the presup-
positions that presently concern us was effectively analyzed in
book 2 of the *Republic*.

The passage in question is well known but open to misinterpretation precisely for the reason that it deals with an original
"state of nature" and a "contract." Now, it is certainly true that
the terms contract (*syntheke*), and nature (*physis*), and by nature,
meaning "originally" (*pephykenai*), occur, but their meaning is
not that given them by an early modern "contract theorist," or
"possessive individualist." In book 2, the topic under discussion is
the opinions, the *doxai*, about justice that the young men, Glaucon and Adeimantus, present to Socrates for analysis. Glaucon
presents three *doxai* concerning justice and injustice, and his
brother indicates the several authoritative sources of them.

Originally (*pephykenai*), said Glaucon, people said doing injustice was good and suffering it bad. But after it was tried for a
while, it turned out that more suffered than benefited; accordingly, people agreed on a covenant or contract and just became
what the law ordained. "This, then is the genesis and nature (*ousia*) of justice; it is a mean between what is best, which is to do
injustice without punishment, and what is worst, which is to suf-
fer injustice without the power of revenge." By this account, doing justice is not loved because it is good but is respected
because of the inability of most people to act unjustly and get

away with it. A real man (*aner alethes*) would be crazy to agree to such a contract.[7]

The first thing to note is that Glaucon presents a *doxa* regarding justice and that this doxa is followed by the Socratic episteme of justice. Dramatically the doxai are presented as sources of corruption of the young; they are therefore meant to be resisted. In the passage just paraphrased, doxic justice results from a utilitarian or pragmatic calculus of advantages and disadvantages. In order to undertake it, the opiner must accept the received opinion as valid—namely that a real man would do injustice because he could get away with it. The doxa, therefore, is in no sense a theory (*theoria*) nor a philosophical or scientific account (episteme) but is, precisely, a kind of lie that is to be resisted as corrupting. More generally we can say that any "contract theory" of justice is the manifestation of a doxic soul. In Platonic anthropology, such a soul can appear at any time so the question of historical continuity need not arise. Glaucon does not present an early version of the "contract theory" and a "state of nature" because such a theory does not exist. In fact, the appearance of such a so-called theory is a symptom of the doxic state of the soul and of society. As Voegelin observed, "We must not let ourselves be overawed by the fact that famous figures in the modern history of political thought, as Hobbes or Locke, entertained a 'contract theory.' For a doxa does not become a theory through the fact that it has a great vogue among modern thinkers of renown."[8] To the names of Hobbes and Locke may be added the name of Ellul.

Ellul's account of nature and society is, therefore, theoretically untenable. It must be considered as a symptom rather than as an account of reality. Likewise, empirical evidence from early civilizations indicates that Ellul's date of 5000 B.C. is far too recent for any meaningful differentiation of "nature" and "society," however those terms are understood. The greatest omission from his scheme, which accounts for its empirical defectiveness, is that it ignores the evidence that expresses the order of prehistoric civilizations, namely the cosmological symbolism that exists, to be sure, around 5000 B.C. but that extends backward in time at least an additional twenty thousand years. Moreover, the notion of an abstract humankind moving through these three milieus is also an obsolete piece of eighteenth-century speculative doctrine. Ellul, like Husserl, was still captivated by a unilinear sense of history even though the evidence points overwhelmingly to a pluralist manifold of differentiating acts independent of one another. Or, if the model of cultural diffusion is retained, it must be placed in a much earlier context. The order of magnitude is immense, fifty thousand years, during which time nearly anything could have taken place.

*

What can be retained of Ellul's argument has no relation to the historical evolution of three milieus. His phenomenology referred only to the technological society—and even there it focused overwhelmingly on its external aspects. It would not be too misleading to use a geological metaphor and speak of levels or strata so that the natural/prehistorical and social/historical levels might be conceived as the foundation of the technological/posthistorical order.

At the same time, however, this image ignored the depth or ground beneath the "natural" stratum. The reason for the omission seems to be twofold. On the one hand, because he was concerned chiefly with externalities or phenomena, he did not address the question of symbolization of the depth or of the ground of being, nor did he concern himself with the experiences of the reality of the depth that are expressed in those symbols. A second reason is that Ellul's awareness of the depth was eclipsed or overbalanced by his response to the spirituality of Christian transcendence.[9] Whether his experience of Christian faith led him to ignore or overlook the evidence of prehistorians or the arguments of political philosophy regarding nature and society, it is impossible to say. It can be said, however, that Ellul's faith did allow him to develop a critical perspective on technology.

Ellul's language was more dogmatic than symbolic, but his meaning was tolerably clear. If the technological order constitutes the milieu of the contemporary world, then no escape from that order is possible within the world. "Only something that belongs neither to our history nor our world can do this." It is, of course, relatively easy to voice fatalistic opinions regarding the probable future course of technology, especially if those opinions are cast in sombre Heideggerian language. Ellul, however, insisted with Augustine (*De civitate Dei* 5.1–5) that fate is not a category of Christian interpretation of existence. In his words, "Something exists that technology cannot assimilate, something it will not be able to eliminate. But this can only be something transcendent, something that is absolutely not included in our world." Ellul "supposed" that the sought-for transcendent reality was biblically revealed in Christ and, on the basis of that supposition or rather, on the basis of its presumptive validity, concluded that Christian faith "gives us the outside vantage point that permits the critique of the system. This also guarantees freedom, because there is no kind of freedom that we can claim to have in relation to technology."[10] From this attitude, technology appeared simply as a phenomenon of the world, useful in some respects, not so useful in others.

The substance of Ellul's insight can be retained even if the doxic and historical speculation within which it is embedded is abandoned. Technology does constitute the specifically novel elements of contemporary life; it does mediate human beings to machines and to each other. So far as the central topic of this book is concerned, however, the essential feature of technology remains that it is a way of thinking, a form of consciousness.

It is, of course, true that the technological society began with the machine, but today the essence of the machine appears as the ideal, image, or norm of efficiency and not just as material hardware. This argument is illustrated convincingly by Jonas's account of the five "stages" that have been traversed in the genesis of the technological society. Each stage has displayed characteristic attributes that recapitulate the dialectic of increasing the richness and the perilousness of life.[11]

Coeval with the industrial revolution was the mechanical stage of scientific technology. Machines were solid; motion conformed to the laws of classical physics. The steam engine, for example, used space as a kind of fuel to produce power by exploiting heat differentials between different local regions of space. The physicists, however, did little to improve the design of engines. Moreover, the only new product was the machine itself, though modes of production were altered. And finally, the old notion that art imitates nature was not obviously refuted, though it may have been more accurate to say that art provided substitutes for nature.

Chemistry changed the terms of human intervention from using natural forces to creating new substances. The intervention into natural structures is deeper and the knowledge that permitted it is finer. Not gross relations of complex fluid volumes to heat but molecules provided the relevant units. The alliance

between scientist and technician was closer: the chemistry laboratory was a small-scale plant, the plant a large-scale lab. Whereas previous technologies, including mechanics, had been conceived and more or less deliberately intended for "the relief of
man's estate," chemistry changed the meaning of that estate. Discoveries were made before any possible use was anticipated. In
the new scientific technological context, this meant that the un-
anticipated possibilities were already imposed on the future by
research discoveries.

The third stage, electromagnetics, continued the direction of
chemistry but increased the degree of dependence on scientific
theory. Chemistry could be linked back to the village forge and
the alchemist's crucible, but electromagnetics had no existence
prior to the increasingly abstract theory that investigated its generation, distribution, and transformation. Electrical technology
was the first to be generated entirely by science. It is, moreover,
the first to be completely unintelligible in terms of concrete
sense experience, as anyone who has tried to explain to a child
what happens when you turn the light on soon enough discovers.

The fourth stage, high-tech electronics, is both more abstract
than electromagnetics and directed to a novel purpose, namely
communications, rather than necessities or motive power. Whereas all lower technologies, whatever their abstraction, could be related to natural human needs for food, clothing, shelter, mobility,
and so on, electronic artifacts are directed solely to satisfy not
natural needs but needs created by the specific form of technological society. Computers are a necessity to high-tech society but
would have been utterly useless in the days of Newton or Watt.
Communications satellites, another high-tech social necessity,
were no more than the dream of a science fiction writer a generation ago. High-tech moves more quickly than its predecessors.
Imitating nothing natural and responding to no natural necessities
it is both wholly artificial or "creative" and inherently directed at
social management. Moreover it is unobtrusive. No dark satanic
mills house either our micro- or our supercomputers, and our
satellites are invisible companions in the ether.

These four stages of intervention may be understood as having
turned back on itself the natural hierarchy of inorganic, organic,
and human being. High-tech social management, which is the
equivalent in the technological society to what justice was in an-

tiquity, depends not on the speeches and deeds of human beings, but on artificial systems and the motions of microunits of transformable matter/energy. Technological consciousness was described as the mode of the human capacity of imagination that permits limitless interventions. This same capacity to contemplate images or forms abstracted from the presence of things perceived gives us access to truth and falseness, to confirmation and disappointment. To human being alone the world appears as an undefined field for understanding. Eventually humans put themselves, or rather, images of themselves, into this same imaginative field. Human self-understanding is coeval with the desire to understand the world—if for no other reason than that humans cannot understand the world without understanding their own place in it. *This* reflective wondering, which human beings undertake about their own being, gives rise to a new and more precarious form of life: humans appear to themselves as irreducible, unique individuals whose words and deeds, whose existence, may be judged and understood in light of a public universal image: an image of the humanity of human being.

The four stages of technology indicated so far may treat human beings "as if" they were matter in motion, statistical probabilities and problems, consumers of commodities and information. That "as if" indicates the hypothetical or ontologically provisional status of the highest of high-tech interventions that was present in accounts of technological society from the start. It is a commonplace for critics or even analysts of technology to observe that, for the most part, the image in light of which the intervention is made is far from elevating. Even so, the potential of human grandeur or even of human piety has not wholly evaporated under the imaginative pressure to strive either for the promised bliss of animal existence or the purity of calculative angels, which seem to be the two major competing images of individuals' humanity in the technological society.

Before the fifth stage, which is indicated by the term *biomedical technology,* lies the transitional phenomenon of the computer. Ontologically, computers are simply artifacts. Like bronze or iron or atomic bombs, computers have helped define an age. Unlike prior technologies, however, the computer provides a whole range of additional images by which humans can understand their own activities with a minimum of metaphorical strain.[12] To say, for example, that human beings are information-processing animals or that psychotherapy is a way of debugging our minds (or souls) is less counterintuitive to "computer-literate" individuals than saying that humans are machines or political animals or stimulus-response systems.

The reason for the metaphorical familiarity of computer imagery lies in the fact that the formal logic employed abstractly by humans is the model for the discrete, finite, isolated, and rule-defined procedures undertaken in the central processing unit of a computer. The success of this form of logic has suggested to many people that it is the preferred way by which mental operations proceed. Following David Bolter we may say that "Turing's man" understands himself (or herself) by means of technological imagery derived from computers.[13] The importance of computers or of the image of humanity evoked by the symbol Turing's man is not simply that computers have furnished a powerful and persuasive imagery but that the imagery can and does sustain a successful practical activity *as well as* a meaningful human self-interpretation.

"Artificial intelligence" (AI), for example, is clearly useful and obviously produces results. Moreover, the imagery is meaningful. If, for example, computers can "think," in the sense defined by the Turing test (or, if "thinking" is what computers do), then good thinking or intelligent thinking must consist in a step-by-step process that takes place over discrete units of time.[14] AI proponents accept the validity of the Turing test and defend it with great passion. The objection to it is that it says nothing about thinking. The point to be made here is not to judge the question but to consider the implications for the self-understanding of technological consciousness or for Turing's man.[15]

To begin with, it would seem, once again, that for Turing's man there is no depth or infinite darkness that cannot eventually be illuminated by operational analysis. What is undefined or what remains as unexplained code does not indicate fortune, variety, or spontaneity but only failure to execute a performance. The self-understanding of artificial intelligence, one may say, amounts to a variation on the modern Machiavellian doctrine by which the wildness of natural being is tamed by clever artifice and enlightenment.

A crucial difference of a practical sort remains. The various spiritual expressions of modernity constitute an equally various congeries of intellectual and spiritual deformation. The deformations involved can be brought to light and analyzed by the critical intellect of a philosopher. In contrast, the purpose of AI or of computers in general is to imitate certain limited human mental processes. But what is the purpose of that? As Bolter said, we are not running short of human beings. The answer, it seems to me, lies not simply in the limited usefulness of computers or AI, but in the meaning of making machines that serve to integrate not merely our labor processes but our self-understanding.

It is for this reason that I have argued that computers and computer imagery constitute a transition to biomedical technologies. Both these later technologies and AI proceed on the assumption that imitative artifice does a "better" job than can be done by human beings as given by nature, where better is understood to mean more efficient with respect to a willed purpose, which is, of course, the defining attribute of technological consciousness.

The term *biomedical technology* in fact refers to a wide category of activity of which three general types may be distinguished according to their specific purposes. First, there are those directed at the control of human death and life, which we may assimilate to the general category of population management. Second are those directed at the control of human potential and, third, those directed at the control of human achievement. All three have introduced novel questions.

The first category is the most familiar. Recent technologies have already increased life expectancies; the promise of organ transplantation and replacement, to say nothing of research into aging as a "disease," indicates that a significant increase in maximum age expectancy is quite realistic. At the same time, however, the results have been somewhat confusing to our understanding of the difference between life and death. The same technology that enables us to prolong life, such as a respirator, induces an ambiguity regarding death. Because traditional life signs, heartbeat and respiration, for example, can be artificially maintained, then new "definitions" of death have had to be invented. For over twenty years permanent unconsciousness or "brain death" as measured by a flat electroencephalogram (EEG) reading, has been employed by medical practitioners.[16] Two questions are involved with the criteria of irreversible coma: first, if life-supporting machines are removed, the person dies by any definition. But second, if a comatose person is kept in a condition that was formerly understood to be alive, a new and separate set of questions arises. It does not take much imagination to see the great utility of these legally dead neomorts, as they have been called. Training, experimentation, testing, manufacturing, harvesting, and banking come quickly to mind.

Novel ethical questions are involved. More to the point, advances in death control generate problems at the other end of the process as well. It is clear that current technologies of birth control involve the promotion both of infertility and of fertility. Moreover, biological and cytological monitoring of fetuses holds out the promise of quality control: prenatal characteristics may be altered at present.

The potentials of fetal alteration lead directly to the second general category, genetic "medicine." Leaving aside currently remote possibilities of genetic manipulation, nuclear transplantation or cloning, and human renucleation of nonhuman cells, current diagnostic techniques can identify fetal genetic disorders. It has been estimated, for example, that in forty years and with 17 million abortions, cystic fibrosis can be eliminated. The great change introduced with genetic medicine is that it treats future individuals by acting on the basis of new definitions of health.

Whatever else may be said of these novelties, they violate the traditional ethical doctrine regarding medicine: *primum non nocere*. The first obligation is not to act but to leave things alone. I can attest from personal experience that this doctrine, which implies that most things are better by morning, is widely practiced by physicians on their own families. The third general area, which aims at controlling human achievement, is still underdeveloped. Even so, chemical and electrical control of the brain has been used to induce pleasure, control rage, and so on. Presumably the relative unpredictability of current technologies in this area reflects the comparative primitiveness of neurophysiology and neuropharmacology.

The principle, however, remains clear: with the advent of biomedical intervention arises the potential of direct alteration of human beings. We may see the difference in another way as well.

The object of biomedical technology is no longer external nature whether in gross or micro form, nor is it the management of human collectives as shepherds herd sheep. The effects of these kinds of technological interventions and actions may be understood as altering the conditions in the midst of which humans live. Biomedical technologies are distinct in that they may be applied directly to the user. Intervention is individual, not collective, and it is micro, not gross. Molecular biology and genetic information transfer promise to alter—which means, destroy—the image of humanity as, figuratively speaking, it has been handed to us. Biomedical technologies offer us the ability to take that image into our own hands and actualize it. With dead-matter technologies and collective human or administrative technologies, we retain the individual capacity to accept or reject them. We can always turn off television, disobey an administrative order, and take the consequences. Biomedical technologies hold out the promise of altering our individual capacity for choice. The great distinction between, for example, propaganda and genetic alteration of human potential is that the first is mediated by language and symbols that convey meanings that must be understood, but also misunderstood, interpreted, criticized, whereas the second kind of behavioral control does not require any mediation of speech. It operates directly on the biological material.

It is true, of course, that the actualization of these new technologies is both partial and intermittent. The principle on the basis of which this activity is undertaken, however, is widely accepted as legitimate. The conclusion to be drawn is this: The world for technological consciousness turns out to be more than an undefined field for understanding; it is also an undefined field for action. Both by contrast with classical thinking and on its own self-understanding, modern technological consciousness is new and open to the new. The technological society may be understood as the unstable institutionalization of novelty.

During the mechanical stage of technological society, hardware was the highest efficiency. Today the organization of hardware (and of software and "wetwear") is the highest efficiency. Ellul's summary description of technology as "the totality of methods rationally arrived at and having absolute efficiency (for a given stage of development) in every field of human activity" clearly indicated this (*Technological Society*, xxv). Several attributes of technology were contained in this aphorism, most notably the triumph of method over purpose or limit and the necessity of efficiency, which is the substantive content of method. Technology is the quest for the one best way. The commonsense question, The one best way of *doing what?* is misleading because the first answer to it is, Anything; the second one is, Everything. The only principle of technology is efficient ordering. Efficient ordering, not fixed purpose, is its guiding image. The result of action in pursuit of efficient ordering is the technological society. The goals according to which the ordering is undertaken, being the product of changing human will, will themselves vary over time and may, indeed, conflict at any one time without in any way challenging the overall technological purpose of society.

In a later work, Ellul referred to the technological system and explained that the later term was superior to the earlier because it directly emphasized the importance of change within the frame of technology.[17] The importance of *system* in describing technology lay in the implication that the reality to which the term referred was an ensemble of mutually integrated elements. Every element in the system implied every other so that a change in one would affect the whole and a change in the whole would have consequences for the integrated parts.

Ellul described modern technology, the limitless multiplication of efficient means, under eight characteristics:

1. The most obvious is calculative rationality. Technology enforces norms of logical organization on sponteneity and creativity by accounting in principle for all activity and by doing so in terms of logic.

2. Technology is artificial in the sense that the meaning of the natural order does not appear on its own within it but is destroyed and reproduced as subordinate. Ellul's example, which was also used by Heidegger, is of a hydroelectric dam that takes a waterfall and leads it into a conduit to produce energy.

3. Technical choices are automatic or self-directing. No one rationally chooses the fifth-best way, so that following the logic of technology ensures human contentment. The condition for this contentment is the reductive transformation of what are initially nontechnological components, such as human beings, into technological ones, such as information processors. The technological society seeks to fulfill the goal of contentment.

4. The automatic elimination of inefficiency means two things: that technological progress is irreversible within any specific society and that it tends to act according to geometric, not arith-

metic, progression. This fourth attribute Ellul called *self-augmentation*. The irreversibility or self-augmenting attribute most clearly expresses the meaning of technological consciousness. Since for technological consciousness, there are no naturally ordered objects, no otherness to nature, it encounters nothing that would enable it to become self-conscious. That is, technological consciousness can never know itself as a form of consciousness because it does not distinguish itself from what it is not. This is why technological improvements call for even more improvements because they will result in greater efficiencies, but improvements that lead to problems and difficulties call for more improvements as well, this time to dissolve the problems and difficulties. In short, technological consciousness is incapable of transcending itself.

5. To say that technology is self-augmenting implies that there is a "self" or at least an entity that augments. It does not mean that there is a presiding genius that directs this entity but only that it forms a whole, a continuous ordering of phenomena within a context that is not the product of any of them. The whole is its use, not the product of its use (because every product becomes a means to further use). The fifth attribute, then, is that technology, and therewith the technological society, expresses a single meaning. Despite secondary variations, the constituent elements of technology "are ontologically tied together; in it, use is inseparable from being" (*Technological Society*, 95). Psychological technologies, for example, have the purpose of adjusting humans to the technological society and so are as much a part of it as telephone repairpersons and TV evangelists. One may reverse the proposition: the technological society is one that requires psychological technicians to adjust the human population to its purposes. Moreover, because technology *is* its use, it makes no sense to distinguish good and bad uses of technology, only more or less efficient uses. Indeed, technology is so far beyond good and evil that if the technician ever stopped to consider those old questions his or her efficiency would be immediately impaired. Technology, to recall Voegelin's term, is a *cosmion*, a little world of meaning.

6. Whatever else a cosmion is, it hangs together. Self-augmentation and wholeness are interdependent: technical problems lead to solutions, which throw up unforeseen difficulties, which demand solutions, and so on. As the technological society

grows more complex, the sixth attribute appears: technologies are
interlinked. The example of psychology as a technology to adjust
humans to the technological society illustrates this. In addition, a
kind of hierarchy of technologies forms. Hardware technologies
from mechanics to electronics require organizational technologies
if they are to be efficiently produced and employed. Commercial,
industrial, and financial organizations constitute the response to
this challenge to efficiency. The physical organization of these
functions, for example, required a new technology, urban planning, with several subordinate operations such as police, fire-
fighting, sewage control, and amusement. Just beyond the
horizon one can anticipate new technologies of population management requiring demographic expectations to be translated into
appropriate abortion and euthanasia rates. A bit further ahead
the effective intervention of various biomedical technologies may
be anticipated. Coordinating all these technologies, practicing
the technology of technologies or, in Heidegger's language, practicing the art of the steersman, cybernetics, is the state. In addition to coordinating these interlinked technologies, the state
introduced its own, which Ellul called propaganda. What began
as material technologies in service to a productive economy
ended with intellectual technologies of adjustment and normal-
ization. All technologies are dialectically interlinked constituents
of the technological society.

7. Technology expands geographically and by expanding tends to
homogenize. These two attributes Ellul called the universalism of
technology. Technological ecumenism does not require "Westernization" or civilization along European lines. The productivity
of Pacific rim countries indicates there is no need for a similar
social context for the technological society to flourish. Moreover,
the spread of technology is attained as easily by "immoral" means
such as war and conquest as by "moral" ones such as capitalist or
communist foreign or fraternal aid. However accomplished, the
consequence is the dissociation of tradition as a configuration of
meaning and its replacement by the aggregation of individuals as
elements of a qualitatively homogeneous order. Efficiency demands homogeneity; expansive efficiency is ecumenic. What differences remain are idiosyncracies subordinate to technological
homogeneity: a preference for vodka over scotch, sushi over
pizza. The true citizen of the technological ecumene would dine
and drink indifferently from the world's produce.

8. Because technology is its use and because the regulative norm of use is expanding efficiency, the most essential feature of technology, the feature that sustains its expansiveness, is autonomy. The technological society is autonomous with respect to economics and politics as well as with respect to social conditions generally; indeed technology elicits or demands economic, political, and social change in order to function according to its own imperatives. Several implications are contained in this last attribute. Autonomy means technology is unlimited by moral considerations. Or rather, the technological society has become the arbiter of what is moral, namely what is efficient. Autonomy means the replacement of human spontaneity, which appears as unpredictability or error, with organization. The technological society aims at a regime of no surprises, which is evidence, precisely, of contentment.

These eight attributes or characteristics of the technological society are mutually supportive. Two features of this complex deserve our special attention because of their specifically political importance, namely the social significance of technological consciousness and its contemporary generative technology, propaganda.

It has become a platitude to observe that, as technology has become increasingly realized or perfected, human existence has become an object for technological use. The most spectacular examples would include the deep but fine interventions of biomedical technologies into the sources and condition of life and of death but also such otherwise bizarre activities as leisure management and self-help exercises. What endows these practices with a single meaning is that they express a certain way of apprehending reality and of acting in the world. We strive, in technological society, to live by objective truth or to participate in it. The act of participating in such a truth imparts to the participant a specific but common attitude toward reality, a common consciousness that expresses a common image of the human being as an object among objects.

In Hegelian language, the content of technological consciousness is a kind of freedom. The subjective certainty of having overcome the realm of natural necessity has resulted from the induction of natural meaning through the conduit of technology. Having ceased to be conditioned by nature, technological consciousness identifies its new condition with freedom. The technology that operates on this consciousness in order to sustain it is propaganda. Included under the category of propaganda are the psychologists mentioned earlier, but also educators, counselors, social workers, advertisers, and state-directed managers of public opinion or "opinion leaders." The combination of organization with pedagogy or therapy aims to normalize the deviant and to mobilize the enthusiasm of the normal. Propaganda has little relation to repression or brainwashing; rather it refers to technologies of eliciting and directing active, voluntary participation in the technological society, which is the intramundane truth, the revealed reality of the present. It is concerned less with attitudes than with behavior; if behavior is modified by propaganda, it is assumed that consciousness will conform to the new reality. If it does not, then more strenuous technologies must be directed to the problem. Specifically, therapeutic technologies can be brought to bear on consciousnesses that do not conform to reality. After all, a consciousness that does not conform to reality is certainly not normal and quite possibly mad.

The central institutions in the propaganda organization are the media of mass communication. The creation of an environment of meaning by mediating the individual to the technological society enables political opinion leaders to communicate to individuals on a mass scale. Reciprocally, individuals experience a sense of participation in the truth of public opinion. There is no refinement of private opinion through debate and exchange of views but only shifts in public opinion that may or may not be managed by opinion leaders. There is no implication of a conspiracy or of direction by a hidden power elite; propaganda, by this reading, is unobtrusive but total and continuous. Indeed, as was indicated earlier, the self-interpretation of technological society is all the more effective for being unself-conscious. A measure of its effectiveness is indicated in the widespread opinion that technology can be used for good or evil when in fact it is beyond good and evil, which is what is meant by the observation that technology is its use.

A concluding implication is that the technological form of politics is bureaucracy. Rational specialization of tasks, including opinion leadership, is required for efficiency. When individuals join the government or a political party they are gradually or quickly transformed into administrators. Parties and the government are correspondingly decentralized into a diffuse but panoptic gaze, a quiet monitoring, the details of which may be left to minor technicians who operate opinion polling enterprises.

\*

Ellul has indicated that the technological order should be analyzed as a pragmatic phenomenon embodying certain advantages and disadvantages for everyday life. According to him, technology is autonomous, which means that the possibility of external action to deflect its course is limited, and it is self-augmenting, which means that external intervention must rely on the instruments of technology in order to be effective, which in turn means that such intervention is not really external. Taking just these two attributes and understanding them as constituent elements of a system, Ellul wondered whether there existed any feedback mechanism by which the system is regulated. He concluded that there was none. Thus, if technological activity is responsible for certain harmful or undesirable results, a properly constituted feedback mechanism would direct our attention to the cause, which could then be acted on directly. Instead, these undesirable consequences are the occasion for additional technological activity. "Ecology," wrote Evernden, "has become a branch of classical physics."[18] If acid rain, for example, is causing fish to die in lakes because acidification removes a vital link in the food chain, the modern technological response would not be to reduce sulfur emissions but to breed plants and fish that could survive in acidic lakes. Technology is not dismantled by these procedures but is augmented. Moreover, one may expect that the new plants and fish will cause additional problems, though we can hardly anticipate what they might be. New problems, however, constitute new opportunities for technological activity. It is for this reason that the language of fate retains some plausibility.

Despite our ignorance of detailed consequences, Ellul considered one thing certain: "the difference and opposition between the development of the technological system on the one hand and society and human beings on the other."[19] The difference between society and technology was implied by Ellul's hypothetical account of human historical development. The conflict between technological and human being, however, was more fundamental. "Human beings," Ellul said, "have an irrational element," which he identified with spontaneity, that made them "unfit" for technology. In consequence, there exists a contradiction between the technological system and the technological society. What one finds, therefore, "is a technological order, but *within* a growing chaos."[20] It is clear enough that order in the sense of organization can be and has been provided by the system. If that order exists within a growing chaos, the chaos must come from the context within which the technological system is located, namely the technological society. Considered as a society, Ellul said, even the technological society is a source of spontaneity or "chaos." And yet, the entelechy of the technological society, considered not as a society but as an organization, is to extinguish human spontaneity in favor of contentment. More radically, it is to displace the social by the system, even at the cost of the social. To the extent that the system induces "chaos" in the society the technological society is inherently unstable, which is another way of expressing the paradox of institutionalized novelty. Insofar as technology tends to become a system, it extinguishes spontaneity; insofar as it remains a kind of society, it sustains spontaneity. Spontaneity, however, appears as "chaos" to the technological system. Hence the instability.

An alternative way to characterize the topic of the relationship of humans to technology is to stress not human irrationality or spontaneity but, on the contrary, human reason. To do so it is necessary to clarify the relationship between technology and reason.

One might begin by distinguishing between two aspects of Western rationality, namely calculative, technical, or pragmatic reason, on the one hand, and noetic reason on the other. Technical-pragmatic reason guides rational action in the sciences of the external world of nature, in technological developments, and, in general, in the efficient and calculative coordination of means and ends. Noetic reason guides rational action in the sciences of human, society, and history, and in the formation or development of the psyche and of social order. Technical-pragmatic rationality is an absolute minimal requirement for the existence of a social or political order, however defective it might be by the criteria of noetic rationality. More specifically, an ideological sectarian government that has effectively destroyed the public visibility of noetic reason is entirely capable of constructing an industrial, technological society. On the other hand, a highly developed sense of noetic rationality within a community does not necessarily entail the growth of technological activity. The Soviet Union might serve as an example of the first kind of emphasis and the Athens of Plato the second.

Having made the distinction, one must immediately add that the separation is not absolute and the realm of technical-pragmatic reason is in fact not autonomous. Recalling the principles discussed in the introductory chapter of this study, technical-pragmatic reason is part of human existence that, in turn, includes noetic reason. The claim to autonomy, which, as Ellul has shown, is a major assumption of technology, amounts to a desire to suppress noetic reason. But noetic reason is what orders the psyche; if it is suppressed, as we know from classical political philosophy, the soul becomes governed by the irrationality of the passions. Because noetic and technical-pragmatic reason are not autonomous, the efficiency of the latter, which coordinates ends and means, will invariably be impaired as the passions (or will) choose ends that cannot be realized, that are self-defeating, and so on. The pursuit of impossible goals does not lend itself to the rational coordination of means. The means will therefore appear inefficient. The usual response to such a situation is not to question the impossibility of the goals but to become even more emphatic about the means, which in turn makes matters worse.

The self-destructive nature of this dialectic has been fully actualized only on the occasion of the establishment of totalitarian regimes. In the technological society, three factors have combined to ensure the triumph of pragmatic reason. The first is a direct consequence of industrialism: the division of labor, the socialization of labor, and the resultant interdependence of members of society have combined to ensure the importance of administrative organization. Accordingly, class membership, ownership of the means of production, and planning have become technical pragmatic questions. Second, the proliferation of nuclear weapons has imposed the necessity of preventing mutual destruction by those possessing them. It is often worthwhile pointing out that nuclear weapons have been used only once in war. Third, these two factors have diminished somewhat the credibility of ideological fantasies. This is not to say that various bureaucratic tyrannies do not rely on ideological rhetoric to justify their own actions at least to themselves, nor is it to overlook the enormous amount of ideological opinion that goes by the name of criticism in nontyrannical regimes; it is to say that even the most ideologically disordered Eastern tyrant or Western intellectual must eventually confront the sobering realities of pragmatic constraints imposed by technology. Recent events in the Soviet empire, interpreted as *perestroika* and *glasnost* and *novoye myshleniye*, illustrate this point clearly enough.

It is proper to conclude, therefore, that the technological society has preserved a minimal requirement of reason, namely technical-pragmatic reason, from wholesale destruction by ideological irrationality. Because the technological society has developed within the context of Western rationality, which includes noetic as well as calculative reason, it is possible to maintain a critical distance with respect to technology equivalent to that which Ellul discovered in his Christian faith. Considering that Christianity has at least as much relation to the formation of the soul as noetic reason, this is perhaps no great surprise.

# 3
# Phenomenalism

The discussion of the technological phenomenon has proceeded on the assumption that a description of appearances
would be adequate to the reality indicated by the term *technology*. It is for this reason that we began with a discussion of phenomenology. In the course of this discussion it became clear that,
insofar as phenomenology also implied an account of consciousness, the Husserlian program would have to be modified in a decisive way: consciousness did not mean only consciousness of
phenomena. On the contrary, the Husserlian intentionality of
consciousness was one subordinate mode of consciousness. The
more comprehensive mode was indicated by the description of
human consciousness as an event within reality. A particular concrete consciousness is aware that it is part of the reality of which
it is conscious; that awareness also carried with it an awareness
that reality is not exhausted by appearance. The venerable philosophical term *substance* and equivalent or near-equivalent terms
such as *nature, essence,* or *meaning* were used to indicate nonphenomenal reality, that is, reality experienced as being expressed through appearance. Alternatively one may say that
phenomena are transparent for substantive reality.

Chapter 2 discussed historical changes introduced by technological activities and novelties posed to human understanding by
those changes. The form of this account was narrative and descriptive rather than analytic. Notwithstanding remarks intended
to indicate the limits of Ellul's account, the descriptive focus has
meant that our concern has been with the surface, with appearance. However, just as it was necessary, in order to understand
Husserlian phenomenology to move the argument beyond the

"apodictic horizon" to a more comprehensive understanding of consciousness, so it was necessary, in order to understand the significance of technical-pragmatic rationality, to refer to the more comprehensive experience indicated by the term *noetic rationality*. This chapter concludes the discussion of the technical phenomenon with some reflections not on technology but on phenomenalism. The intention of the argument is to indicate the limitations of the discussion to this point but also to make explicit a heretofore unspecified assumption that undergirds the technological phenomenon.

*

By phenomenalism is meant the preoccupation with the phenomenal realities of the world and a corresponding atrophy of attention to the substantive realities of human beings, society, history, God, and the world.[1] At the extreme, phenomenalism indicates an exclusive preoccupation with phenomena and a lack of awareness of substance. The linguistic and historical complications associated with the use of this term may be indicated briefly. Historically, phenomenalism has been associated with scientism, by which, following Hayek and Voegelin, we mean the opinion that mathematized science is the model science to which all others must conform.[2] Moreover the whole question of phenomenalism and scientism has frequently been identified as materialism. The reason for this identification may be found in the magnificent achievements of the science of material phenomena, namely physics. The distinction between substance and phenomena with respect to the science of physics is indicated by the observation that, with physics, the substance for which the phenomena have been substituted is matter.

The distinction between phenomena and substance has been made with unsurpassed clarity by Pierre Duhem.[3] There are, he said, two ways of answering the question, What is the object or aim of theoretical physics or of physical theory or, more simply still, of physics? The first, he said, is to explain a group of theoretically established laws. By "explain" he meant "to strip reality of the appearances covering it like a veil, in order to see the bare reality itself." What the physicist observes is physical phenomena, but such observation "does not put us into relation with the reality hidden under the sensible appearances, but enables us to apprehend the sensible appearances in a particular and concrete form." Duhem used the example of music, which appears to our sense of hearing and is elaborated by common sense in terms of pitch, octave, chord, and so on. That account may be contrasted with acoustic theory, which explains our commonsense notions in terms of the amplitude and frequency of periodic vibratory motions. In turn, these vibratory motions can be sensed with our fingers. Most of the time, however, physical laws cannot be sensed and so cannot be confirmed with the experiential certainty of acoustics. They are, accordingly, hypothetical or abstract.

Several implications follow from this conclusion that bear on the question of interpretation of observation.[4] First, in order to judge whether any set of propositions in fact constitutes a physical theory, one must ask whether the logic connecting them expresses (in hypothetical or abstract form) the real composition of matter or merely represents a universalization of perceived phenomenal properties. Only the former alternative can be a physical theory in this first sense because it expresses a reality distinct from appearances. Science, therefore, necessarily employs a reductive hermeneutic of suspicion.[5] But in order for the work of suspicious scientists to make sense, they must affirm that the reality they seek is distinct from appearances that are revealed to our perceptions. The second consequence, therefore, is that this required affirmation is external to the procedures of experimentation. Indeed, in this context experimentation amounts to a means of obtaining sense experience, as, for example, readings that can be observed on instruments.

Having granted that the purpose of experimentation is to obtain a certain kind of sense experience that, in turn, expresses, or is transparent for, a distinct reality to be explained, "it is impossible to recognize that we have reached such an explanation until we have answered this next question: What is the nature of the elements that constitute material reality?" Now, the means to answer that question transcends the methods of physics, as was also true of the affirmation of a reality distinct from appearance. The resolution of such questions is the aim or object not of physics but of a science beyond or after physics, literally of a metaphysics. "Therefore," Duhem concluded, "if the aim of physical theories is to explain experimental laws, theoretical physics is not autonomous science; it is subordinate to metaphysics."[6] If that is so, physical theory does not attain "a form to which the greatest number of minds can give their assent." Rather, "we limit its acceptance to those who acknowledge the philosophy [that is, the metaphysics] it insists on."[7]

Given the well-known disagreements among philosophers or metaphysicians for a science that, in principle, seeks universal agreement, the dependence of physics on metaphysics would seem to be an insuperable objection to universality. Accordingly, one might anticipate encountering a wide range of physics dependent for its validity on a wide range of metaphysics. And, indeed, historically there have existed a Platonic physics, an Aristotelean physics, a Thomistic physics, a Newtonian physics, and so on. More broadly, terms such as *Aristotelean science, Christian science,* and *Newtonian science* have been employed to describe a class of experienced realities.

In the face of this variation, Duhem proposed a second account of the object or aim of physics that was autonomous or independent of metaphysics. By this second alternative, a physical theory would not be an explanation but "a system of mathematical propositions, deduced from a small number of principles, which aim to represent as simply, as completely, and as exactly as possible a set of experimental laws."[8] The balance of Duhem's book was devoted to the elaboration of the implications of such an understanding of the aim or object of physics. The present concern, however, is with the criteria used to distinguish physics from metaphysics.

According to Duhem the distinction has existed since antiquity.[9] "The Greeks," he said, "were acquainted, properly speaking, with only one physical theory, the theory of celestial motions." In their discussions of the theory of the motions of the stars, they "clearly distinguished" between "what belongs to the physicist—we should say today the metaphysician—and to the astronomer." It was up to physicists (or metaphysicians) to say what "the real motions of the stars are" on the basis of their cosmology. "The astronomer, on the other hand, must not be concerned whether the motions he represented were real or fictitious; their sole object was to represent exactly the *relative* displacements of the heavenly bodies."[10] In terms of the distinction between substance and phenomena, the astronomer was concerned with phe-

nomena and the physicist with substance. The relative motion of
the heavenly bodies required a cosmology to make sense of that
motion.

Duhem's claim[11] that the distinction was unanimously maintained until the fourteenth century has been questioned by contemporary historians.[12] It remains true, however, that this
distinction, or a distinction very much like it, recurs among analysts of scientific operations. And so, for example, one finds
Heiko Oberman making the following observation: "The goal of
the natural sciences," he wrote, "is validity in the sense of *accu-
racy*, whereas that of the humanities, particularly of philosophy
and theology, is validity in the sense of *truth*."[13] More simply
still, Bush has distinguished the metaphysicists' question,
"Why?" from the physicists' question, "How?"[14] It is the burden
of the present discussion to indicate that a denial of these kinds of
distinctions was of fundamental importance to the establishment
of phenomenalist science and thereby to the development of
modern technology.

It is of more than historical importance to uncover the reasons
why this venerable distinction was eclipsed, forgotten, or overcome. In Duhem's view physics "does not grasp the reality of
things; it is limited to representing observable appearances by
signs and symbols."[15] In the language favored by Duhem, it is
"positivist."[16] It does not follow that Duhem was a positivist in
any sense other than his understanding of the aim and structure
of physics. Indeed, he was a Christian and in no sense a sectarian
"positivist" in the Comtean sense.[17] His "positivist" physics followed from his acceptance of the autonomy of physics with respect to metaphysics and theology. Gurwitsch has made the
identical argument using phenomenological language. Following
Husserl, he argued, "The mathematical conception of nature
is . . . not essential to the human mind." The question of
whether nature is or is not mathematical should be replaced by
the Duhemian notion "Nature lends itself to mathematization."
Duhem, moreover, would agree with the phenomenological conclusion: "The resulting universe is the product of a methodological procedure, a tissue of ideas (*Ideenkleid*), which must never be
mistaken for reality itself. Reality is, and always remains, the life-
world, no matter how vast the possibilities of systematization and

prediction that have been opened up by the development of science of the Galilean style."[18]

It follows from this understanding of physics that metaphysics, or better, first philosophy, has as *its* aim and object the knowledge of essence or substance insofar as it is the ground or "cause" of phenomena and the basis of laws. As with the term *substance*, cause is also a philosophical concept of great antiquity. A medieval commonplace declared, "scientia est cognitio per causas." Scientific knowledge implied knowing that something was as it was because it could not be otherwise; it could not be otherwise because of what caused it to be so. This Aristotelean formulation was of historical importance for the development of modern science after the recovery of the *Posterior Analytics*.[19] For Aristotle, causes are explanatory factors that permit scientific accounts (*epistemai*). Within science, Aristotle distinguished knowledge of facts from knowledge of reasoned facts, with the latter's being the more scientific because it accounts for why the fact is as it is.[20]

Aristotle admitted four types of cause, named by medieval scholars as formal, material, efficient, and final. The details of Aristotle's argument[21] are less important than the principle that scientific methodology can be applied to the whole range of beings found in the world, including human consciousness, and thereby the ground of the being of the world and the experience of the reality beyond even that being. As with the earlier analysis of the confining "apodictic horizon" of Husserl, the process of consciousness transcending what is given to it, a process of searching for more comprehensive meaning, cannot be limited beforehand.

In the example of Aristotle, this did not mean that mathematics was eliminated from physics. On the contrary, Aristotle employed mathematical arguments in the *Physics*, in *On the Heavens*, and in the *Meteorology*. In the latter work in particular, Aristotle provided a very "modern" treatment of the phenomenon of the rainbow. Whether what modern physicists recognize as Aristotle's "mathematics" would be so recognized by him may be doubted.[22] Indeed, Aristotle often indicated that the direct application of mathematics to physics amounted to a kind of "category error." Even in the *Meteorology*, he concluded the work with the words, "We know the cause and the nature [or substance] of a thing when we understand either the material or formal cause of its generation and its destruction, or best of all when we know both, and also its efficient cause."[23] No mention is made here of a final cause as a source of explanatory knowledge of material being because, he said, "the final cause is least obvious where matter predominates."[24]

The conclusion to be drawn is this: any account of nature, of natural being, of being simply, will consider phenomenal being but also substantive being, being that might properly be treated by mathematics and being, such as human being, for which distinctive nonmathematical but coherent and, in Aristotle's sense, scientific accounts are required. Likewise a specific language is required to consider the being that is symbolized as being beyond being.[25] Traditionally, philosophers and metaphysicians have symbolized their experience of the distinctiveness of the modes of being by means of a hierarchy. The terms have varied, but the structure of the argument indicates that what is given to the senses is one kind of reality and what is suprasensory is not only another kind of reality but one that is more real, more true, more meaningful. In the language we have been using, substance is not only other than phenomena: it is above and beyond phenomena in the sense of being more true, more real, and more meaningful.

Traditionally, that is, substance and phenomena (or alternative but equivalent terms) have been linked as a distinction essential to thinking philosophically. Nietzsche provided a gloss on his description of the madman who announced the murder of God by indicating that the term *God* was equivalent to the metaphysician's notion of substance, reality, or, to use his term, the true world. The metaphorical murder of God, that is, was equivalent to the abolition of the true world, what we have called substance. "We have abolished the true world. What has remained? The apparent one, perhaps? Oh no! With the true world we have also abolished the apparent one!"[26] Likewise, Democritus's dialogue between the mind and the senses indicated the unfortunate results when the true world or substance abolished the apparent world or phenomena. Sense experience, said the mind, is mere appearance and convention (sweet and bitter, hot and cold), but by true nature there are only atoms and void; the senses replied: "Wretched mind! Do you who get what is trustworthy [*tas pisteis*, evidence] from us yet try to overthrow us? To overthrow

us will be your downfall."[27] In this respect at least, Nietzsche and
Democritus agreed: if either the sensory phenomenal world or
the suprasensory substantive world is imaginatively abolished,
the distinction between the two is also eliminated and, as Hannah Arendt observed, "The whole framework of reference in
which our thinking was accustomed to orient itself breaks down.
In these terms, nothing seems to make sense any more."[28]

*

The origin of phenomenalism may be traced to the latter half
of the sixteenth century. Having said that, however, one must
quickly add by way of qualification that what is involved is a subtle and complex series of shifts in the cultural atmosphere or climate of opinion. These meteorological metaphors are intended to
indicate a change in sentiment and tone rather than the creation
of a new systematic doctrine of the human being, society, God,
and the world. The new doctrinal form, namely ideology, was not
achieved until the Enlightenment.[29] However, the theoretical or
philosophical issues involved were systematically debated three
centuries earlier.

Several well-known historical events conditioned the aforementioned shifts. First, the replacement of the medieval church with
a plurality of churches entailed a plurality of responses: mysticism, toleration, skepticism, indifference, agnosticism. Second,
the humanist recovery of the learning of classical antiquity immediately introduced the problem of a plurality of civilizations and
likewise stimulated several responses to the new knowledge. On
the one hand, antiquity might be mobilized and deployed against
the disintegrating complex of Christianity, but on the other, it
might be rejected as the dead hand of the past. Third, the recovery of ancient texts led to the famous advancement of learning,
which at its best meant a kind of Bergsonian opening of the soul
to the full amplitude of reality experienced, but also to an exclusion or spiritual closure with the acceptance of Hellenistic astrology as an important element in an unstable astrological-Christian
syncretistic creed. Fourth, and in reaction to this syncretism, one
finds protestations in the name of Christian spirituality on the
one hand and of the secular human dignity on the other.

Despite the complexity of these patterns, and bearing in mind
the focus of this study, a point of convergence appears to exist in
the notion that human being is the origin of meaning in the

world, that the existence of meaning in the world owes its being to having been evoked by humans. The movement from the closed cosmos to the infinite universe was not merely an astronomical hypothesis. It contained as well the rejection of a stable world of divine creation and of a providential history leading to the eschatological transformations of the last days. For these evocations of medieval Christianity were substituted the spatial extension of the universe as the projection of the human mind and the temporal extension of history as an intramundane process conditioned by the same natural forces that operate on individual humans. On their own terms, these evocations were called discoveries, the substitution of truth for untruth, reason for superstition. Retrospectively, they seemed to moderns to be the first victory over the ancients.

The initial event that cast grave doubts on the providential course of history was the rise to power of the Osmanli Turks. Beginning with the settlements of the midfourteenth century, continuing through the disastrous defeat of the Western Crusaders at Nicopolis in 1396, to the conquest of Constantinople in 1453 and the seige of Vienna in 1529, the advance of the Turkish threat was interrupted only by the conquests of Timur the Lame, or Tamerlane. By comparison to the contemporary European battles of the Hundred Years War as well as to those famous battles of antiquity, the victories of the Turks were grandiose and magnificent. The heroism of him who defeated the Turks appeared to the Europeans as of a different order entirely. Moreover, since to the Europeans Timur seemed to have emerged from nowhere, it was relatively easy to evoke his name as an index of demonic power that might erupt mysteriously in history and vanish just as mysteriously.[30] Of equal importance to the appearance of demonic power was the invocation of the goddess Fortuna to explain these events.[31] This Hellenistic divinity, prominent in Polybius, evoked the notion of historical rhythms that are themselves subrhythms of the cosmic order.

At the same time as the Western European powers were expanding exuberantly from the Atlantic seaboard, the shadow of the Eastern menace began to plague the humanist scholars. They found the same conflict of East and West present in the opening paragraphs of book 1 of Herodotus's *History*. The combination of Western expansive optimism and pessimistic anxieties about the

threat from the East has not yet been removed from popular consciousness. The first element in the shift, then, consisted in the
alteration of the providential course of history.

The addition of demonic interruptions of providential history
or of the introduction of Fortuna to the list of interpretative tools
available to historiographers did not leave the inherited Christian
accounts unmolested. Specifically, political events, of which the
appearance of Timur was a spectacular example, were interpreted
in light of natural or cosmic rhythms. Louis LeRoy, "one of the
most intelligent commonplace minds of his day," for example, argued in the late sixteenth century, that new eras were founded by
great conquerors: Alexander, Caesar, and Tamerlane.[32] These
conquests were regularly followed by civilizational flowering in
the form of inventions (LeRoy was impressed with gunpowder,
the mariner's compass, and the printing press) and learning (here
LeRoy compared Petrarch to Hercules, and especially to his
cleaning of the Augean stables). Whatever else was implied—certainly a low opinion of the products of scholastic philosophy—the
era of Christ was no longer the great division of history.

Precisely because LeRoy was both intelligent and commonplace, his views may be taken as widely diffused among the
educated humanists of his day. The restoration of ancient learning included a revival of Hellenistic cosmology and especially
of astrology.[33] In the early reaction to astrology or to the
astrological-Christian syncretism, the several issues involved were
clarified. A century before LeRoy, both Pico della Mirandola and
Savonarola protested, the one in the name of the secular dignity
of humankind, the other in the name of Christian spirituality. Savonarola's criticism is more important for present purposes because it focused on the decisive issue, the nature of nature. For
the "orthodox" Christian, nature was closed within itself; the
meaning of its externality included the drama neither of the fall
and redemption of the individual soul nor of humankind. In contrast, the nature that was evoked to account for historical influences on individuals was capable of causally altering both the
human body and its spirit. This contrast between Christian "or-
thodoxy" and various shades of heterodoxy is somewhat over-
drawn.[34] The direction of the understanding of nature, however,
was toward a kind of respiritualization, to be followed by a second

despiritualization in the eighteenth century along with an even more radical anti-Christian intellectual movement.

As a postscript to this sketch of the historical context in which phenomenalism originated, we might consider the attitude of the church. By the late sixteenth century astrologers were no longer welcome at the Vatican. In 1586, a *Constitution* was published "against the exercise of the arts of judicial astrology." Judicial astrology, as distinct from natural astrology (which was more like the practical lore of the *Farmer's Almanac*), was condemned because God kept human beings ignorant of the future in order to restrain their pride and ensure proper veneration of the divine majesty. Accordingly, if people nevertheless insisted on prying into the future, this was evidence not of the power of astrology but of aid by demons who, because of their refined intelligence, and unlike humans, were capable of such foresight. Bodin made a similar argument in his *Démonomanie* (1581). Moreover, Augustine had indicated another objection: if celestial phenomena could be reliably predicted, they must be assumed to be of unalterable regularity. But this must mean either that God has freely limited His ability or that miracles are impossible. Astrology, thus, contained an implicit challenge to divine omnipotence.[35] A second *Constitution*, published in 1631, condemned judicial astrology used to predict the deaths of popes and other eminent persons. In addition to the reasons given in 1586, the *Constitution* of 1631 added that such predictions caused needless anxiety to princes and might arouse an unstable public to turbulent actions. Similar objections regarding the effects of publishing public opinion polls during the course of an election campaign have been raised.[36]

The foregoing remarks indicate the general complex of sentiments and ideas that constitute the context within which the new cosmologies, associated with the famous sixteenth- and seventeenth-century astronomers, were developed. To reiterate: the Christian providential meaning of history, which stretched from the creation of the world to the end of days, was undermined by a recrudescence of ancient fatalism based on various myths of nature. More specifically, the recovery of ancient sources resulted in the flowering of astrological speculation. The process by which astronomy and phenomenal science disengaged themselves from the humanist understanding of nature began with the publication of Copernicus's great book, *De Revolutionibus Orbium Colestium*, in 1543. Accordingly, this inquiry into the genesis of phenomenalism must include an account of the significance of Copernicus's cosmology and of the background to his great achievement.

*

Two elements may be distinguished in Copernicus's evocation of a heliocentric cosmos. First is the desire to simplify the assumptions regarding the observations of the sky. Second is the choice of the heliocentric model to do so. Now, the second factor existed as an option in antiquity and was familiar to any well-educated "humanist gentleman."[37] And, indeed, the shell of the Copernican cosmos was still the Hellenic sphere of the fixed stars. Accordingly, attention to the first component, the desire for simplicity, indicates the chief importance of the new evocation.

The meaning of simplicity, however, is not simple. To begin with, Copernicus's method of calculation in fact led to results that were no more accurate predictors than were Ptolemy's. Second, because he wished to retain a circular model of planetary orbits, the complexity of his calculations equaled that of the Ptolemaic model and some operations were of greater complexity.[38] Third, there is no contemporary evidence that the question of comparative calculative simplicity ever arose.[39] The simplification achieved by Copernicus was, in any event, not calculative but conceptual. As Gingerich argued, a cosmology of "fixed symmetry" (*certam symmetriam*) unified the scales of the planetary orbits, which indeed entailed a great simplification over Ptolemy's model. This was, he said, "a new cosmological vision, a grand aesthetic view of the structure of the Universe."[40] Copernicus's simplification was important for our purposes because the resulting model could easily be seen as real.

The next question is to determine the nature of this reality. Osiander's foreword to *De Revolutionibus* restated the traditional doctrine regarding hypotheses as a means to save the phenomena.[41] But as numerous historians have pointed out, *De Revolutionibus* saved the phenomena because, in Copernicus's mind, it was a *true* hypothesis and not merely an aid to computation.[42] That is, Copernicus believed he was describing the physical universe and not offering a useful model. In modern terminology, he was a "realist" rather than an "instrumentalist." Diurnal and annual motion of the earth was, for Copernicus, a fact; its facticity was attested by the "fixed symmetry" of the universe that the account brought to light. The circularity of the argument is indicated easily enough by a scholastic question: since God could make a world that was as complex as He wished, why must the hypothesis of "fixed symmetry" be true? Copernicus's own answer was that it was easier to believe.[43] But why should God have made it easier rather than more difficult to know the divine Creation?

Such questions may be meaningless to modern astronomers, but it is by no means obvious that they would have been meaningless to Copernicus. Moreover, we have the evidence of the great controversy between Bellarmine and Galileo to indicate that the issue was very much alive two generations later. In that seventeenth-century controversy, as well as in Copernicus's day and before, questions regarding the substance or nature of the divine creation were not the province of astronomy. At the close of his letter dedicatory to Pope Paul III, Copernicus admitted as much.[44]

How these questions bear on the topic of phenomenalism has been indicated in a general way by Benjamin Nelson. Like Kepler, who, however, abandoned the common prejudice in favor of circles, Copernicus was against "fictionalism" as well as "probabilism."[45] The former term referred to the tradition of saving the phenomena by means of hypotheses; the latter to the Averroist doctrine of "two truths," according to which the truths of theology alone were absolute and indubitable as a result of their sacred origin. The truths of metaphysics or of natural philosophy were only probable because they were derived from natural human capacities of memory, induction, and reason, which were flawed and capable of error.

In contrast to fictionalism and probabilism, Nelson argued that Copernicus and the other great pioneers of the sixteenth and seventeenth centuries were convinced that "objective certainty and inner certitude were the indispensible signs of science, true philosophy and just belief."[46] The desire for certainty and certitude began in the area of moral philosophy and theology and expanded to the cosmological topics discussed by Copernicus. Now, Averroism, or rather a series of Averroist propositions derived from an interpretation of Aristotle that carried heterodox or perhaps even anti-Christian implications, had been condemned by Etienne Tempier, bishop of Paris, in 1277.[47] Because the condemnation proved unable to arrest the destruction of Aristotelean natural philosophy, Duhem considered it to be the starting point for modern science.[48] It was, so to speak, the catalyst for the anti-Aristotelean reaction. Averroism was more than a solution to Aristotelean doctrine. It also expressed a complex of sentiments that were constituent elements of scientific phenomenalism. The subjective significance of the "two truths" doctrine, of which Duhem's "positivism" is a late example, was not that those who held it were insincere in their profession of Christian as well as scientific faith. On the contrary, it is more likely that the separation of matters of faith and matters of reason was entirely sincere and, on the basis of the separation, entirely reasonable. However, it was precisely the reasonableness of the separation that Bishop Tempier questioned and judged in the condemnation. The scholastic solution, formulated early in the thirteenth century, to the problems associated with the introduction of Aristotle and his Arabic and Jewish commentators was to declare philosophy to be the handmaid (*ancilla*) of theology; theology was the queen of the sciences and the others must wait on her as servants; nature must pay tribute to grace. In general one may say that the understanding of divine things, to the extent that it was analogous to natural understanding, was such that it would be impious for natural understanding to seek to know what only faith could grasp. For this reason, one must interrogate the sentiments expressed in the Averroist doctrine and not merely the claim to be reasonable.

This may be done by considering the alternatives. On the one hand Thomas Aquinas (some of whose views were condemned in 1277 as being dangerous) was able to harmonize not the surface doctrines of reason and faith but the underlying experiences. On the other, Ockham avoided doctrinal conflict entirely by removing the realm of revealed faith from the domain of knowledge. The condemned Averroism shared with Ockham's teaching a critical stance regarding certain aspects of Christian dogma, but unlike Ockham, the Averroists developed a counterdogma of reason in light of which the separation from faith could be justified. Of course, Ockham's solution, nominalism, had its own problems.[49] However that may be, it remains true that the alleged conflict between faith and reason so warmly embraced by medieval and modern Averroists is only partly a conflict between the critical intellect and Christian doctrine; more fundamentally it is a conflict between two dogmas.

The outcome of the condemnation that Duhem rightly saw as so important for the birth of modern science was the defeat not only of Tempier's episcopal dogmatism but of a philosophical concern for substance. The first was no more than an indication of defective or imprudent ecclesiastical statesmanship. The second led not only to a diminished concern for questions of substance posed in Aristotelean language but also to an eclipse of evocations of Christian substance. If, for example, the Christian drama of fall and redemption, which expressed the substance of the individual soul, was beyond the scope of the critical intellect, then a new one, more compatible with it, would have to be formulated. Initially these new doctrines drew on the complex of emotions expressed in the astrological speculations mentioned earlier. Subsequently they took on the form of "critical reason" and were advanced as deliberately anti-Christian. In short, the sentiments expressed in the Averroist doctrine that separated faith and reason established the sovereignty of the speculative intellect. Without a nominalist reminder of its own limitations, such an intellect was free to elaborate an interpretation of human being, nature, and society without any reference to the divine or, more particularly, to the transcendent spirituality of Christianity.[50]

The dissociation of faith and reason, therefore, presupposes for its intelligibility the sentiment of dogmatic counterdogmatism. It is this pretheoretical constitution of a specific attitude toward human being, nature, and society that is important for understanding the meaning of technology. The rejection of probabilism and fictionalism, in the context of the Averroist doctrine, led in the direction of certitude and certainty, to be sure, but the range of reality experienced was confined to phenomena apprehended by the dogmatic critical intellect.

As Nelson observed, the new science claimed "that there could be some set of truly trustworthy assurances based upon the evidence of the senses concerning the plan and pattern of the 'Book of Nature.' "[51] Those trustworthy assurances were found not in any evidence of the senses but in the extraneous assurance that the Book of Nature was written in numbers, not words. Numbers, unlike words, do not lie nor are they ambiguous and so in need of interpretation according to any doctrine of two truths.

With the acceptance of the Galilean view that the Book of Nature is written in mathematical characters, the last step in the abandonment of Aristotelean substance, or rather, of a concern for substance expressed in Aristotelean language, was taken. E. A. Burtt pointed out many years ago that this mathematical account was also a metaphysical one and that the metaphysics was associated with the name of Plato. A short time later, Edward W. Strong attacked Burtt's interpretation on the grounds that "mechanical knowledge marches by method, not mathematics." According to Strong, substantive speculations on number are not mathematical inquiries. Such activities as are deserving of the name mathematics are "operational and autonomous in the sense that their distinctions are working distinctions and their definitions and concepts take their meaning from the limited method and subject-matter of their [phenomenal] science. They are pragmatic in their approach and in their work."[52] This was, of course, an emphatic restatement of Duhem's "positivism."

A few years later Alexandre Koyré, whose philosophical astuteness was equal to that of Duhem, restored the balance in a series of articles that argued that Galileo's "Platonism" was indeed a kind of mathematical metaphysics.[53] The present concern is less with the controversies of historians of science than with the adequacy of the objection to a mathematicized Book of Nature.[54] Here Koyré's observation was entirely to the point. Against the Galilean dictum, two objections can be raised: (1) The Book of Nature is *not* written in mathematical characters, and (2) it is dangerous to think that it is. The danger lies not in any Whiteheadian fallacy of misplaced concreteness, but that habits of mathematicized thinking conduce to an inability to apprehend the nature of reality. "The more a mind is accustomed to the precision and rigidity of geometrical thought," Koyré said, "the less it will be able to grasp the mobile, changing, qualitatively determined variety of Being."[55] Once committed to a geometric or mathematicized world, the combination of certainty and certitude would prove irresistible. In modern philosophical language, a geometricized ontology is stabilized with the epistemological buttresses of certainty and certitude. In theological imagery, if

God wrote the Book of Nature in mathematical characters, it was an act of piety to decipher the text and prove the pattern of the design. If the world was a mechanism, the individual could participate in the divine creation by an act of cocreation, which meant by the development of scientific-technological mechanisms. By the twentieth century, the piety implied by the privileged status of humanity as a self-chosen cocreator had become a platitude and the mood had changed to Promethean revolt. As early as the sixteenth century, however, sustained philosophical objections were raised against the new phenomenalist dogmas.

*

Let us recall the theoretical issue. Put boldly, it is not self-evident that mathematical simplicity is "more true" than mathematical complexity. Of course it may be conceptually simpler if the origin of the mathematical coordinates is declared to be the sun and not the earth; this was Copernicus's great achievement. But the "truth" of the matter is that the motion of the heavenly bodies is relative to one another, however it is described. More to the point, the heliocentric model in no way alters the experience central to the humanists' concern, namely the meaningfulness of cosmic rhythms; the sun rises in the east, spring follows winter, cold winds blow from the north, the equinoxes precess. If one were concerned with the meaning of those cosmic realities, that is, with questions of substance, and if one used nature as a guide to interpreting events, then a mathematical account of the sky would be of no interest. And, indeed, several of Copernicus's near contemporaries were quite unimpressed by his achievement.

For example, in his book, Copernicus used a quotation from the *Aeneid*: when the ship leaves port, the town and home fall away. That is, the ship, not the town, moved (*Aeneid* 3.72). Accordingly, Copernicus favored the "truth" of spaceship earth. However, as Bodin remarked a generation later, "How does it serve to correct the tables of the celestial movement [of the ancients] whether the earth be mobile or immobile? Whether there be epicycles or no? By placing the sun at the centre? For that the pilot leaves port for to course upon the high seas, and if he thinks that the port moves off and that his ship moves not, as the poet says, *urbesque domusque recedant*; there will ever be the same distance from the ship to the port as from the port to the ship."[56]

Bodin's methodological point was clear: one could assume a heliocentric cosmos in order to simplify calculations, but if one were not initially interested in calculations, nothing would be gained thereby.

In fact, Bodin was interested in nature as substance, as a source of meaning, and as a reality to be apprehended through contemplation; he was not therefore concerned with nature as an object of mathematical investigation. The task of the philosopher, he argued, was to indicate the order of nature so as to compel the assent of faith in God.[57] The significance of Bodin's mystical penetration of cosmic order is indicated by the contrasting arguments developed by his seventeenth-century successors. The central theological or substantive question concerned the presence of divinity in the cosmos. Bodin sought divine presence in nature as the ground of religious experience beyond the dogmatic wars of Christianity. Grotius dealt with the same question by assuming a natural code of ethics. Likewise Hobbes's naturalist evocation of the Leviathan to master the effects of pride, chiefly of religious pride, was followed by Spinoza's proposal of governmental imposition of a minimum dogma. Locke exiled the whole question of religious experience to the confines of private practice. The course of political philosophy from Bodin to Locke was, in this respect, a kind of spiritual dilution. Increasingly the experience of the divine order of the cosmos atrophied. The end point is a kind of double vision: we see with our eyes that the sun rises in the east, but we see in our minds that the earth revolves about the sun. In the words of the modern cosmologists Lennon and McCartney:

> But the fool on the hill
> Sees the sun going down.
> And the eyes in his head
> See the world spinning round.[58]

In his evocation of the divine order of the cosmos is found the greatness of Bodin's spirituality. Bodin conceived of a spiritually animated cosmos hierarchically ordered, a *cosmos empsychos*. For Bodin the order of the cosmos was the thing about which human beings could be most certain. Now, certainties are in demand for the purpose of overcoming uncertainties, which, in turn, are accompanied by anxieties. The source of uncertainty for both Bodin and his dogmatic phenomenalist opponents was

Christianity. Indeed, one of the essential features of Christian experience is uncertainty. When the gods of the world are dismissed as demons, as had been done by St. Augustine, communication with the God beyond the world exists only in the experience of faith, "the substance of things hoped for, the proof of things not seen" (Heb. 11:1). "The life of the soul in openness toward God," wrote Voegelin, "the waiting, the periods of aridity and dullness, guilt and despondency, contrition and repentance, forsakenness and hope against hope, the silent stirrings of love and grace, trembling on the verge of a certainty which if gained is loss—the very lightness of this fabric may prove too heavy a burden for men who lust for massively possessive experience."[59] Moreover, the greater the institutional success of Christianity, the greater the likelihood that significant numbers of nominal Christians would lack the spiritual strength and integrity needed for a Christian life. By Bodin's time, Christian spirituality had, for a sufficient number of nominal Christians, ossified into a dogmatic creed useful as the pretext for holy slaughter.

Bodin's recovery of the order of the cosmos in the face of the disorder, both spiritual and pragmatic, of the Christian dogmatists was a splendid achievement. The easier solution to political disorder based on dogmatic conflict, a solution followed initially by the Averroists and subsequently, nearly without exception, from Grotius to Locke and to Locke's enlightened successors in the present age, has been to propound a counterdogma, a final dogma to end the dogmatomachy. The contemporary version of this solution is called the end of ideology. Since the form of this solution is still dogmatic, it is no surprise that the "end of ideology" has itself been criticized dogmatically as yet another ideology. There is no dogmatic escape from dogma: ever since the separation of dogmatic and mystic theology during the thirteenth and fourteenth centuries, the only escape from the one has been the other. Bodin's mysticism was a means to avoid dogma; the toleration that it sustained was a counsel to end religious warfare; indeed, the noetic rationality by which it was expressed indicates his greatness as a philosopher.

The immediate political response to the disorders of dogmatic religious wars was not, however, the recovery of Bodinian experiences of cosmic mysteries. The issue between Bodin and Copernicus, to repeat, centered on the significance of mathematical calculation. The seventeenth-century successors of both men sought the "massively possessive experience" of political as well as astronomical certainty in mathematical or quasi-mathematical calculation of natural regularities. The speculative political analogue to calculative astronomy was based on the hypothetical assumption of a "state of nature," variously described, on the basis of which certain conclusions might be reached by logical deduction. The appeal of these modes of reasoning came from a series of new factors whose weight began to be felt in the last quarter of the sixteenth century.[60]

The cosmos of both Bodin and Copernicus was, we said, in its essential feature, the Hellenic sphere bound by the fixed stars. In 1572 a new star appeared in the constellation of Cassiopeia, a region where generation and corruption were not supposed to occur. Tycho Brahe interpreted this event as a sign that God's free creation of the world was not over and that corresponding terrestrial changes might be anticipated.[61] Moreover, the appearance of a new comet in 1577 added to the disturbance. Tycho's calculation of its parallax, or rather of the relative absence of parallax, indicated that it was not sublunar but ethereal.[62] That is, it passed clean through the rigid crystal spheres that had, by the Hellenic model, supported the heavenly bodies. It appeared that these spheres had not been shattered by the comet's passage. Anomalous events such as this one contributed to an atmosphere of readiness to accept the famous "paradigm shift" that we associate with the astronomical revolution.[63]

Over the past generation, scholars have examined in great detail the transition from the Hellenic cosmos to the mathematical universe. The issue involved in that transition was formulated with great clarity on the occasion of the controversy between Kepler and Fludd.[64] One might almost say that, for Kepler, as for Duhem and Strong, mathematics was quantitative measurement not numerological harmony. Qualification is necessary because Kepler was also keenly interested in numerological harmonies, astrology, and so on.[65] The difference between the two was described by Debus as follows: whereas Fludd "sought mysteries in symbols according to a preconceived belief in a cosmic plan," Kepler "insisted that his hypotheses be founded on quantitative, mathematically demonstrable premises."[66] In terms of the distinctions used in this study, Fludd undertook a meditative exegesis of the substance of reality experienced, whereas

Kepler sought to find the correct mathematical expression of celestial phenomena.

"Ubi materia," said Kepler, "ibi geometria." This modern commonplace implied, however, a difference, narrow but deep, from the combination of alchemy, natural magic, and a new medical teaching that Fludd had advocated. To begin with, astrology, which had constituted the numeric bond of the empyrean, the celestial, and the material world, was suddenly a pseudoscience. Causality was defined mechanically rather than by means of subtle psychic influences. Ontology was no longer derived from the Aristotelean opposition of identity and alterity but from the difference between plus and minus. There were no absolute opposites for Kepler, only mathematical continua of variation. Thus, for example, there could be no light bodies, only heavy ones of different magnitude. Kepler's assumptions contained the implication (not made by him) that, if nature could adequately and exhaustively be described by mathematical continua, there exists no substance of nature beneath or behind what appears in mathematic description. Fludd, like Bodin, was not interested in calculative measurement but in measure, in the meaning of nature or in its substance.

The purpose for which Fludd sought this knowledge, as Yates has indicated, was probably Hermetic.[67] And Hermeticism, at least for men such as Fludd, implied not the vulgar and odious arts of necromancy but a precious spiritual discipline that combined philosophy, gnostic magic, and "Egyptian" wisdom. The Hermetic adept, like the Christian, believed that the human being was made in the image of God and had been given dominion over all creatures by God. In addition, however, humans partook of divine creative power in a kind of junior partnership with the creator-demiurge. Moreover, humans had voluntarily taken on their bodies in preexistence and thereby had voluntarily submitted themselves to the influence of the celestial bodies. In contrast to the Biblical drama of fall and redemption, then, Hermetic doctrine indicated that the divine substance had been retained unimpaired within the soul. All that was needed to apprehend that substance fully was to overcome the influence of the body. Because the body had been obtained voluntarily, it was considered possible to do this by appropriate acts of will. The procedure was equivalent to the Hegelian or Marxian move from

consciousness to self-consciousness; it involved not merely a metanoia, however, but also the practice of ascesis.[68]

Through acts of purification, the Hermetic adept was able to
recover what in Christian terms would be innocence. The ascesis,
in Christian terms, would amount to pushing the cherubim away
from the tree of life (Gen. 3:22). Once purified, the adept became again innocent—or rather, evil and sin had been overcome
and the magus gained a gnosis of God, of nature, and of truth.
This gnosis enabled the adept to use the powers of nature for
beneficial purposes, rather like Prometheus, the *philanthropos*.[69]
Modern Promethean philanthropy, from Shaftsbury through
Goethe, Shelley, and Marx, reinterpreted the Hesiodic and Aes-
chylean original, who was stricken with a great *nosos*, or mental
sickness.[70] For the moderns, Prometheus symbolized the human
being who is superior to destiny. The original "modern"
Promethean, as Jonas pointed out, was the ancient alchemist
Zosimos.[71] The philanthropic purposes of the gnostic operations
to control nature are supposed to excuse the Promethean sickness
of revolt against the divine order.

The initial impetus of Hermeticism, however, may be understood best as an attempt to know nature sympathetically rather
than to dominate it operationally. In the exchange between Kepler and Fludd this aspect is emphasized. Fludd: "Mathemati-
cians are wont to talk about the quantitative shadows; the
alchemists and hermetics grasp the very marrow of natural bodies." Kepler: "I grasp reality by its tail, as you say, but I hold on
to it; you may try to reach its head, if only in a dream. I am
satisfied with the effects, that is, with the movements of the planets; if in their causes themselves you can find such intelligible
harmonious relations as I have found in their revolutions, it will
be only fair if I congratulate you on the discovery and myself on
understanding it—as soon as I am able to understand it."[72] In
short, for Kepler the substance, the "marrow" of natural bodies,
had disappeared from his horizon of attention, leaving only mathematical relations, albeit "mystical" ones.[73]

Kepler's system of relations existed only as the intramundane
mediation between the motion of matter and the human intellect.
Fludd's desire for access to the marrow of natural bodies by way
of alchemy and Hermetic operations, although not science in any
sense of the term, nevertheless did express the experience that

nature was spiritually meaningful. In Voegelin's language, nature
for Fludd was transparent for its divine ground, even if the divinity involved was not Christian. Once the Keplerian version became accepted as the standard of science, the spiritual experience
expressed by the losing side, namely Hermeticism and alchemy,
was cut loose from nature conceived as a cosmos. The result, surprising in other respects, was to liberate the sentiments and emotions attached to alchemical and Hermetic practices and leave
them free to operate elsewhere.[74] In our own times we find a
congeries of ideological movements inspired with an activist mysticism, the objective of which has been to liberate human beings
from the bondage of matter, of materialism, of a materialist society, and so on. These several varieties of liberation have as their
common experiential core a faith in intramundane salvation that
simultaneously overcomes the evils of nature without spirit. The
immediate result, however, was the wedding of the Galilean doctrine regarding the mathematization of nature with the Hermetic
desire to dominate.[75] Such are the emotionally primitive roots of
modern technology. Jonas's discussion of Zosimos, to say nothing
of Eliade's analysis of certain Paleolithic symbols, indicates the
historical primitiveness of such operations.[76] Unlike our Stone
Age predecessors, however, contemporary technological alchemists seem unaware they are practicing magic.

*

Beneath the absurdity of the later developments a real issue
exists between the mathematization of science, with or without
the addition of gnostic/Hermetic/alchemical emotions, namely the
rehabilitation of *curiositas*, and the older philosophy of nature.
The thinker who gave the most precise account of the issue was
Giordano Bruno. In developing his distinctions between the science of phenomena and the science of substance, the significance
of phenomenalism was indicated with great clarity. In the past his
fame has been vouchsafed by enlightened historiographers who
attributed his misfortune at the hands of the Inquisition to his
defense of Copernican heliocentrism, and thus of "science,"
against the obfuscations of superstitious religion. It is true that
Bruno agreed with heliocentrism, but it is not true that he ad-
mired without reservation Copernicus's intention of mathematical
simplification. As recent studies of Bruno have indicated, he considered mathematical knowledge inferior to knowledge gained by

meditative contemplation.[77] Mathematical knowledge was concerned only with accident and not with substance. "Substance
and being are distinct and independent from quantity, and in
consequence, measure and numbers are not substance but are
relative to it; not being, but incidental to being."[78] Accordingly,
"substance in its essence is free of number and measure." Bruno,
like Bodin was concerned with substance and depth, not with appearance and surface. "And so," he said, "if we think into the
depths of things with the philosophers of nature and leave the
logicians to their conceits, we find all that effects difference and
number is mere accidence, mere shape, mere complexion."[79]
Like Fludd and the natural philosophers, Bruno sought the "marrow" of nature, its meaning for human existence.

For Bruno, Copernicus had simply been a "timid" cosmol-
ogist.[80] The new cosmology should best be seen as having asserted that the human mind was the determinate center of human knowledge. This act of assertion by Copernicus had the
effect, felt as late as Kant's own alleged "Copernican revolution,"
of liberating the intellect from dogma.[81] For Bruno, that is, Copernicus's "revolution" was incomplete. Not only was the sphere
of the fixed stars left intact; everything beneath that finite canopy
had to submit to mathematical laws. Bruno's own speculation on
infinity would, he thought, complete what Copernicus had begun. As Drake observed, the Copernican features of Bruno's
speculation were limited to the notion of uniformity of nature and
relativity of motion, not heliocentrism, "and the same demand for
freedom in philosophizing untrammeled by irrelevant criticism"
as was found in Copernicus's preface to *De Revolutionibus*.[82]

The cosmos within which Bruno lived was not, however, the
mathematical universe of science but the *cosmos empsychos* of
the alchemists and Hermetics. Unlike them, however, his concern was not with the "marrow" of specific natural substances but
with the "marrow" of the cosmos as such. The means to obtain
understanding of the cosmos was not through the various asceses
of the magi, but immediately by way of the psyche. If the cosmos
was *empsychos*, the psyche, the human spirit, was the sensorium
of its meaning. This was a splendid solution to the question of the
difference between substance and phenomena. On the one hand
he avoided the magic operations of the alchemists who attempted

to penetrate to the "marrow" of nature by operating on phenomenal realities; on the other, he avoided the fallacies of scientism, which operated on human spiritual substance as if it were phenomenal reality, which is also a kind of magic.

The details of Bruno's formulation may be overlooked in order to summarize the results. To the question, What can be known of the cosmos? Bruno offered the following response: (1) the substance of the cosmos is spirit; the cosmos is a cosmos empsychos. (2) The spirit that animates the infinite manifold of natural forms is God, which is itself unknowable; God is beyond the infinite manifold. (3) We can ascend from matter to spirit because it is in this way that we know the cosmic substance is psyche. (4) This substance is, nevertheless, unknowable as determinate because it is infinite, whereas the human psyche is finite. (5) What we know as determinate and finite is the trace or shadow of the cosmic substance created by God; what we know is like an image in a mirror. (6) The infinite manifold of forms is, with respect to God, accidental; of these accidentals, the phenomenal, determinate accidentals are known by mathematicized science. (7) Thus, to know the cosmos by way of natural, mathematicized science is to know only the accidentals of the accidentals, the image in the mirror. (8) But to understand the greatness of the cosmos, the natural philosopher must contemplate the primary cause by way of the infinity of its cosmic appearance. (9) This can be done by the imaginative expansion of consciousness from finite, determinate experience analogically into the infinite. (10) The result is an image of an infinity of space filled with an infinity of worlds; that image, which, if taken literally rather than imaginatively, contradicted Christian doctrine, was the production of the human mind and an icon of the substantive infinity of God.[83] Copernican astronomy, therefore, was a kind of parable whose meaning would be evident to philosophers or philosophical mystics such as he. Only such persons could see in the infinity of worlds the unity of the divine.

From this summary of Bruno's mystical evocation two conclusions that are central to the analysis of technology may be drawn. First, as a methodological analysis of the distinction between substance and phenomena, Bruno's insight cannot be improved. Second, Bruno's ontological insight may be taken as equivalent to those made by von Uexkuell with respect to the tick or by Kohak regarding his porcupine. In Bruno's account of the unity of spiritual substance in the cosmos, nature is spiritualized. Because of that spiritualization, the human psyche can understand it. Bruno transcended von Uexkuell and Kohak, however, by his understanding of the relationship reciprocal to that of spirit in nature. At the decisive conjunction of human existence, psyche is a manifestation of nature. He transcended them as well in his expectation that by unifying science, philosophy, and theology he would help heal the schisms of Christendom and end the religious wars. In this he was at one with both Hermeticists such as Mornay and Patrizi[84] and philosophers such as Bodin.

One can see the delicate balance achieved by Bruno by referring to the even more precarious balance achieved by St. Francis of Assisi. In his great canticle *Praises of the Creatures*, St. Francis began by praising God, the heavenly bodies, the elements, the earth, which sustains fruits and flowers, and the humble who forgive and peacefully endure. The significance of this text is that it expressed the joy experienced in beholding mute creation. Creaturely existence, by itself, glorified God because it was a meaningful part of the world. This apprehension of the dignity of nature and of the human dignity of the most wretched and despised was both the strength and the weakness of this great saint. Francis's understanding of the dignity of the creatures and of creation was resumed in a later language by Bruno. The weakness of St. Francis, which also expressed his sanctity, was that his attention tended to be limited to the meaning of creation. In the language of Christianity, St. Francis's imitation of Christ, conformed only to Christ's humanity; that was the significance of Francis's receiving of the stigmata. What fell into relative neglect was the balancing symbol of Christ the cosmocrator and triumphant head of the mystical body of humankind. Those neglected emotions were readily absorbed by the scientific-technological adepts.[85]

Bruno's philosophical language was more easily controlled by noetic canons of intelligibility than was that language of St. Francis. Both attempted to redirect human sentiments toward the natural world; both attempts contained the potential of conflict with Christian authorities. With Bruno the conflict was direct; with Francis, it came a generation later with the "spiritual" wing of the Franciscans. Political events and interests and the requirements of order and obedience all played a part in these conflicts. But so too did the Christian understanding of nature whereby it appeared as external being indifferent to the salvation of the soul or, worse, as an unredeemed reality against which the soul must strive in order to find fulfilment. Bruno's experience of the identity of nature and psyche sustained his argument about the hierarchy of reality, from the unknowable God beyond the infinite manifold of animal and vegetable forms to the accidentals of the accidentals, studied by the new mathematicized sciences. In this way he avoided both dogmatic pneumatocentrism and dogmatic phenomenalism.

He did not, however, avoid the attention of the Inquisition. His Hermeticism has been thoroughly documented by Yates. If that were insufficient to establish his heterodoxy (if not his heresy), then "his path of triumphant defiance on behalf of *curiositas*" would certainly have brought him into conflict with ecclesiastical authorities.[86] Two additional reasons may be suggested. As one who accepted the truth of Copernicus's account, so far as it went, the sun was really at the center of the, or rather, of this universe. Jacob Klein has suggested that, to the church, heliocentrism looked a great deal like ancient sun worship. Bruno's younger contemporary, Campanella, for example, wrote *The City of the Sun* (1614) in direct opposition to Augustine's *City of God*.[87] Second, his postulation of an infinity of universes seems to conflict with the doctrine of the infinity of God. How, doctrinaire churchmen might ask, can there be two infinities? As a matter of fact, the image of *many* universes separate one from another is easily conceivable; it is like an enormous Swiss cheese, with the holes being the several universes and with fixed stars at the outside of the holes. Bruno wished us to imagine an infinite Swiss cheese.

*

Despite the soundness of Bruno's methodological principles and of his metaphysics, the next two centuries belonged to the mathematicized sciences and to the quasi-mathematical philosophers. Bruno's speculation on infinity, which bore a family resemblance to the Hellenic symbol of the apeiron as well as to more orthodox Christian notions of the contrast between creaturely finitude and divine infinity, simmered down to a question of working out solutions to problems of transfinite numbers, indefinite series, and, of course, to integration and differentiation in the calculus of Newton and Leibniz. From Descartes to Kant the attempt was made under the category of epistemology to deal with the problems thrown their way by the sciences of phenomena. The indirect effects of these sciences on politics were felt in the areas of present interest: nature became increasingly despiritualized, and the sciences grew increasingly "applied," resulting in the changes outlined in the preceding chapters. The transition from a concern with a spiritual order of existence to a material standard of living is probably the best known ingredient of modern society.

We may conclude this chapter with a few summary definitions of the matters just treated. By phenomenalism, first, is meant the tendency to consider phenomenal relations of things as the substantive order of meaning. Once phenomena are treated as if they were substantive meanings, the result is the creation of a "phenomenal reality." This twilight mode of reality has been identified by Voegelin (following Robert Musil) as "second reality."[88] Notwithstanding its imaginary status in terms of substantive reality, phenomenal reality can be treated as if it were substantive. It can be an object of speculation and of emotional projections that can even turn obsessive. More to the point, phenomenal reality can serve as the basis for human action, which is the topic discussed in part II.

PART II

# *Modern Worldlessness*

# Introduction

The novelty of the technological phenomenon was indicated by the analyses of part I. In order to establish the technological society some aspects of human experience were intensified and others were diminished or eclipsed. The discussion in part I indicated that phenomenal realities and attention to them have increasingly overshadowed nonphenomenal or substantive realities of meaning. The result may be summarized by the observation that the human capacity for action has been enhanced. In addition, however, part II describes alterations in the human condition that the capacity for action has achieved when it is undertaken on the basis of a phenomenalist understanding of nature and, indeed, of reality as a whole.

The central text to be examined in this section is Hannah Arendt's *The Human Condition*.[1] The purpose is not to provide an exegesis of Arendt's political philosophy but to examine her formulations with regard to the insight they bring to the topic of this study.[2] The general direction of her argument was indicated by her teacher, Karl Jaspers. In 1930 he wrote *Man in the Modern Age*, completing it just prior to the first electoral victories of the National Socialists. It was, among other things, a reflection on the significance of technology. Technology began, according to Jaspers, as a means to furnish the masses (themselves a new social category) with necessary commodities. Eventually, however, human beings lost touch with nature; everything was turned into a commodity to be used, or rather, to be used up and discarded; the human habitat became machine-made rather than handmade, and the surrounding environment grew despiritualized. The result: "Man was, as it were, bereft of his world."[3] In the following sentence Jaspers indicated that the loss of a world was equivalent to the reduction of authentic human being to a function.

101

*Modern worldlessness,* the title of part II of this study, is meant to indicate first of all a complex of sentiments and experiences that is expressed in the platitude that history has accelerated, in the sense that all things are in movement, that all is process and change. The perplexing aspect of this modern kind of change is that it does not appear to take place within a stable framework. We cannot step into the same river twice because we, unlike Heraclitus, are convinced that both the river and human beings change. It is as if we were travelers through a landscape that is altered as a landscape by the fact of our passage. Heretofore the world has been a semipermanent structure that stood between human beings and the anonymous changes of nature. The world in this sense consists of things made, of use objects but also of human social institutions such as the family, and of political institutions too. To the extent that human beings have been at home in the world, to the extent they feel that "all's right with the world," they know where they are. "Here" is our place; if you do not find this place to be a "here," it is because you are from someplace else, from "there." That is, a sense of worldliness was the expression of particularity; it meant that human beings shared the space of the world by distinguishing themselves as communities and societies from others. The world both distinguished human beings as communities and united them as possessors of a share of the earth.

The argument of part II is intended to indicate how modern technology has obliterated the world by destroying sentiments of stability and meaning and replacing them with those of process and function. The most significant political expression of worldlessness under conditions of technology is totalitarianism. The argument is not intended to prove that the technological society is totalitarian, a notion that is both romantic and careless. Nor is it intended to indicate that totalitarianism was simply a means to obtain "the goal of rapid modernization,"[4] but simply to indicate the continuity between the two modes of modern worldlessness.

*Modern* worldlessness is to be distinguished from premodern or medieval or, better, from Christian "otherworldliness." The world, to medieval Christianity, was to be invested with the sentiment of "contempt." In book 10 of his *Confessions,* Augustine distinguished three sets of things to be held in contempt: lusts of the flesh; lusts of the eyes, which were connected to the flesh by reason of dependence on sense experience; and pride of life. The first category included the expected excesses of gluttony, greed, drunkenness, and sexual pleasure, but also an aesthetic love for art; the second included the aesthetic loves but also the craving to examine nature for no reason but from curiosity to know it; the third included the expected evils of envy, pursuit of riches, vainglory, praise, and honor. The biblical passage that inspired these reflections, 1 John 2:15–16, was connected as well to the temptations of Adam and of Christ.[5] The world and the things of the world hindered human beings in their search for spiritual union with God. That is, the world was filled with temptations.

This did not mean, at least not to Augustine, that the world was simply sinful nor that it was evil. The world was not sinful because it tempted humans; sin is an act as well as a condition. According to Augustine, the act of sinning begins as suggestion, is followed by delectation, and ends as consent. Our sins are therefore voluntary and we, not the world, are responsible for them. Nor is the world evil. Because God created the world, and because God is good, His creation is also good. But it is not so good as God, whose goodness is immutable. Accordingly, the goodness of the world, Augustine said, is mutable.[6] What it did mean was that the *imitatio Christi* included the renunciation of the world. Most notably this renunciation was expressed in the monastic vows of poverty, chastity, and obedience, all of which were understood as aids in the act of "dying to the world."[7] The sentiment is in some respects equivalent to Plato's expression in the *Phaedo* that philosophy is the practice of dying.

The chief area of equivalence may be described as balance with respect to the range of human experience. It seems obvious enough to common sense that an active love of worldly goods will mean that one runs out of time, to say nothing of inclination, actively to love God. Augustine's great existential symbolism of *The City of God* was of the two loves: love of God to contempt of self or love of self to contempt of God. What made the juxtaposition of alternatives so arresting was that it appealed with same immediacy to the soul as did Plato's discussion of eros in the *Gorgias*, the *Republic*, and the *Symposium*. By the twelfth century the Augustinian balance that instructed the faithful to avoid the things of the world insofar as they were sources of temptation, but also to use them properly for justice, order, and salvation, had been altered. This should not be surprising: much had changed in Christendom from the days when Alaric sacked Rome, seven hundred years earlier.

Reference has already been made to the new spirituality, expressed through Gothic cathedrals and scholasticism, through courtly love, vernacular poetry, the growth of towns, and translations from Greek and Arabic. It was expressed as well through a hardening of the meaning of contempt. The emphasis turned to the more aggressive sentiments of scorn and disillusionment. The locus classicus is *De miseria humanae conditionis* written toward the close of the twelfth century by the great church statesman Innocent III. He began with an account of the indignity of birth and ended with the putrefaction of corpses and the punishments of hell: not a balanced portrait of human life nor of the world.

By the fourteenth century a new imbalance was introduced, as was discussed in a different context in chapter 3, with humanist historiography.[8] Earthly glory was the means by which to attain a kind of immortality as remembrance, a legitimate reward for greatness. Lust of the flesh was called love; lust of the eyes was called productivity; pride of life was called honor and reputation. Moreover, "because fame was conferred by writers, by chroniclers, historiographers and poets, learning and literacy became a necessity in the courts of princes."[9] Power and wisdom began to converge. From an Augustinian perspective this meant increased attention to the world; at the same time, however, it entailed a destruction of the world as the stable home of human beings.

*

The structure of Arendt's argument reflects our contemporary predicament as heirs, among other things, to the fourteenth-century changes in Western spirituality. Her procedure was first, to describe the topic; second, to show how it had been historically understood and misunderstood; third, to show how the reality to which the topic referred had been destroyed, transformed, or altered so as to account for the understanding/misunderstanding. Central to her argument is an awareness of the importance of making distinctions. Making distinctions is not the same as making up definitions. By analogy with a right to one's opinions, it is often said that one has a right to define one's terms. Such a "right" is spurious and indicates only that words have "lost their common meaning, or that we have ceased to live in a common world where the words we have in common possess an unquestionable meaningfulness" (*PF*, 95).

The end of a common world is sometimes described as the decline of tradition or the decline of authority. In fact, the two have declined together, harnessed like a team of faithful Percherons. What gave the past its authority was that it was handed over as tradition. For Arendt, however, the break with or in our tradition is a fact; the events that challenged and destroyed tradition were indicated by the terms *scientific* or *technical* or *industrial revolution*. The utter ruin of the Western tradition was unmistakably achieved in totalitarianism. The interpretation that sustains this claim was that these events altered, reversed, or destroyed the inherited framework within which understanding and judgment had been carried on.[10] Loss of tradition, therefore, was not part of the "history of ideas" but of the history of the world. Moreover, the loss of tradition was not to be lamented—which would have been futile anyhow. The absence of tradition enables us to look on the past with a directness and freshness that our predecessors lacked precisely because they had the authority of a tradition to guide them. Arendt's work demonstrated that the disintegration of tradition has also opened up a space for thinking.

In the more differentiated conceptual vocabulary of Voegelin, the term *tradition* belonged to the category of derivative or second-order terms. It was a doctrinal symbol rather than a signifier of reality experienced. The contextual reality within which the term was significant was historiogenetic myth, a single time line that was held to be meaningful or, in Arendt's language, a "thread."[11] By arguing that tradition had been "dismantled," Arendt indicated (in Voegelin's terms) that the term was opaque for the reality experienced as "thinking." It is important to be aware of the status of Arendt's terms so as not to be sidetracked into futile exercises such as disputing whether or not tradition has "really" been dismantled.

An important way to observe the actual birth of new things, especially in politics, where speech is supreme, is to notice when the word that is attached to the phenomenon first appears. A new appearance requires a new word, which may be either the extension of an old word to a new meaning or the fresh minting of a neologism. This understanding of the relationship of words and things accords priority to things, to the realm of experiences and events and facts. The "history of ideas," according to which ideas follow and generate one another in temporal succession, makes sense only by assuming the validity of a conceptual context akin, in principle, to Hegel's system. So far as Arendt was concerned, crossing the "rainbow bridge concepts" (Nietzsche) to the ethereal land of *Geistesgeschichte* was as much a confession of homelessness and worldlessness as the outrageous nominalism of insisting on the right to define one's terms.

The opacity of traditional concepts of political science meant, for example, that totalitarianism cannot be assimilated to traditional forms of government, such as tyranny, with which it had a certain affinity. The tendency to draw analogies is comprehensible but misleading when we seek to understand novelty. That is why Arendt insisted, often in the face of considerable opposition, that one could "understand the essence of this new form of government [namely totalitarianism] only by an analysis which insists on making distinctions."[12] What was true for this particular novelty, the final reversal of the Western tradition, was true as well for an understanding of earlier events and earlier "reversals."

Assimilating the unknown to the known, understanding the unprecedented in terms of precedents, were excusable errors when the events for which understanding was sought were as horrible as those that comprise the story of totalitarianism. Two other factors, which amount to no more than prejudices, help account for the reluctance of social scientists to make distinctions. The first follows less from the fact that terminology is conceived historically than that history is conceived as a process or a stream of development where "everything can change into everything else." Distinctions thereby become meaningless because they are instantly obsolete as the great historical stream rolls over them.

A second, perhaps more widespread reason is the result of the functionalization of concepts and ideas. Functionalization proceeds on the assumption that social science is unconcerned with substance and meaning. Its concern is directed, say, at the function that religious or ideological phenomena play in society. In order, for example, to treat religion as an ideology it must be considered as a social phenomenon that performs certain functions; the substantive content or meaning of religious experience, however, must be neglected, ignored, or reduced to a functionalized concept. Accordingly, religious self-understanding for a social scientist such as Marx becomes an ideological "superstructure" of the real underlying historical process, which for Marx was the process of production. The substance of religious experience could thereby be exhaustively understood in terms of the historical and social functions that religions performed. But ever since Karl Mannheim pointed out, in *Ideology and Utopia,* that Marxism was an ideology, Marxism could be functionalized too: it is the opiate of the intellectuals (Aron). Marxists, of course, avoid this embarrassment through the same sort of metaphysical exceptionalism noted earlier regarding technology: they exempt themselves from the presumptive universality of their argument.

Considered from the standpoint of common sense, functionalism seems to be an elaborate device to prevent analysis of what appears in the world. It operates by translating the contextual focus of discourse from factual experience, across the rainbow bridge, to a realm of conceptual abstraction and imaginative logical wordplay. There is, furthermore, a close connection between the desubstantialization and functionalization of categories of analysis and the fact that human beings have increasingly become functions of mass technology. One of the consequences of that fact has been to deprive most members of the technological society of a sense of wonder at that which is as it is. Making distinctions is a first step in seeing what is there in the world, a seeing from which the experience of wonder might spring. Making distinctions is a requirement for the discrimination of meaning or of substance. Only a prior commitment to phenomenalism allows one to ignore real differences or differences in reality between, for example, religious experience and the experience of constructing a self-serving excuse that relies on religious language but is intended to justify highly questionable activities.

However that may be, it is the factual, worldly aspect of Arendt's analysis that is of present concern. She was not concerned with the "history of ideas" but with factual history. The modern age is not part of the "history of ideas" but a factual event that can be dated by specific events that interrupt routine procedures and processes, that introduce innovation. In order to see events as interruptions and not as elements in a routine process, one must make distinctions. But if distinctions are not made-up definitions, the question arises, On what basis do we make them? Like good Platonic butchers (*Phaedrus* 265e; *Statesman* 287c), we must aim to carve at the joints. But how can we feel where they are? Arendt's reply was that we must look to the world, and especially to language.

The prologue to *The Human Condition* began with a reflection on our first little traveling companion, *Sputnik*. "This event, second in importance to no other, not even to the splitting of the atom" was greeted with a "strange statement" and an "extraordinary line," namely that the earth was a place to escape from, that it was a place where humans were bound, a house of bondage. Heretofore such sentiments belonged to science fiction; now they were commonplace. Not only had people turned away from God, who was their Father in heaven; they also repudiated "an Earth who was the Mother of all living creatures under the sky," and the "very quintessence" of the human condition. Only the earth provided a habitat where humans could move and breathe without effort and without artifice. Our imaginative repudiation of the earth as a habitat for life has been accompanied by a rebellion against life as it had been given to human beings. Instead of accepting the naturalness of life, a gift, secularly speaking, from nowhere, human beings have worked hard to exchange it for one they have made.

The significance of the new technologies to fabricate life or extend it beyond the span of three score and ten is that we have begun "a rebellion against the very factuality of the human condition" (*OV*, 13). This rebellion, moreover, is not an imaginative Sturm und Drang, a metaphorical storming the heavens, but an active reality, a real activity, significant, as *Sputnik* was significant, because it is an event. The beginnings and current justifications for biomedical technologies may have appeared to be Promethean philanthropy; the result, however, shares much with those deplorable new regimes of this century.

Practically speaking the most immediate and impressive technological achievement is to have developed nuclear weapons. These devices serve not victory but deterrence and have thereby altered the significance of the military virtue of courage. Thus, any future military action that employed nuclear weapons on a large scale would consist more in revenge than protection. Moreover, the fact that the vengeance exacted would be futile and out of all proportion to any conceivable political goal means that warfare, the immemorial arbiter of international disputes, has lost its effectiveness as well as its glamour (*OR*, 4–5; *OV*, 3). About all that nuclear weapons can reasonably do is serve to demonstrate but not enact massive destruction. "Hypothetical warfare," was, in fact, discussed in relation to the A-bombing of Japan in 1945. The impressive and practical potential of killing all humans is new. To the extent that the past of humanity is retained as memory, the destruction of all humans would destroy former as well as future humans. As one A-bomb survivor put it: "Such a weapon has the power to make everything into nothing."[13]

No less significant is the theoretical consideration that the destructive explosive force is carried out by physical processes that do not naturally occur on earth but on the sun, even though we measure the strength of the devices in terms of the explosive force of TNT. Indeed, the processes of certain newer weapons apparently occur naturally only in outer space.

One of the first points to bear in mind about technological worldlessness is that the release of natural forces is more characteristic of recent developments than the constant improvement of methods of production. Moreover, the release of these forces, or the ability to release them, has decisively shifted the emphasis of technology from production to destruction. Arendt was sanguine enough to believe that human beings had a choice regarding the destructive versus the productive use of technology (*HC*, 3), even though her own argument indicated that the productive use was also destructive. The difference was that it did not entail the spectacular and apocalyptic destruction of war.

Whether productive or destructive, technological changes involve political questions of the first order. Technology is political not simply because, as is often said, it may be "used" for different purposes, which is a pious hope that is in no way self-evident, but because speech is involved. Wherever the relevance of speech is at stake, matters become political by definition, for speech is what makes human beings political. Accordingly, if we adjust our speech and "culture" to the achievements of technology, it will reflect the imperatives of technology. This is evident, as we said, in our use of the imagery of computers to interpret our daily life.

A less obvious but related consequence appears as a crisis within the natural sciences. This crisis is twofold: First, the truths of modern science can be proved empirically only by technical activity. "The thinking of our science," said von Weizsaecker, "proves itself only in action, in the successful experiment."[14] When Kant discussed the antinomies of reason, and in particular the conflict of morality and freedom with scientific causality, the difficulty was, so to speak, merely theoretical. No longer. Here I would mention the second side of the crisis in natural science, namely the everyday observation that scientific truths can be demonstrated theoretically only by mathematics and not by normal expression in speech and thought. The paradoxical "speech" dealing with subatomic physics, for example, was a consequence of our ability to act, as von Weizsaecker said, but to do so as if we were incorporeal dwellers in the universe. Commonsensical expression in speech and thought reflects the fact that we dwell on the earth, where the sun rises and sets. If nevertheless we act as if we were not at home on the earth but angelic observers "freely poised in space," then mathematical signs, not commonsensical language, are the appropriate means to express the truths opened up but also produced by such a perspective. When we try to "translate" such mathematicized "speech" back into commonsense speech, the result is nonsense. Or, to be more precise, it is as meaningless as Nietzsche and Democritus promised it would be.

To use the language of the preceding chapter, what science and technology have done, to speak most broadly, has been to force open the ground of appearance with the objective not of apprehending substance but of accounting for appearance in terms of numbers. Yet, human being is fitted both for phenomena and for substance so that the results have been perplexing. The consequences of combining abstract scientific phenomenal assumptions and technological activity is that we are unable to understand, that is, to think and to speak about things, that nevertheless we do.

This is highly significant. We cannot understand what we do because we cannot think or speak about it. We cannot think or speak about it because we lack a coherent language. Gadamer has made a similar observation. It was, he said, "ultimately significant that science not only does not think . . . but also does not really speak a language in the proper sense." Because science "has liberated itself from language" by developing its own system of signs, "are we not heading toward a future in which language-less, wordless adaptation makes the affirmation of reason negligible?"[15] The political problem of speechlessness, which is also the problem of worldlessness, is akin in one respect to that faced by St. Paul when dealing with glossolalia: there may be truths beyond ordinary speech and they may be highly significant to individual men, but they are utterly irrelevant to men as political beings. That is why, if holy gibberish cannot be interpreted into ordinary speech, the community can ignore it (1 Cor. 14). The problem of scientific-technological speech is politically significant because humans in the plural, that is, human beings insofar "as they live and move and act in this world, can experience meaningfulness only because they can talk with and make sense to each other and to themselves" (HC, 4). Scientists, however, take pride in objectivity, in a lack of care for their own stature or place in the world. But precisely for that reason their political judgment cannot be trusted. As a scientist, one has no care for the world, however much one may warn against the consequences of one's own actions when speaking up as a citizen. Various "coalitions of concerned scientists" are not simply collections of guilt-ridden hypocrites, though there is something faintly comic about their posturings. What remains true, however, is that we can not act on the basis of paradoxic or commonsensically contradictory speech. Otherwise, we would never build or operate our colliders and supercolliders. The difficulty lies in discovering what such actions mean.

Some hints are found in literature. *Gulliver's Travels,* for instance, considered at least some of these problems. Gulliver in Brobdingnag recapitulates Aristophanes' observations on the scientific interest in the size of a gnat's anus with his description of Brobdingnagian breasts. Lack of proper perspective turns what is naturally or humanly attractive into something ugly and repulsive. More important, however, was Gulliver's visit to Laputa, a flying island ruled by scientists.

Again there is no concern for the intermediate range of perception: The Laputians have one eye on the zenith and one eye looking inward, like perfect Cartesians. They study astronomy and music and understand the world only by way of those two sciences; they are lacking in ordinary sense experience and one gets their attention by beating them. They cut their food into geometric shapes and admire women insofar as their several parts resemble conic sections. They have no poetry and are unerotic; they overlook their wives' adultery even when it takes place in front of them. They have no understanding of politics, but Gulliver is astonished to report that they are greatly interested in it and think of themselves as having a special right to rule.

The power of the Laputians is based on science: their flying island is kept aloft according to the principles of Newtonian physics. Moreover, they threaten to cut off the sun or to crush the cities below them if they are refused the tribute necessary to ensure the scientists' leisure. Their power, Swift said, is nearly unlimited and their responsibilities are none. Accordingly the rulers of Laputa require neither virtue nor prudence. Swift's point, it seems to me, is that if the new science is allowed to flourish without restraint, it both destroys the natural perspectives of human beings and establishes a tyranny.

Both Aristophanes and Swift saw that science was indifferent or hostile to the commonsense questions that for most people inform politics. Aristophanes criticized the scientific study of a gnat's anus because it was both ugly and useless and so politically unimportant. Modern scientists have, so to speak, discovered the utility of measuring a gnat's anus: malaria control, for example. More importantly, the moderns have discovered the importance of power. Modern Laputians demand to be left alone by political men, and in exchange they allow political men to use their devices as they see fit. More to the point, even if modern Laputians wished to use the results of their science, they have no knowledge of what those results should be used for, at least none that is grounded in their science. For example, when a great scientist witnessed the first atomic explosion all he could do was identify himself with the image of death in the *Bhagavad-Gita*, hardly a source of political prudence.

Evidence for the atrophy of experiences of meaning in nature are several hundred years old. Bruno and Bodin were concerned with analyzing and resisting the problems that the new phenomenalism brought with it. A century and a half later the practical implications were still sufficiently remote that Swift could engage in satire. Today reality is sufficiently grotesque to make satire impossible: after all, how could it be exaggerated?

Let us turn now to another decisive and, for our society, perhaps threatening event, automation. Again technology has been central in modifying a fundamental aspect of the human condition, namely the toil and trouble of labor. Freedom from labor, which automation may provide for the many, has previously been accorded only the few. It might appear that all that automation promises is to achieve for all what, in the past, was the privilege of a small minority. The problem, however, is that, in the past, labor was despised as meaningless, whereas the modern age has brought with it a glorification of labor, the factual result of which is that the whole society, both the many and the few, however they are distinguished, has been transformed into a laboring society, or rather, a state/society of jobholders. Accordingly, if a laboring society is freed from the pain of labor by technology and lacks members who know of more meaningful activities than labor, it is hard to imagine a more miserable social order. Robots are symbols of the anguish of a society of jobholders because they extinguish what had already been degraded, namely labor. Factually, a laboring society freed from labor's toil and lacking anything more meaningful than a job to do (whether that job be king or plumber or cop on the beat), has largely relied on technologies of leisure management and television to fill up the empty time when one is off the job and neither sleeping nor eating. Hannah Arendt's importance here lies in raising the question, What is the meaning of what we are doing?

To begin to answer such a question Arendt proposed a reconsideration of the human condition in light of recent experiences. What we are doing, our activities, is within the capacities of all humans, alive or dead or yet unborn. For this reason Arendt called them "the most elementary articulations of the human condition" (HC, 5). Thinking, in contrast, is able to transcend the conditions of human existence, but only mentally, never in the reality of the existing world. It is a task to which she and all human beings are called when, as Tocqueville said, "The mind of man wanders in obscurity." The extent of the obscurity involved was indicated by an earlier observation, that we live in an age of obsessive phenomenalism.

The historical context within which phenomenalism grew has already been indicated. One way to see the luxuriant results in our own time is to consider the peculiar genre of literature produced in response to it: science fiction. From Mary Shelley's *Frankenstein* to contemporary cartoons and commercial advertising, one can follow the transformation from fiction to obsession on a large scale. An intermediate or ambivalent position might be held for a time by a text such as *Brave New World;* on its publication it was unclear whether it was supposed to be a satire on phenomenalism as an obsessive stupidity or a warning about the effects of science on human society. Things have progressed since Huxley's book first appeared; respected, or at least well known, scientists now expect to make contact with creatures in outer space and flying saucers have been sighted with at least the same regularity that our medieval predecessors encountered horned demons with claws and a tail. The reason for our contemporary obsessions, it seems, is the same commitment to a phenomenal world that was discussed earlier as evidence of philosophical illiteracy. The difference, however, is that we must now consider the matter as a mass phenomenon.

Looked at in this fashion, the achievements of technology, magnificent as they have been, are also obsessional. As evidence one need only observe the widespread argument that we must do what we can do. One may say that this characteristic of technological consciousness constitutes the main objective of the technological society. The results, from atomic weapons, to population management, to a cure for AIDS, all signify the same process: purposes become devoid of substantive content and are determined only by available technical implements. In the language developed earlier, phenomenal obsessions have replaced spiritual order. In Arendt's terminology, such obsessions indicate that technological consciousness has no care for the world.

We know that the end of the road has been reached in the politics of this century. Looked at from the longer perspective, indicated by references to medieval Christian thinkers from Augustine to Innocent III, the chief characteristic of the present age is that Christian eschatology has been eclipsed by notions of infinite processes operating in history and in nature, themselves no longer understood as substantive orders of meaning but as closed phenomenal streams. With such assumptions directing the understanding of nature and history, "research" has come to mean investigation leading to the discovery of the "laws" that govern the several processes. Moreover, the world is no longer "this world." Accordingly, it can no longer be "renounced" so as to gain a world to come. In an immanentized world cut off from eschatological fulfillment there is nothing to tempt us and there is no sin. We cannot, therefore, be Augustinian pilgrims toward the Heavenly City. And yet, as Howard has observed, just "when the world becomes Man's permanent abode [that is, when the experience of a world-transcendent beyond has atrophied], the *idea* of the world is shaken. It is shaken by technology."[16] The paradox of modern worldlessness is that it presupposes the triumph of what for Augustine or for any Christian thinker would have been "worldliness." The starkest manifestation of the destruction of the world through the imaginative introduction of phenomenal processes into stable substantive order has been the totalitarian regime. By contemporary technical standards, this combination of the slaughterhouse and the lunatic asylum was deformed only by its inefficiencies.

# 4
# The Modern Human Condition

The term *human condition* sounds vague. As with her illustrious predecessors, Innocent III and Montaigne, Arendt meant something precise by it. "Whatever touches or enters into a sustained relationship with human life immediately assumes the character of a condition of human existence"(*HC*, 9). There are three basic conditions under which life has been given to humans on earth. Human beings are alive, having been born and having to die. They are therefore limited by birth and death and must labor in order to live (Gen. 3:16). Second, they are born into a world they never made, but they can modify it in order to make themselves at home. Third, they are they, not one. They are roused to action in order to find their own place among their fellow beings.

The world is first of all a world of appearance, of phenomena. Every creature born into it is born well equipped to deal with a realm where being and appearance coincide. They are fit for worldly existence because they are not just in the world, as ink is in the pen, but are of the world. They are both subject and object, perceivers and perceived. Arendt was not following Heidegger or the later thought of Merleau-Ponty in these formulas, but Aristotle: "What appears to all, this we call being."[1] Such words carry no implication that we are exclusively of the world. As has already been indicated, for philosophers, for whom philosophy is the "practice of dying" (*Phaedo* 67d–e), and for Christians, for whom exclusive love of the world meant estrangement from God (1 John 2:15–16), there was an order of meaning that transcended the world. In a sense, estrangement from the world

116

was a necessary condition for trust or hope (*pistis*) in the divine order.[2] Arendt was not concerned focally with experiences of world-transcendent realities but with human worldliness. In this and following chapters, the question of world-transcendent reality is largely ignored as well. This does not mean that Arendt was unacquainted with world-transcendent experiences. On the contrary, her first book, on Augustine's concepts of love, dealt extensively with the central experiences by which consciousness transcends the world.[3] The limits of Arendt's perspective will be suggested in the Conclusion to part II. Considered solely within the context of worldly experience, the ability of scientific technology to force open appearances in order to substitute for them a mathematical or quasi-mathematical algorithm is to be contrasted not with the meditative apprehension of substance, an experience with a world-transcendent dimension, but with common sense. Human worldly affairs are guided and interpreted by common sense. Accordingly, whatever the potency of scientific technology in establishing and acting on phenomenal reality, common sense insists that regarding human things, being and appearance are indistinguishable. To all appearances, then, we are fit for earthly life. The conditions for human existence, namely life (natality and mortality), worldliness, and plurality, correspond to three fundamental activities, labor, work, and action.

All three conditions and activities are interrelated. Labor produces vital necessities and sustains the life processes of the human body. Work produces things that make up the world. Action produces nothing but appearances and new beginnings; it occurs, without the mediation of nature or of things, directly before others. All are related to politics in one way or another, but action is preeminently political because plurality is preeminently the condition of political life. All three activities are connected to the general condition of human life, namely birth and death. Labor ensures both individual and species life; work provides a measure of permanence, a frame within which the otherwise futile life processes can operate; action, so far as it founds and sustains political bodies, sustains history and thereby the possibility of meaning.

In addition to the conditions under which life has been given to humans on earth, they are conditioned by the consequences of what enters the human world of its own accord and by what is created in it by humans: either way the impact of the world conditions existence. (Reciprocally, the things of the world would be unrelated, that is, would be a nonworld, if they did not condition existence.) What is striking about technology, considered as a general condition of modern existence, is the degree to which synthetic conditions have been substituted for natural ones. The most radical changes in the human condition to date were indicated or alluded to previously: a few human beings have temporarily emigrated from the earth in order to dwell in space or on the moon. Perhaps an even more radical possibility involves not forsaking the earth as habitat but altering the nature of its inhabitants through biomedical technologies. In this case new species made or partially made by human beings would, or could, roam the planet.

Human beings are not totally conditioned by the world. This is made evident, among other ways, by the "little miracle" of lying (*PF*, 250). In order to lie, one must be sufficiently free of conditioning circumstances so as to be able to imagine that they might be different. From the point of view of the world, the chief characteristic of imagination is that it is invisible. The imagination can recall and recollect what is no more and anticipate what is not yet, provided that it withdraw from the world and the world's present urgencies. It is possible, however, to make present urgencies so great that imaginative capacities are paralyzed. This is called total domination, a condition that has been experimentally achieved in concentration camps, though not in the world at large. It is actualized when human beings, normally a mixture of spontaneous and conditioned being, have been transformed into entirely conditioned beings whose reactions, under any circumstances, can be fully and accurately calculated. In the ordinary language of fabrication, the goal of total domination is to transform human beings into bundles of reliable reactions or patterns of behavior. The means by which it is done is terror. Total domination, achieved by terror, has the effect of making invisibility and withdrawal from the world impossible by extinguishing human internality. This is what makes those places unfit for human habitation.

The experimental conditions achieved in concentration camps are, happily, rare events in history. What the very extremeness of these phenomena shows is the degree to which not "human nature" but the capabilities and the mutual relationships of human beings can be altered. These changes are most easily observed in the changing self-interpretations of human being, or rather in what might be called the changing interpretative hierarchies of the human condition. Such interpretations are expressed by well known tags, usually in Greek or Latin, prefaced by the phrase, "man is": a *zoon politikon* or *noetikon*, an *animal rationale* or *laborans*, *homo faber* or *ludens* or *furens* or *viator*. The fact is, human beings "are" all of these things because each referred to an aspect of the human condition.

What has changed historically is the understanding that human beings have of the relationships of these several capabilities. For this reason Arendt spoke of reversals. These reversals did not involve the human condition, except in the case of concentration camps, a condition, to repeat, for which humans were not fit. The reversals were reversals of understanding or of interpretation of the constituent elements of the human condition. Reversals in interpretation are important for purposes of this study as well, but not all interpretative changes are reversals.

\*

*Politics* is a Greek word, akin to *athletics*. Athletics is what athletes do just as politics is what *polites*, that is, citizens, do. *Society*, in contrast, is derived from Latin. The chief meaning is that of an association with a specific (and not necessarily political) purpose. For Aristotle, humans were "social" in the sense of being gregarious, but so were termites and dolphins. "Social" companionship was not so much a mark of human existence as a necessity imposed by the needs of biological life. As the first book of the *Politics* makes clear, the center of biological life and its needs was the family and the household, the *oikia*, from which our term *economics* is derived. Outside the household and its necessities stood the citizen doing politics, which for the most part meant speaking up, speaking his mind, exchanging views, refining his opinions. Sometimes it meant fighting. Politics was a way of life, a *bios*, whose chief activity was public speech. What took place in the household, which was, of course, very important, took place in private, hidden from other citizens. Moreover, family life was not employed with the making of speeches that exchanged opinions but with speeches that made rules articulate, performed religious duties, instructed children and slaves.

Politics was related to household affairs only in the sense that as a matter of course, the necessities of life had to be taken care of before one could literally step across the threshold into the public world. Necessity ruled the household. Or rather, the household was, of necessity, managed by violence so as to liberate (some) human beings from its pressing cares and enable them to lead what Werner Jaeger called a kind of second life, in freedom. Aristotle called doing politics the good life. What made it "good" was that it was not bound to the necessities of biological life processes. Moreover, being "good," political life could become "excellent." By definition, excellence is public: one can excel, that is, distinguish oneself, only in public. The Greeks expressed this activity in a characteristic verb, *aristeuein*, to be best of all.

The term *public* signifies two distinct but related things. First, it means that what appears in public can be seen by everybody. The presence of others is required not simply to enable human beings to excel but to assure them of the reality of the world. Second, the term signifies the world itself, the things humans possess in common that relate and separate them one from another. This public space endures and might as easily be called a public time. Or rather, the public world is both the space of appearance of this generation and the enduring link across the generations that enables the institutions of the dead to influence the present and enables the living to endure in memory. Theoretically speaking, the public realm is the space-time of earthly immortality in the memory of generations of human beings and of relative permanence.

Because the public world both relates and separates, its reality depends on the presence of several perspectives. These perspectives are all distinct so that there can never be devised a common denominator or an objective meaning to it. The common world is a meeting ground, but a meeting ground of people who have their own distinct locations. The plurality of perspectives ensures that there will be many versions of the historical truth. On the basis of those partially evident truths or partially completed stories, human beings begin to act, and so do others, who may become opponents. Inherently, therefore, the plurality of perspectives on a common world constitutes political reality.

The political expression of public life is the equality of citizens before the law. Two points follow from this: those who have no place in the public world, who cannot be seen or heard, have no standing before the law. Second, equality before the law (or before God, for that matter) is always an equalization of differences, which in turn reflects the condition of plurality.

The distinction between public and private was perhaps optimally present in the polis life of the Greeks. For Aristotle the difference between politics, the activities that related men to, and within, a common public world, and economics, the activities of household management connected to the necessities of life, was quasi-axiomatic. It is not so for contemporary citizens, for reasons to be discussed. Nevertheless, the distinction is not arbitrary even in the contemporary world. Consider, for example, the status of children. The most fervent supporter of "children's rights" would, one hopes, have second thoughts about granting infants the responsibilities of citizenship. By nature, one may say, children seek the obscurity of the family and are in any case unfit for the merciless exposure of public life.

Maintaining the distinction between public and private is essential to the maintenance of the world. The main characteristic of the world with respect to the individuals who share it is that it is more permanent than they. In consequence, there arises a conflict between the interests of individual mortals and the interest of the common world they inhabit. The origin of this conflict, for the individual, lies in the immediate urgency of self-interests that protect the life process. A modest amount of persecution is all it takes to ensure that individuals will be incapable of forming a public space. Persecution puts pressure on individuals and constricts the inner space of their world. It produces a warm glow in the dark, heat from huddled bodies, but no light by which to see and care for the world. It even produces a natural compassion in outsiders, but "the humanity of the insulted and injured has never yet survived the hour of liberation by so much as a minute." This does not mean that compassion is insignificant, because in fact it makes insult endurable. Politically speaking, however, "it is absolutely irrelevant" (MDT, 16–17). Politics, the public realm, the world, becomes distorted when used as a theater for spiritual or psychological therapies. And correspondingly, the souls of human beings are also distorted when politics is transformed into an inner experience. Let loose on the world,

compassion devours every structure. Social revolutionaries beginning with Robespierre have demonstrated the fact time and
again.

Modern technological societies are not threatened by outbursts
of revolutionary compassion. Nor are great economic sacrifices
and corresponding acts of courage required to liberate citizens
from the care for mere life. Rather, the boundary between public
and private, and thereby the world, is challenged in a different
way by a lack of privacy. The primary condition for privacy is
ownership, not property, and ownership is respected by neither
capitalists nor socialists. Both practice expropriation and both respect acquisition because both have given their primary commitment to technology. The absence of privacy in mass technological
society implies that equality is not equality before the law, or still
less, before God. It is a kind of equality of opportunity, but opportunity is limited to wealth and power, neither of which allows
for resistance to technological expansion. On the contrary, both
provide greater opportunities to consume by increasing the range
of commodities available. Simply put, affluence is a measure of
degrees of equality and inequality that does not challenge the
requirements of the mass technological society. Accordingly, affluence has become the measure or standard of living. And affluence, as Borgmann pointed out, "has an undeniable glamour. It is
the embodiment of the free, rich, and imperial life that technology has promised."[4] The glamour that accompanies affluence is,
by nature, a phenomenal reality. There is adequate evidence to
indicate that it can easily become an obsession. More important,
it means that, just as poverty, persecution, and misery pose a
threat to the world, so too does an affluent society.

*

Antique and medieval Latin sometimes rendered Aristotle's
zoon politikon as animal socialis. Modern social reality, which is
neither public nor private, strictly speaking, added greatly to the
linguistic difficulties involved in sorting out various meanings and
in describing the historical realities to which they refer. What for
Aristotle was a clear and obvious distinction in reality has become
a question of great conceptual subtlety. Ernest Barker once remarked that, for Aristotle, "political economy" was a contradiction in terms; for many of our contemporaries, that term best

describes the scientific discourse involved in describing and pre-
scribing the administration of the state, the organization charged
with large-scale public housekeeping.

The existence of society and of the state has radically changed
the meaning of the old distinction between public and private.[5]
No longer is privacy tied to privation; unlike Pericles, we do not
think that "private men" are less than fully human, though we
have preserved at least something of the connotation in our word
*idiot* (Thucydides 4.2). The reason for this change, according to
Arendt, is that modern privacy is as much opposed to the social
as it is to the political. The most important function of modern
privacy is "to shelter the intimate" against "society's unbearable
perversion of the human heart" (*HC*, 38–39). The heart, unlike
the household, has no visible place in the world; nor does society, against which it must be protected, have a definite locality.
There are no thresholds between the heart and society, no walls
to shelter what is private from the public gaze. Arendt no less
than Aristotle saw the advantages of human gregariousness.
When social ties are cut, life is much more difficult. Morality, for
example, is more easily maintained in the context of an explicit
social status. But society is more than a confirmation of "moral
standards" and evidence of gregariousness. It demands of its
members that they act as though they had but one opinion and
one interest. It smothers the heart, which then, with a sense of
its own individuality, indignantly rebels at the demand it conform. It starts to whine and turns romantic. Romantic individual-
ism, however, is hardly a political position at all. Moreover, it
cries out for the discipline of the state.

Originally the "social question," which has become so important in the modern world, was independent both of politics and
of technology. Prior to the modern age, the Aristotelean distinction between the few who one way or another liberate themselves
from poverty and the many who labored in poverty was assumed
to be inevitable. What cast doubt upon those convictions, or
rather, what demonstrated they were false, was American colonial
experience and the contrast it made with European monarchies
that carried on their housekeeping in public but without in
any way altering the economic circumstances of the poor. In this
way, "America" became the symbol of a society without poverty
long before the technical means had been invented that could

actually abolish the want and misery that long had been thought unchangeable.

The "reversal" in the understanding of poverty was politically far more important than the initial technical discoveries and the application of them to the process of production. Poverty was abject because it put human beings under an absolute bodily necessity, known immediately to everybody (because it is shared with animals) and the condition of life itself. The example of America indicated that poverty was not a historical necessity as well, from which the conclusion was drawn that political action could remove its curse. Unfortunately, as is indicated later, the meaning and purpose of politics are perverted when it is transformed into a means or a technique to achieve a goal.

Poverty and the cares and worries of the body belong to the sphere of the household. If they are a matter of public concern they can be dealt with administratively, by the state, rather than by the process of persuasion and decision. In the end, the desire for a general liberation, not from tyranny but from biological necessity, seems inevitably to result in the imposition of an administrative necessity. State and society are, in this respect, two sides of the same coin. For Aristotle, the distinction between household rule or administration and political freedom was substantive. The legitimate source of rulership lies in the desire to be rid of life's necessity and to have others bear its burden. Slavery was justified by that desire; technology, including the administrative technology of the state (and certainly not political ideas), has demonstrated the untruth of the Aristotelean view that only violence, only rule over others, could make some humans free. Abolition of the violent rule of masters over slaves has meant the substitution of administrative rule for it, not the abolition of rule.

No revolution has ever solved the social question. In France, which became the model for nearly all subsequent revolutionary upheavals, the attempt to liberate people from want led to the terror that sped the revolution to its Napoleonic end. In America, as compared to Europe or Asia, the social question can scarcely be said to have existed. To the extent that poverty was related to politics at all, it was an incidental consequence of the "mild government" the colonies enjoyed under the British crown. After the successful separation from Britain, the ambiguity of the revolutionary purpose became more visible. To this day it is not clear whether the purpose of the U.S. government is prosperity or freedom. A commercial republic, for all its advantages and virtues, is still an ambiguous political reality. Many early nineteenth-century immigrants were, in fact, political refugees. Later, as Emma Lazarus's verses on the pedestal of the Statue of Liberty proclaimed, came the tired, the poor, the huddled masses, "the wretched refuse of your teeming shore." This new type of immigrant came for economic reasons, was not politically minded, and had little knowledge of the meaning America held for Western European political thought as the land of freedom and self-government. The new immigrant saw America as a land of opportunity, where opportunity meant material well-being rather than republican political forms. These poor, having grown rich in America, did not necessarily turn to politics. Many simply became richer. Such prosperity, it bears repeating, is fully compatible with the demands, constraints, and opportunities of the mass technological society. It consists in the possession and consumption of the most refined and various commodities. At least, it appears that way from below, which is the place from which it is seen by most people.

It is certainly true that freedom can come only to those whose needs have been satisfied. It is also true that it will never come to those who seek only the satisfaction of biological desires. As Aristotle also pointed out, they simply prolong needlessly the process of overcoming need. Whatever else it may be, the *tableau vivant* of conspicuous consumption is not politics. In *Democracy in America*[6] Tocqueville argued that in 1835 America had still maintained a balance between "the most selfish greed" and "the most lively patriotism." At the same time he warned, "A human heart cannot really be divided in this way." Arnold Gehlen commented on this passage: "What does Tocqueville depict here? Did he foresee the cities teeming with millions in the welfare states of the rich affluent societies? Did he address the conditions that prevail when all of politics comes to revolve around vast arrangements for the administration of everyday existence?"[7] Many observers have answered these rhetorical questions by arguing that economic growth does not necessarily entail political liberty nor constitute proof that political liberty exists This is not to say that affluence is, by itself, a political evil, which would be absurd, but that the activities necessary for life in an affluent society may undermine the continued existence of political freedom.

There are several reasons why affluence may pose a danger to political life, the most obvious of which is that it promotes mass conformity. In the polis, one-man rule was the organizational device of the household; in early modern society, one-man rule was repeated, this time on the grander scale of the "national family." In both instances, the opinion of a single man governed all, and so, in a way, there existed a kind of unanimity. Moreover, in Europe, as distinct from North America, the monarch was a national monarch, the ruler of self-conscious people attached to a particular homeland, the product of past labor, on which history had left its traces. For European nations, the homeland was the milieu into which one was born, to which one belonged by right of birth. North American societies, because they are immigrant societies, could not possibly be national societies in the European manner.[8] But this has simply meant that social conformity is based on something other than nationality, not that the danger is absent. The reason why conformity is a danger is that, in the end, it destroys the world.

In order for there to be a world, things and individuals appear in a variety of ways without changing their identity. Sameness appears in diversity. The common world can be destroyed, then, either by dissolving it into sheer diversity or by congealing it into sameness. Politically speaking, dissolution into diversity is the objective of tyranny, a regime where no one can agree with anyone else because they have nothing in common, trusting in neither the world nor one another. But equally the public world may be destroyed if sameness no longer appears in several aspects. If everyone prolongs and reinforces the view of everyone else, the result is a singular experience innumerably multiplied, not plurality. Without a world to separate and relate them, individuals are turned into members of a "lonely crowd" (Riesman) or they are compounded into the intensified isolation of Lazarus's huddled mass. These are equivalent social forms inasmuch as neither contains a public or private space. Accordingly, no exchange of views is possible; the world is invariably degraded. Moreover, with the application of the appropriate techniques of propaganda, the two forms of lonely crowd and huddled mass can be easily changed into one another. The administrative objective, a well adjusted population, necessarily consists of depersonalized individuals. Only such persons can be considered as reliable data for the application of disciplined planning technologies.

If early modern societies can be thought of as national housekeeping under the supervision of one person, the monarch, late modern societies are supervised by nobody. This "no-man rule," the rule of interconnected bureaus, is certainly not no-rule. In a fully developed bureaucracy there is no one with whom one can argue or dispute, no one on whom the pressures of power can be exerted. Rules are rules, period. It is, Arendt said, "a tyranny without a tyrant" (OV, 81), the chief drawback of which is that it is a form of tyranny for which the desperate remedy of tyrannicide is necessarily excluded. Any particular bureaucrat is simply a functionary.[9] As Gadamer observed, "In a technological civilization, it is inevitable in the long run that the adaptive power of the individual is rewarded more than his creative power. Put in terms of a slogan, the society of experts is simultaneously a society of functionaries."[10] Functionaries function; they do not act and so are in no respect irreplaceable. Just the opposite: the whole purpose of functional organization as Alfred Krupp explained with respect to his own steel operation, is that anyone, good or bad, stupid or intelligent, could make it go.

So far as opinion is concerned, the same assumption applies to bureaucracy as applied to the ancient household or to national monarchy: society has a single opinion and a single interest. This opinion is expressed by being processed through the correct channels; the corresponding interest is guarded, fostered, and implemented by administrative decisions, which are invariably rendered in the imperative mood. Action is completely excluded from bureaucratically regulated society, just as it was excluded from the ancient household. Instead of action, society expects normal, disciplined, and consistent behavior, behavior that conforms to the rules, whatever they may be.[11] In the early days of "high" society, behavior was regulated by rules that reflected social rank; in the bourgeois society of the last century, behavior conformed to class expectations; in today's mass society, behavior reflects job and function.

Society is greatly aided in its search for smooth functioning by the transformation of political parties from representative bodies that enabled citizens to participate in political life into bureaucra-

cies representing nobody except the members of the party machines that staff them (CR, 89; OV, 81–82). Even those who do
not behave, delinquents, for example, perform a function: they
keep the police and social workers busy and so, in a sense, they
do behave. The absence of public action, one hardly need add,
means an end to excellence as well. Political leaders, under these
conditions, are also functionaries with a job to do. The less flam-
boyant are simply managers of public opinion; the others are, in
Robert Eden's words, "career demagogues," who use the public
stage for their own, not public, purposes.[12] For them, the world
is a tool and they are opportunists, a fact that is quite properly
recorded in survey data that reflect the public's opinion of political leaders.

The normal social self is a disciplined being whose behavior is
predictable. Such a self conforms to expected patterns and regu-
lar statistical frequency distributions. Now statistical laws are
valid only for large numbers of items and long periods of time.
Meaning, however, is disclosed only in those rare events and acts
that light up, usually quite briefly, our everyday, normal existence. The statistical analysis of politics, therefore, obliterates its
own subject matter by turning rare and significant events into
error variance. As David Luban observed, "In politics to control
the variables is to erase the data."[13] The ridiculousness of the
"behavioral persuasion" in politics has a grimmer side. The only
reason to study politics is to understand the meaning of events,
not to predict or control—for which it would be necessary to
make people predictable and controllable. Statistical uniformity is
not, therefore, the harmless ideal of technological maniacs but
the political ideal of a disciplined society that has entirely sub-
merged itself in the routine of everyday living. It is, accordingly,
fully reconciled to the technological-scientific outlook inherent in
its existence (HC, 43). A perfectly anonymous and uniform society is an administrator's ideal.

Though it might have horrified him, Engels's old dream, that
the governance of people be replaced with the administration of
things, has partially been realized in modern technological mass
society. Moreover, the constant increase in leisure for the masses,
characteristic of all industrialized countries, approximates the
"utopian" expectations of the German Ideology. But it is also true
that free time is not the Greek skole, which also had the form of

an active verb meaning "to do leisure" or "to leisure," a notion that is nearly unimaginable in modern languages. Modern "leisure" is just leftover time, time available after the job is done, the meals are down, and you have had enough sleep. Vacant time nowadays is a gap in the biologically conditioned cycle of labor that entertainment and hobbies are designed to fill.

*

The modern human condition is that of jobholder in a mass technological society. Society and the state are concerned with public housekeeping, with the affairs of biological life, and in particular with the consumption of commodities. With the admission of housekeeping activities to the public realm, society has grown, devouring first the older realms of public and private, initially (through the process of expropriating property) by eroding the border, the difference maintained by law, between them. More recently, the sphere of intimacy has also been invaded by society. Any bookstore, for example, is filled with technical manuals on self-manipulation, the object of which is to adjust the manipulee, the "heart," to the social norms of the day. Society, the public domain of the life process, apparently has an irresistible tendency to be fruitful and multiply, like life itself. The result is the affluent society characterized by the extensive consumption of an ever-growing range of commodities. And the state is indeed its executive committee. The end of the violent rule by masters over slaves resulted in the rule of nobody, that is, administrative rule, over everybody. Efficient administration requires a predictable population; proper planning can hardly be undertaken and carried out in the absence of mass conformity and anticipated but marginal deviance.

It is difficult to raise substantive questions regarding the modern human condition because doing so entails abandoning the phenomenalist understanding of human existence. Economic prosperity, for example, is sustained by a productive technological society and an efficient state. Moreover, it is justified by an elaborate theory of economic phenomena. Productive power is coupled to phenomenal knowledge. The theory of economic phenomena, for example, is concerned with making certain assumptions about economic rationality, individual self-interest, laws of supply and demand, and so on. The objective would be to indicate the mechanisms whereby the rational economic actions of a

collection of individuals would result in the maximum production
of goods and services for the whole society.[14] Assuming the validity of the assumptions of the science of economics, nothing can
be inferred regarding the nobility, justice, or desirability of a
political regime with a legal order established in such a way as to
maximize economically rational action and, therefore, productivity. The substantive question to be raised concerning this topic
would be; Is the maximum production of commodities the most
worthwhile activity for human beings? Are the required sacrifices
in terms of spiritual, ethical, political, and aesthetic realities
worth the increases in productivity?

Such questions are not addressed by economics, and there is
no intention of requiring that they should be. Like Duhem, we
can all be "positivists" on this question with a minimal loss of a
sense of reality. On the other hand, we may speak of phenomenalist obsession when the theoretical laws of economics are
turned into standards of action. The usual "right-wing" version of
this obsessive deformation is to hold that the theory of economic
relations constitutes in the substance of justice and right order.
According to this deformation, any attempt to intervene in the
economy in the name of a higher or more comprehensive vision
of human existence must be resisted.

The justification for this resistance is the theory of economics
itself, according to which the maximum long-run productivity of
the society is ensured by the operation of the market. Short-run
inconvenience must, accordingly, be sacrificed. The contrast between long and short run, however, is highly questionable. Considered in terms of human substance, the short term is real,
concrete human existence, and the long-term is purely imaginary.
When the anticipated future, which serves as a focus in view of
which the concept of the long-term makes sense, becomes substantively actual, as it must do through the efflux of time, what it
substantively *is*, is again the short-term presence of real human
beings living at that point in time, namely the former focus of the
long term. Equally questionable is the substantive assumption regarding the being of *homo economicus* as producer and consumer.
In Arendt's language, obsessive economic phenomenalism is evidence of the triumph of *animal laborans*.

Criticism usually comes from the "Left." It tends to center on
the brutality of the action entailed by a consistent and single-

minded pursuit of commodity maxima. To use familiar ideological language, economic liberals are vulnerable to the criticism that they have cold hearts as well as cool heads. The fatal flaw in this criticism is that the proposed remedy, planning by the state, a remedy most emphatically applied by the national socialists of Germany and the international socialists of the Soviet Union, is itself a manifestation of obsessive phenomenalism. Moreover, just as the brutality of the liberal market subordinates the individual to the economic mechanism so too do the several varieties of socialism treat the individual as a function of the plan. As the two regimes just mentioned indicate, when the administrative apparatus of the state is charged with formulating and applying the plan, the brutalities of the liberal market fade into insignificance.

As for "social democrats," as they call themselves, two observations may be made. First, either they are serious or they are not. If they are serious, it is difficult to see what distinguishes them from the totalitarian murderers beyond a squeamishness made evident in their equivocal use of words. If they are not serious, they are no more than moralizing romantics, beautiful souls whose first principle is to maintain a pure heart. Since most social democrats would be unlikely to accept either unflattering characterization as pertaining to them, a second comment is in order. If social democrats can advance their view regarding the brutality both of the liberal market and of the totalitarian planners, and without considering themselves to be whiners, it is because they presuppose the existence of a substantially existing democratic social order. In that case what remains questionable is their silence regarding the nature of the social order, whose existence they uncritically assume.

The expansion of the life process in advanced technological societies is simply an intense and concentrated form of an ecumenic phenomenon. Humankind, which began as an eschatological symbol of human universality and was transmogrified into a symbol of humanist aspirations, has become a kind of everyday reality as a consequence of the technological development of the Western world. Europe and North America did not simply unite the world through technical cleverness; they exported at the same time the domestic processes of their own disintegration.

From a theoretical rather than a pragmatic perspective, the danger inherent in the new reality of humankind, considered as an ecumenic society and based on technologies of administration, communication, and violence, is that it promises to destroy all particularity, all local and national traditions, and thereby obliterate the genuine origins of common meanings. Even if it were true that these transformations of particularity were necessary for the mutual understanding of all people, the result would be a shallowness that would also transform human being beyond recognition. It would be more than mere superficiality; it would be "as though the whole dimension of depth, without which human thought, even on the mere level of technical invention, would simply disappear" (*MDT,* 87). Such an outcome, the global affluent society, would have the effect of transforming all the historical pasts of all nations, tribes, and hordes, in their vast disparity, diversity, variety, and bewildering strangeness for one another, into temporary obstacles to a unity at the lowest common denominator. How low, how common, is difficult to imagine.

# 5
# Modes of Active Life

The opening words of the three central chapters of *The Human Condition* are an engaging understatement: "The distinction between labor and work which I propose is unusual" (*HC*, 79). As has already been noted, distinctions are central in Arendt's work: between public and private, politics and economics, the social and the intimate affairs of the heart. If this particular distinction between labor and work seemed arbitrary, decisive evidence against such a judgment lay in "the simple fact that every European language, ancient and modern, contains two etymologically unrelated words for what we have come to think of as the same activity, and retains them in the face of their persistent synonymous usage" (*HC*, 80). Now, Arendt has argued at length that in language "the past is contained ineradicably, thwarting all attempts to get rid of it once and for all" (*MDT*, 204). The language we use and the historical depth of changing usage are worldly phenomena. Distinctions based on etymology and historical usage are therefore based on the evidence of the world as surely as stratigraphic correlations are based on trilobites.

More than the reliability of the world and the world's languages guarded against the danger of making arbitrary distinctions. With respect to labor and work, the distinction between the two activities depends not on differences within the process of production but on the worldly durability of the product. The difference between a table, which may last generations, and bread, our daily bread, the staff of life, which endures but a day (and is best fresh from the oven), is greater than the difference between a carpenter and a baker. That is, language is inherently world-oriented, whereas the theories spun to make sense of the world are human-oriented. The differences that bear on our understanding of the world are visible only from the point of view of the world. Distinct from both use objects such as tables and consumer goods such as bread are the worldly "products" of action and speech, namely human relationships, the reality of which depends on the presence and testimony of others. Acting and speaking are manifestations of thought, which is an activity that need not be manifest at all to be real. Considered by itself, thought is even more unworldly than action and speech. To become in any way worldly, thoughts must be transformed, first into the sheer appearance of speech and deed; these then must be remembered and finally turned into things, sayings, books, monuments.

From the standpoint of the world, laboring is destructive and devouring; it tends to consume all worldly things as if they were good things of life. From the standpoint of nature, work, not labor, is destructive since it removes matter from nature without swiftly returning it. On the contrary, work reforms nature as a thing. Technology shares characteristics of both kinds of destruction. Like labor, it destroys worldly things quickly, but like work, it does not return them to nature. It reforms what it destroys in order to destroy what it reforms. Technology shares the process character of labor but also the formative character of work. Unlike work, technology does not stop when the work is done; unlike labor, technological processes are not guided by nature.

Considered on its own, labor produces not new objects for the human artifice but rather objects whose consumption ensures the reproduction, and more, of the producer. By oppression and exploitation, that is, by violence, or by technological multiplication, starting with the division of labor, the laborious efforts of some can sustain the life of all. Both because its products are quickly consumed and because the naturally fertile activity itself concentrates on the maintenance and growth of life, labor is oblivious of the world. Its productivity is always measured against the biologically necessary requirements of the life process for its own reproduction and "not in the quality or character of the things it produces" (HC, 93). Indeed, in an affluent technological society, all use objects that might give stability to the world are treated as consumer goods. In this light, the greatest consequence of technology is to have increased productivity by removing the only element of stability in the production process, skill itself. Specialized workmanship has everywhere given way to the divided and coordinated organization of labor into a smooth production process consisting of simple but endless tasks.

Labor is the central activity of society. This is why the theoretical justification for a society of laborers came first from the economists; what they called it was the right to accumulate wealth, which was rightly seen as the life of society. Any attempt to check or control wealth was understood as an attempt to destroy the life of society. Under such circumstances, the privacy of property can only be a restraint on the relentless growth of social wealth. Indeed, there seems to be no economic reason why very wealthy societies should not be propertyless, with individual incomes proportioned in terms of contributions to the total income of society. It is certainly clear that the production of wealth, but not the safeguarding of property, is inherent in the operation of the technological society.

That wealth and property are only contingently related is evident in the change of society from one of property holders to one of jobholders. For example, Locke's notion of property was that it was chiefly a refuge from the public realm even while it was a base from which the common wealth could be appropriated and increased. It both was connected to the common world and was itself a worldly institution. When interest shifted from property to the growth of wealth and the process of accumulation, a minor "reversal" took place. Property then appeared as an impediment to the growth of social wealth precisely because it was owned and owners eventually died. The life of society, however, is unlimited by the human condition of appearing into, and disappearing from, the world. For this reason, the life of society can be the subject of unhampered accumulation and infinite wealth. Social life, apparently, can be worldless.

The question of worldlessness alters the significance of automation. From this point of view the much deplored mechanization of natural life and increasingly pervasive articificiality are less important than the possibility that all human productivity might be integrated into an intensified life process that would follow automatically, without pain or effort, its own ever-recurrent cycle. The chief consequence would be to erode even more rapidly the durability of the world. Nonlabor time, empty time, would increasingly be spent consuming not the necessities of life but its superfluities.

Earlier it was observed that nothing could be worse than a society of laborers who had virtually no labor to perform. Now it is clear why. The triumph of the modern age over necessity and the apparently eternal curse of toil, hardship, and poverty was achieved by the emancipation of labor. In Arendt's words, that emancipation "forced open" the boundaries that distinguished and protected the world from the biological processes of nature. As a result, "the always threatened stability of the human world" was abandoned and delivered over to natural processes (*HC*, 126). Independently, animal laborans knows only the life processes, the endless rhythm of exhaustion and regeneration, the pain of toil followed by the pleasure of relief. It seems, moreover, that a life of pleasure without the experience of pain and effort would also reduce what had served to compensate pain, namely pleasure. The widespread, if not universal, unhappiness of modern society can in part at least be traced to the joyless quest for joy (Strauss) that seems inevitably to be a consequence of the emancipation of labor from necessity. Its only achievement has been to devour the world.

\*

Nature and the earth generally present a different aspect to homo faber than to animal laborans. The earth conditions life, including human life, by providing it with an abundance of good things. For homo faber, however, these good things are merely the provision of raw material whose value lies in the work he or she performs on them. The things of the world, not nature, constitute the condition under which specifically human life can be at home on earth. This is why mass technological society, where the individual as social animal rules supreme and where the "green revolution" could guarantee the survival of the species, is at the same time threatening humanity with extinction by destroying the things of the world, and thereby the worldliness of the world.

The activity of work fabricates the things of the world, the totality of which constitutes the human artifice. Using things the way they were intended does not cause them to disappear as consumer goods. Accordingly, things give the human artifice stability and solidity necessary to house mortal (and so, unstable) humans. The durability of things is not absolute: use uses up. Even so, destruction of use objects is incidental to use, but inherent in consumption. The most durable objects of all are not use objects but objects of art. The durability, or rather the permanence, of art represents the stability of the world, the human artifice as such. The increase in durability, particularly of the highest products of homo faber, gives the individual a greater dignity than animal laborans. Whereas animal laborans remains nature's servant even though master of all living things, homo faber "conducts himself as lord and master of the whole earth" (HC, 139), and of the regions beyond the earth. Politically speaking, homo faber acts as a god capable of creating and destroying reality itself.

Considered from the perspective of the world, beauty is connected to durability. Without the power of endurance, things cannot be beautiful or ugly. But by appearing as beautiful or ugly, things thereby transcend their sheer usefulness. A thing is never judged simply in terms of its utility but also in terms of its adequacy or inadequacy to what it should look like, to how closely it conforms to the image or idea that is visible to the inner eye and that preceded the genesis of the thing and survives its degeneration. This is one interpretation of the experience that survived in Plato's use of the term *idea*. In general, therefore, the human artifice becomes a home for mortals only because it transcends the functionalism of things produced for consumption and the sheer utility of use objects and becomes a place of beauty.

Whereas the process of laboring is endless—one labors to eat and eats to labor—the process of making has a definite beginning and a definite end. (In contrast to them both, action has a definite beginning but no end.) The instruments of homo faber are so intensely worldly that we can distinguish, for instance, the Bronze and the Iron "Ages" by using instruments as a criterion. In a society of laborers, including mass technological society, instruments constitute much of the world. They condition human life by reversing the relationship of human and tool. The most delicate tool neither guides nor replaces the hand that uses it. The most crude machine guides the human body and demands that bodily motions be adjusted to mechanical rhythms. Eventually the human body is replaced altogether.

The process of making is governed by the categories of end and means. Once produced, a use object is judged as a means because it can show its usefulness only by actually being used—by being used *for*, which is to say, by becoming a means. Lessing's famous question, What is the use of use? signifies the rapidity with which utility turns into meaninglessness when the standards that guide the genesis of the world are prolonged to the governance of the result. Matters are not improved by declaring something to be an end in itself. Every end is an end in itself insofar as it guides the process of fabrication. Once the process comes to its end, the result is an object, an object among other objects from which homo faber selects means to pursue additional ends.

The stages of technological development discussed earlier were distinguished in terms of the degree of impact on the world and on the activities of homo faber. When natural forces, which come into being by themselves, are channeled into the world, they destroy its purpose, which is to keep natural forces outside the world. Arendt's formulation of the question concerning technology, then, was not so much whether humans are masters or slaves of machines but whether machines serve the world and the things of the world or whether the automatic motion of technological processes has begun to rule and thus to destroy the world and things in it. Technology, it seems, has reversed the fundamental purpose of homo faber: fabrication has come to destabilize the human artifice. Increasingly products are designed not to be useful or beautiful, which are worldly standards, but to fulfill certain functions in accord with the capacity of an artifice to produce them. In this situation the distinction between end and means no longer makes sense because it is the means, the capacity of the artifice, and not the end that determines the shape of the product. That is, the product is essentially conditioned by the process that created it. The result, again, is an increase in worldlessness even though it is accompanied by more of the good things of life.

Life in its biographical, not biological, sense, life as the time line of appearance between birth and death, manifests itself in action and speech. Without homo faber in his or her highest capacity, as poet and monument builder, historian and artist, the stories human beings enact and tell would not survive after the moment of action and speech. Animal laborans needs homo faber to ease labor and remove pain; mortals need homo faber to erect a home on earth. One recalls that the Laputians had no poetry. Consequently, when humans no longer care for immortality they no longer care for the world. This could be stated the other way around as well: if humans believe that the world, a product of mortal hands, is as mortal as its makers, they will no longer care about being remembered by the yet unborn. This may reflect the sentiment "All is vanity." But equally it may be a device to enhance the enjoyment of consumption: eat, drink, and be merry for tomorrow not only do we die but the world comes to an end. Arendt captured the vulgarity, stupidity, and thoughtlessness of the sentiment with aphoristic pungency: "Worldlessness, alas, is always a form of barbarism" (*MDT*, 13).

Kant once made a joke—or perhaps he borrowed it from Hume. He said: war is like two drunks fighting in a china shop. The serious implication was that the world (the china shop) is not taken into account during a war by the warriors. Even when the drunks grow sober they may be unable to put the pieces back together. This is even more true when war would have the effect not simply of dismantling the world but of destroying it utterly. Modern technology, at least prior to its most recent phase, has been the slow destruction of the world, the deliberate smashing of the plates and cups and saucers one by one. Nuclear and biomedical technologies, in contrast, are more like loose bulls. To see why, one must analyze a third mode of activity, action.

*

Plurality, the condition of action and speech, has the twofold character of equality and distinction. Distinction is more than otherness or alterity because it expresses itself, whereas alterity universally exists in sheer multiplicity. With human beings, distinction is expressed in speech and in this way is transformed into uniqueness. There is, therefore, a kind of hierarchy of appearance: all things possess alterity; all living things possess distinction; all humans possess uniqueness. In terms of communications, all organisms can communicate because they perceive and because they include a dimension of internality that was identified earlier as the capacity for emotion. Lower organisms characteristically communicate unreflective meanings: attraction to the light or butyric acid, fear, hostility. In addition, human beings can communicate themselves. Unlike labor and work, speech and action are not optional: the impulse to begin, to initiate, and so to disclose arises from our being born. To the questions, Why did God make human beings in time? Why did the eternal create new things? Arendt answered, with Augustine: in order that there be novelty, a beginning existed. The creation, *principium,* of the heaven and the earth, which simultaneously created time, did not constitute a beginning, *initium,* because the living creatures made prior to the human being lacked will and therefore lacked initiative and individuality. Augustine might as easily have answered: in order to bring individuality into being.[1]

If, following Augustine, the creation of human being coincides with the introduction of beginning (and freedom) into the cosmos, then the birth of individuals, who are new beginnings, reaffirms the original nature of human being in continuity with the original "in the beginning." At the same time, the fact of memorable continuity of beginnings over the generations ensures the existence of history as the story of beings that are characterized by the capacity to begin. Because it is the "nature" of human being to be a beginning, each human is something new and, from the point of view of the world, quite unexpected, a "miracle." Moreover, human beings know that they are each a beginning, that they can act, and that they will have an end, that the human beginning is the beginning of the end. Animals lack this self-consciousness and so, properly speaking, lack a beginning and an end. Animals are truly species beings. Humans are created in the singular, as unique individuals, and so as new beginnings, by virtue of their birth. By analogy with Homer's term, they are "natals" as much as they are "mortals." From the perspective of the world, the death of an individual means more than just a disappearance: an irreplaceable voice has been stilled.

Taken together, speech and action reveal a "who," the actual individual that has appeared in the world before others and with them, not on their behalf or against them. In contrast to production, for example, the production of art, action without a name is meaningless. Anonymous art is not; a thing of beauty remains a joy even if its author is unknown. Or, consider the contrast, an extreme one, to be sure, between Homeric and modern warfare. Homer's heroes were not simply opposed to one another and did not employ violence to the task of producing enemy corpses and a large body count. Before fighting, they made speeches; the audience was not only the enemy but the gods and the allies as well. In this way they disclosed the who that was prepared to die. The opposite to all this self-disclosure is found in the appearance of unknown soldiers whose tombs were first built after World War I. Recollection of what has been lost may account for the cinematic careers of Clint Eastwood or Sylvester Stallone, though the speeches of the latter are hardly Homeric.

"Many, and even most acts," Arendt said, "are performed in the manner of speech" (*HC*, 178). For the most part, these speeches are not the bombastic self-revelations of Homeric heroes but express a concern for what lies between humans: the world of things, their inter-est. The speeches *about* this in-between world constitute a second, intangible in-between that consists in what humans say *to* one another independently of what their speech is about. This second in-between Arendt called the web of human relationships. The disclosure of a who through speech and the initiation of a new beginning through action always occur within this already existing web composed of innumerable intersecting and interfering intentions, purposes, and wills. Altogether they represent the world into which each act is cast. The reason action almost never achieves its intended goal is that any initiative alters the entire web; there can be no ceteris paribus, because simultaneously every doer is a sufferer, every agent a patient.

Initiative calls forth a response, which is not simply a reaction but a new action. Accordingly, action is boundless because it is unpredictable. It is, Arendt said, an "enacted story," which is not the same as one that is made up; an enacted story is not made at all. But *telling* a story of the actions and speeches of another is precisely how one reveals not who has acted and spoken but the meaning of those deeds and words. Meanings, the meanings of deeds and words, are not "made" but rather are revealed or disclosed in stories. Just as it was argued earlier that substance and meaning were near-equivalent terms, so too are storytelling and philosophy. The relationship between the two was indicated by Aristotle's remark "The lover of myth is in a sense a lover of wisdom" (*Metaphysics*, 982b18–20). Outside the self-manipulation and self-making of therapeutic technologies, no one has ever tried to "act meaningfully" because meaning cannot be the aim or purpose of action.

Historically, the polis and its verbal arts most perfectly actualized the in-between web of action and speech. Not all the inhabitants of the Greek towns and cities appeared in the polis, that is, in the public realm, the space constituted among men by speech. Slaves, women, foreigners, and barbarians were excluded in antiquity; in premodern times, laborers and craftsmen were excluded not from the polis, of course, though from that public space of meaning where I appear to others as they appear to me; in the modern, technological world, functionaries and jobholders—which means, just about everybody—are excluded.

The public realm is kept in existence by power, which in turn exists only where words and deeds have not split apart, where words disclose rather than hide realities, and where deeds are not brutal and destructive but establish new relations and create new realities. But just as people can always lie and deeds can always be brutal, so is power always a potential, a potency, and never a possession or a thing. At one point Arendt said it was the "lifeblood" of the human artifice (*HC*, 204). The metaphor rightly conveys the meaning that, without speech and action before others, the world would be a collection of unrelated things and human affairs would be a wandering futility.

The conviction that the greatest human achievement is to appear before others is by no means uncontested. Homo faber believes it to be the creation of a beautiful and useful world; animal laborans says it is a long and comfortable life. From the point of view of action and the world, these other modes of activity do not fully disclose the individual; the stories told are not very interesting. The death of a salesman lights up much less of the human landscape than the death of Caesar or Macbeth. Work, undertaken in isolation, can never produce an autonomous public realm but only a marketplace, a collection of boutiques, not a plurality of initiators. Even so, homo faber is still connected to a space of appearance and to the world by tangible things he or she has produced, which are, if not unique, at least stylish and highly individual. Animal laborans is both alone and worldless, alone with the body and taxed only with keeping it alive; with others, of course, but those others are just other examples of an organism, as animal laborans is. He or she may be distinct, like a dog or a butterfly, but chiefly animal laborans is a specimen, a species being, a radically equal example that, at the extreme, loses even the quality of otherness: the lonely crowd is created in order to be transformed into a huddled mass.

So far as homo faber is concerned, the great defect of action is its boundless unpredictability. It has no goal or specific aim and it never attains any end. In terms of cognition, the political actor never really knows what he or she is doing. This is a drawback, however, only for the activity of fabrication. Power and action are not justified by what they achieve, because they achieve nothing and at most can serve as the source of stories. They are, instead, legitimated by the initial act that brings together a plurality of people (OV, 52).

Human beings have always been tempted to overcome the general haphazardness of political acting by substituting doing for it. Doing, like fabrication, starts with the assumption that the author of an "act" cognitively knows or, like Lenin, claims to know "what is to be done," to know what the objective is, so that the sole problem is to find the appropriate means to achieve the sought-for ends. The world is to be ordered according to a single meaning, if necessary by a single will. Under such conditions, words do not find their purpose in stories but are, as Lenin also said, "weapons." Doing, in fact, is acting in the mode of making. However, by substituting the deeds of one actor for those of many, the essential requirement for the space of appearance, namely the existence of a plurality of actors, is destroyed. The substitution of making for acting amounts to the abolition of politics and the institution of rule: by one, a few, many, or nobody. The desirable results, or at least the results for which rule is instituted, are stability, security, and productivity; the inevitable loss is power. In its place, keeping with the activity of fabrication, is violence brought to bear on "human material." This modern metaphor is much more radical than the one current in antiquity, which spoke of rule as akin to the taming of savage animals. Lenin's "party of steel" was staffed with men and women whom Stalin called "engineers of human souls."

Modern political activity has been enormously aided in its understanding of action as fabrication by the notion of "making history." This strange idea rests on two highly questionable assumptions. First, it assumes that the end of history is known so that the history maker can freely choose the correct means. This assumption is at least doubtful because it denies the possibility of continued initiative and so violates or ignores the human condition of natality. Second, it assumes, with doing, that cognitive knowledge of the results of action is possible in the same way one can have knowledge of the results of fabrication: by beholding the product. But the consequences of action are, in fact, unpredictable. In order for them to seem, in principle, to be predictable, a further and imaginary phenomenalist transformation is required. History, and nature too, must be visualized as a process; research has the task of discovering the laws of its operation; once discovered, those laws may be amended by appropriate human action and, with effort, repealed. But at the same time, acting undertaken in terms of making, especially if one wishes to "make history," must be violent. Moreover, because the phenomalist process is imaginary, the violence will be endless. In political terms, any doctrine that justifies the transformation of political action into the making of history can serve as an ideology for totalitarianism. The most popular and well known doctrine to have done so, of course, is Marxism.

History, according to Arendt, is not a process or a stream in which all things blend, but a "space in which certain forms of government appeared as recognizable entities."[2] This does not, of course, mean that it is improper to "make" patterns and examine history to see how closely events conform to them. Empirical generalizations of this sort may prove useful in formulating prudential advice to political leaders, for example. They are not, however, meanings, which, as has been indicated, can only reveal themselves and are not made or made up.

The difficulty with really doing something, that is, with acting in the mode of making, is that it combines the boundlessness of action with the violence of fabrication. Making means using violence to do whatever one has in mind, and if things do not work out, violence is used to undo as well. An unsuccessful work—a cracked clay pot, for example—is simply destroyed. Humans have always been able to destroy what they have made. Left to themselves the things of the world eventually decay on their own anyhow. In addition, thanks to technology, humans can even destroy what they did not make, Tasmanian tigers, passenger pigeons, and perhaps even the habitat of the earth. Far more important in this connection than the arresting imagery of apocalyptic annihilation is the ordinary and prosaic fact that humans have never been able to undo the processes they have begun by action nor even reliably to control them. There are many ways to hide the origin of an act—by lying, for example—but there is no way to prevent its consequences. By the same token, we can never reliably foretell the consequences of action even if we know what moves the actor. The great strength of the process of action is that it is both irreversible and unpredictable. And that is also its great burden, for it makes actors responsible for consequences that never were intended.

We have argued that there exists a sort of natural hierarchy among the human capacities of labor, work, and action such that the higher redeems the lower from futility and meaninglessness. This is why the pain and trouble of animal laborans, the imprisonment of the human being in the cycle of laboring and consuming, is relieved by tools and by the making of a durable world. Likewise, homo faber is saved from meaninglessness by the capacities of action and speech that are the source of meaningful stories. In each case what saves and redeems comes from outside (or above, but in any case, beyond) the respective activity. But how to relieve the predicaments of action? How to wash away the guilt the actor acquires simply by acting and thereby becoming responsible for consequences unseen and unintended? How to control the chaotic uncertainty of the future that action commences, to say nothing of sheer human mendacity?

Theologically, the predicament is overcome by God's promise of forgiveness to the faithful, and punishment for the wicked. *Homo viator* redeems *homo politicus*. On earth, politically, the same two powers are involved. Forgiving, like punishing, puts an end not to the consequences of an act but to the blame that attaches to it and thereby enables a new initiative. The one who acted is forgiven though the deed can never be undone. Deeds are judged, but persons who commit them are forgiven or punished. In contrast, making and keeping promises, the capacity to deal with the future as if it were present, stabilize human unreliability and introduce an element of constancy into the future. Most important for our present concern, both forgiving and promising depend on the condition of plurality, for no individuals can forgive themselves, and no individuals make promises only before themselves. Usually such apparently solitary promises are made after God has been invoked as witness.

The means-end category of doing and making excludes the capacity to forgive as a matter of course and alters the meaning of promise from mutual agreement to imposed plan. Applied to acting, the means-end category is quickly transformed into the murderous making of the totalitarian fabricators. Even more significant is the question of acting into nature, an activity that carries irreversibility and unpredictability into a realm where no possible remedy exists to forgive or to undo. Modern technology can do in the realm of nature what Vico thought could be done only in the realm of history. Technological human beings have shown themselves capable of starting natural processes that would never have existed without human initiative. Technological action has the inevitable consequence of carrying human unpredictability into that realm of being that used to be conceptualized in terms of inexorable laws such as the law of gravity. The final and puzzling consequence of acting into nature is that we have succeeded in "making" nature. By reproducing universal or cosmic processes the habitat of which is beyond the household of earth-bound nature, these processes have become part of what is happening on earth. Where recombinant DNA-technologies are involved, this aspect of modern technology is even more obvious.

In contrast to the other schematic definitions of the human being as a political or a rational animal, as homo faber or even animal laborans, modern technology has indicated that humans are chiefly acting beings. Yet, both modern "history making" and modern "nature making," which are in fact both ways of acting, are initiations that exclude plurality. In both instances, the greatness of the human power to initiate begins to destroy the conditions under which life was granted to humans. If human beings could really "make" history, all further action would be impossible; indeed, such experimental "makings," which constitute the activity that goes on in concentration camps, simply destroy humans. Second, "making" nature has the effect of undermining the stability of the world, the human artifice, and then the habitat of the earth itself. To state the obvious, that this was not intended simply affirms once again the unpredictability of human action.

*

The beginning of the modern age has been dated in many different ways. Usually a particular event or innovation has been

taken to symbolize a complex configuration of change. One might
focus on the new astronomy, for example, and consider the substitution of the science of phenomena for the science of substance
to be symptomatic of modernity. Machiavelli's political teaching
has often been seen as a fundamental break with the tradition of
political philosophy stretching back to antiquity. Similar claims
have been made for particular inventions: the stirrup, the mull
board, movable type, synthetic urea, the transistor. Arendt argued that the reversal of the relationship between the *vita contemplativa* and the *vita activa* constituted the great watershed. It
was certainly important for the question of technology because it
entailed several additional substitutions or reversals.

Considered in terms of conceptual modes, the first activity to
replace the stillness of contemplation as the highest principle of
human existence was making. The primacy of homo faber shared
with the earlier primacy of contemplative life the by no means
self-evident assumption that one human preoccupation must inform and order the whole of human existence. Second, the activity of making and the inactivity of contemplation both overcame
the instability of action, though in different ways. Moreover, making uses a kind of contemplation, as when the makers behold an
eternal model or plan by which to construct their own product.
Neither the inner affinities between fabrication and contemplation nor the dependence of people on instruments and tools
proved decisive in the substitution. The structure of experimentation did.

Experiments imitate under controlled, artificial conditions the
process by which a thing came to be; it produces its own phenomena in accordance with human design. From the start, experimentally produced truth depended on human productive
capacities. Experimentation shows how a thing came to be, not
what from all eternity it is. Knowledge is therefore not of things
but of genesis, of the process by which the thing, perhaps temporarily, came into existence. For the premodern artisan the production process was simply a means to the fabrication of the
product. However, for the modern scientist who fabricates in experiments in order to produce knowledge, the material product
was a side effect and nothing more. When the priority of the
product over the process of its production was reversed, the last
vestige of contemplation was removed: making as an activity

became more important than what was made. Neither the thing made, which can be visibly beheld, nor the nonexistent, eternal pattern, which can be beheld by the mind's eye, mattered any longer. So far as homo faber was concerned, the reversal was disastrous. Without the possibility of a quasi-contemplative apprehension of permanent and fixed standards as a guide, homo faber had neither directions for doing nor criteria for judgment.

The emphasis on process is connected to the functionalization of society and the increasing meaninglessness of the modern world. The argument was made that the image of history as a stream or development in which everything can become everything else implied that the concrete particular, the single thing or event, was no longer considered meaningful itself but only as part of an invisible movement. Events, those singular, unexpected, and exemplary occurrences, have thereby been degraded from beacons of meaning into functions of a process, which is to say; Events must be ignored. The chronological reforms of the eighteenth century that distinguished B.C. and A.D. added to our perplexities by creating a twofold temporal infinity without beginning or end, the subject of which was expressed in a late-blooming flower of Averrosim, the "de-eschatologized" symbol, "mankind," a sort of immortal organism or species being (Marx). Immortality became a process in a biological stream of generation, and eternity became a process in the order of nature. All things were seen to be part of these processes, which meant that "things" came to have no integrity of their own. To use the language introduced earlier, things became functionalized. And as for the ersatz eschatalogical symbol, humankind, it quickly proved incapable of sustaining the meaning with which it had been burdened. Under the direction of various bands of saints and members of vanguards, the revolutionary events that were supposed to actualize "humankind" by transforming or remaking mere human beings turned into little more than occasions for a change of regime accompanied by large-scale killing.

The movement from the postulate of infinite natural and historical processes to mass killing was mediated by the brief moment when "research" was turned to the discovery of the laws of movement of whatever process held one's interest. Even before the enterprise was under way, Pascal expressed his reservations in his famous remark that he was frightened by the eternal silence of the two infinities stretching before and after the short duration of his life. Less mystically inclined thinkers could hardly have been reassured. So far as secular history was concerned, living within an infinite process might be expected to have the effect of dampening eschatological expectations. Instead, the accompanying anxiety of meaninglessness seems to have displaced genuine eschatological experiences with pseudo-eschatologies smuggled in by way of fabrication imagery. People can make patterns to discover the "thread of progress" (Turgot) but only because, following Vico, they believe they can know only what they have made, namely history. Knowing that, they know as well they have made it all up. Just as anything could serve as a function, so anything could serve as a pattern. Moreover, just as functionalization turned events into meaningless occurrences, patterns deprived of meaning everything that preceded the present, during which the pattern was discovered, or the future, when it is supposed to be fully actualized. From Turgot to the totalitarians and their intellectual successors, the bewildering succession of patterns in modern history shows nothing so much as the meaninglessness of the entire business. In contrast to Arendt, for whom "history is a story which has many beginnings but no end,"[3] modern progressive intellectuals who fabricate imaginatively within its infinite process, it has no beginning and a single end: the one their pattern proposes.

The modern concept of process has engulfed both experimental natural science and historical or social science. Technology, the ground on which the two realms of history and nature have met and interpenetrated, is scarcely more than a celebration of a world-immanent or intramundane process.[4] In one respect at least this also may be found in the degradation of Descartes's meditation into the activity of introspection. When the medieval and Christian experiential context atrophied into divine external "hypotheses" needed to bridge the ontological gap between res cogitans and res extensa, the mathematical structures of the mind were no longer the contents brought up by introspection. All that introspection can bring up, besides consciousness of itself, is the biological process. William James, for instance, reported that the "stream of consciousness" amounted to the sound of the rhythm of his own breathing. Biological life, the process of metabolism with nature, appeared to be sufficient to connect the individual to the outside world. Laplace explained with pride to his political master precisely that he had no need for the "hypothesis" of God. He could not explain with what he replaced God.

That the sheer biological process of life is the only being that can be discovered by introspection seems obvious enough. But that does not explain why, for that reason alone, it should have become the highest good. The reversal of contemplation and action need not have been world-destroying; one can conceive of a world, however dreary, where fabrication and the virtues of honest workmanship, teamwork, and utility were considered the highest good. What was crucial, according to Arendt, was that this reversal took place within a Christian society. "For the Christian 'glad tidings' of the immortality of individual human life had reversed the ancient relationship between man and world and promoted the most mortal thing, human life, to the position of immortality, which up to then cosmos had held" (*HC*, 314). Neither the world nor the ever-recurring cycle of life, and certainly not humankind as a "species being," is immortal, but only the single living individual, made by God *ad imaginem et similitudinem nostram* (Gen. 1:26). The Christian belief in the sanctity of life, that the human being was the *imago Dei*, the belief in the life eternal, could not but bestow an enormous importance to life as such. Life on earth may simply be a preparation for a higher life, but still it is life, and without it there can be no higher life. Death is indeed the wage of sin for Christians. But the sanctity of life was in no way a glorification of the biological processes that maintain it. On the contrary, labor, like all modes of the vita activa, was unquestionably subordinate to the vita contemplativa. However, the combination of the reversal of doing and contemplating, following the Christian reversal of life and world, established the conceptual departure point of the modern world. Only with the disintegration of the vita contemplativa could life become fully active; only because the vita activa remained bound to life could the laborings of humanity unfold completely.

*

Doubt, now torn out of its meditative context and turned into a sarcastic dissolution of dogma, brought an end to the Christian belief in the certainty of immortal life and the human being again became a mortal. But unlike the mortals of antiquity, the world for modern mortals was no longer their immortal home. Having lost hope in a world to come, modern mortals have not fallen back on "this" world. (To speak of this world without tacitly assuming there is an other world makes no sense.) On the contrary, modern mortals are unsure the world is real since they have the ability to view it from anywhere. Having doubted the other world, humankind lost this one too, which, to recall an earlier remark, was just as Nietzsche (and Democritus) said it would be. What was worse, however, modern human beings did not gain "life" even though they considered it the highest good. Rather modern consciousness grew introspective. The sole contents of introspection were bodily urges, biological processes; the sole hope for immortality was the life of the socialized individual, the species being. The thought of an absolute mortality apparently no longer troubles modern human beings; the old alternatives of individual immortality in a mortal world or mortal life in an immortal world are no longer meaningful.

With so many modern vulgarians searching for "meaning," the earlier observation, that modern society is pervaded with an absence of meaning, sounds like a piece of cheap moralizing. It follows directly, however, from the modern connection that we can know only what we have made, on the one hand, and the confusion of ends and meanings on the other. It is certain that we undertake projects and produce things and that these things are the end for which the project was begun. But once they are made the project itself ends and the things, which we say gave meaning to the project, simply become means to further projects. Even more discouraging is the fact that, under present circumstances, almost any hypothetical end can be declared meaningful and acted on in such a way that the sequence of results not only makes sense logically but in fact actually works. In this way, for example, walking around on the moon is supposed to be meaningful, both "one step for a man" and a "giant leap for mankind."

The rhetoric used on the occasion was appropriate. The actual human being who took the first lunar step was less important than "mankind" that had made the giant leap to the moon. Behind the symbol "mankind" lay the unthought ontology of phenomenalist species being. More immediately, however, sat "armies of skilled technicians" with the astronauts themselves being "as interchangeable as the parts of their machines."[5] The celebration of the efforts of armies of technicians to achieve a

representative act of "mankind" means "quite literally that everything is possible not only in the realm of ideas but in the field of
reality itself."[6] Our modern conviction that truth and meaning
are made, are products of the human mind and human action,
seems to ensure only that meanings will never reveal themselves.
The reason seems to be that pride in the accomplishments of
"mankind" is celebrated along with contempt for the individual
human being.

The most striking feature of life in the modern world, by this
account, is not simply the loss of contemplation but the sheer
impoverishment of human experience. First, modern human beings are surrounded with a veritable avalanche of fabulous instruments and commodities, which means that it is increasingly
unlikely that we encounter anything in the world that is not artificial. The great symbol here is the moon walker whose words
were quoted earlier: he cannot encounter his actual environment
without instantly dying. Moreover his practice, the hours logged
in the simulator, were so much more rigorous than the actual
flight that Tom Wolfe described it all as a prepackaged experience. Second, however, the apparent necessitousness and autonomy of the process of technological innovation, which have
effectively transformed the human artifice from a stable home for
humanity into a kind of liquid movement, has had an effect on
humans not dissimilar to the old fears of ruin at the hands of
nature or the devil. If individuals decide to become a part of nature they turn themselves into blind tools of natural laws whose
course is set beforehand. By so doing they have renounced the
capacity to prescribe their own laws to nature, to call a halt to its
eternal rhythms. Technology is akin to nature as the source of
fear insofar as it seems to follow its own law, swallowing more and
more of the world and inducing a futile melancholic search for
meaning. The third aspect of our impoverishment, then, is that
the one mental faculty that is suited for the search for meaning,
namely thought, has been excluded almost entirely from the
modern technological world. In place of thought, logical reckoning has been substituted, though computers are far better at
reckoning than humans, or we have substituted cognition, the
highest criterion of which is scientific and technical truth. These
substitutions are not replacements.

Work is still done; people still fabricate. But the faculty is exercised increasingly only by those few artists who understand their task as imitation rather than creation. Accordingly, the experiences of worldliness are confined to smaller and smaller numbers of people. People still act, in the sense of releasing processes. But this faculty is exercised increasingly only by scientists and technicians. Unfortunately, their actions are nearly meaningless because the stories they generate are not very interesting. By acting into nature rather than into the web of human relationships, next to nothing is revealed. This is why, for example, official histories, company histories, histories of administrative institutions either are unbearably dull or else are revelations of the ambitions, desires, failures, in short, the action and passion, of the individuals who make up the institutions. But then they are aggregated biographies, not institutional histories.

Only thought, it would seem, is still possible. But thought requires neither the presence of others nor a common world for its actualization. In fact, its most characteristic feature is that it withdraws from the world. This does not mean, however, that it is indifferent to political freedom. If the widespread sense of meaninglessness in technological society and its accompanying moods of melancholia and regret are connected to thoughtlessness, then it seems clear that, even if we cannot immediately identify the mass technological society with tyranny, the two show elective affinities with one another. Both technology and tyranny strive for worldlessness, though the means used to achieve it differ. There is no comfort to be found in the observation that traditional tyrants did not have modern technologies at their disposal. All such observations mean is that modern, technological "tyranny" wears a disguise and that a hermeneutic of suspicion is required to understand its significance. We may bring to light the face of this new regime by following Arendt's account of its first actualization, totalitarianism.

# 6

# The New Regime

Hannah Arendt's first book in English was on totalitarianism. As one recent reviewer noted, *The Origins of Totalitarianism* "is a lengthy book concerning crimes of enormity. It cannot be understood from a single perspective. Therefore, any single study will be guilty of sins of omission. This is as it should be."[1] In this chapter our concern is with the relationship between the phenomenon of totalitarianism and the phenomenon of technology.

The importance of novel usage for Arendt's political science has already been indicated. According to the *Oxford English Dictionary*, the term *totalitarian* was not used in English before 1928, when the *Contemporary Review*, after Mussolini's earlier usage in Italian, remarked that, by contesting an election, Fascism had renounced its function as a totalitarian regime. A year and a half later the *Times* identified both the Fascists and Communists as totalitarian and contrasted this type of regime with a parliamentary one. Totalitarianism, however, was not simply a novelty; it was also a great and terrible evil. Indeed, if there is a single overwhelming image that summarizes the historical experience of the Second World War it is the extermination camp. (The atomic bombing of Japan, so much closer to our present concern with technology and so much a part of our current symbolism of fear, seems quite distinct from the imagery of Auschwitz or Kolyma.) The significance of totalitarianism is not simply that it introduced a new form of government, a novel regime, but that it is an ever-present danger. The destruction of Nazi Germany and the internal transformation of the Soviet Union following Stalin's death have not altered the danger or the potential. Today the memory of those criminal regimes persists as the generally implicit (and

154

occasionally explicit) standard by which unacceptable political activity is measured. Analysis of a criminal regime, notwithstanding its being a standard, is surrounded by unusual methodological problems.

Dionysios of Halicarnassus said of Thucydides' great work on the Peloponnesian War that what he wrote about was inglorious and should never have happened or, failing that, since it did happen, it should have been ignored and consigned to silence and oblivion. Arendt made a similar observation: because "all historiography is necessarily salvation and frequently justification," there was, accordingly, a major problem: "how to write historically about something—totalitarianism—which I did not want to conserve but on the contrary felt engaged to destroy."[2] Her answer was not to write a history of totalitarianism nor even a history of its origins,[3] but "an analysis in terms of history; I did not write a history of antisemitism or of imperialism, but analyzed the element of Jew-hatred and the element of expansion insofar as these elements were still clearly visible and played a role in the totalitarian phenomenon itself."[4] In addition, however, Arendt was moved by a sentiment expressed most forcibly in Santayana's aphorism, that those who cannot remember the past are condemned to repeat it.

Arendt faced this question in the preface to the first edition. "Comprehension does not mean denying the outrageous, deducing the unprecedented from precedents, or explaining phenomena by such analogies and generalizations that the impact of reality and the shock of experience are no longer felt. It means, rather, examining and bearing constantly the burden which our century has placed on us—neither denying its existence nor submitting meekly to its weight. Comprehension, in short, means the unpremeditated attentive facing up to, and resisting of, reality—whatever it may be" (OT, xxx). Her writing, which aimed at providing readers with an understanding of the meaning of totalitarianism, constituted an act of resistance. Ellul, it may be recalled, expressed the same sentiment with respect to the technological society.[5]

*

Arendt's concern for the distinctiveness of worldly phenomena and for the modes of the vita activa may have originated in her exposure to, and subsequent study of, totalitarianism. The great impediment to "a proper understanding of our recent history," she said in 1950, "is the only too comprehensible tendency of the historian to draw analogies."[6] But Stalin and Hitler were not like Tamerlane or Chinggis Qan, and were not simply worse than other great killers, but entirely different. Several times Arendt insisted on the novelty of the regime, often in response to sociological or psychological analyses that showed it to be a more radical version of something well known and well buffered by scholarly discourse.[7] The fact of novelty is itself remarkable, which is why it has not always been readily acknowledged. Nevertheless, the evidence is convincing, namely the inability of traditional terminology to account adequately for the political phenomena.

The phenomenon of totalitarianism was evidence of the breakdown or disintegration of the Western tradition. The extent of the breakdown varied with time and place, and, more important for the present question, the dimension varied as well: "Politically speaking, it was the decline and fall of the nation-state; socially, it was the transformation of a class system into a mass society; and spiritually it was the rise of nihilism, which for a long time had been a concern of the few but now, suddenly, had become a mass phenomenon" (MDT, 228). The present focus is on the first two constituent elements. In the next section the nature of the experience of totalitarianism is discussed.

Historically speaking, the nation-state was the successor to the old regime. The internal or domestic premise of the new body politic was that all nationals were to enjoy conditions of equality. The symbolic expression of this premise was found in the abolition of hereditary rights and privileges. But at the same time new inequalities based not on caste or status but on class were introduced. Only in the United States was there anything approaching a genuine equality of condition. In Europe there existed only equality before the law. Accordingly, a contradiction existed between legal equality and social inequality that impaired the development of republican forms and a genuine political, as distinct from social or economic, class. In nineteenth-century European society, the status of an individual was defined by social or economic class membership and not by position in the state. The major exception to this generalization was the Jews. A second and more important contradiction, expressed grammatically by a hyphen, existed between the nation and the state. The premier nation-state has been France because that country most fully embodied the necessary requirements: a homogeneous population with a sense of rootedness in the soil and a legal order that embodied the principles of liberty, equality, and fraternity.[8]

The balance between formal and legal principles and specific and particular language, history, and ethnicity constitutes the substance of the conflict and harmony of public and private in the modern world. The whole sphere of the given, of bodily shape, of gender, of mental talent, is relegated to private life in modern society. The private sphere is based on difference and differentiation. It is inherently unequal and particularist. In contrast, the public sphere is based on equality, which is not given, but is the result of human action guided by a sense of justice and principles. In this context, "nature" may be said to indicate the limit of the human artifice; nation-states seek homogenous populations in order to minimize the political appearance of that limitation. Under such conditions, the "alien" becomes a symbol of difference and otherness, of the aspect of reality that human beings cannot change and so have a tendency to destroy. The balance between the particularisms associated with "nature" and the principled universality of the law is precarious. A great deal can go wrong with such a political arrangement in a comparatively short time.

Nationalism, for example, is a permanently threatening disturbance to the nation-state. The original Western, French-style state was an instrument of law. Nationalism perverts the purpose of the state by turning it into an instrument of the nation. The proper relationship between the state and society was established by classes of people who understood themselves as liberal individual atoms. The state had the double task of protecting the nation from disintegration but also of maintaining social atomization. Class conflict was kept under control by centralized bureaucratic administration, and nationalism became the glue binding the centralized state to the atomized society. Eventually nationalism turned out to be the only connection between individuals and the state. But it was also highly unstable, even where the trinity of people-territory-law traditionally existed. Where it did not exist, in Central and Eastern Europe after World War I, for

example, the imposition of states on the territory identified by
C. A. Macartney as the "belt of mixed populations" was simply a
recipe for disaster.

The succession states were anomalies on two counts. First they
were internally heterogeneous, and second, that heterogeneity
was recognized in the Minority Treaties, which in turn constituted an implicit violation of their sovereignty. The significance of
the Minority Treaties lay in the fact that they said outright what
had up to that time been implied: that only persons of the same
national origin could enjoy the full legal status of citizenship, and
that exceptions needed exceptional laws, at least until they were
fully assimilated. In principle, the transformation of the state
from an instrument of law to an instrument of the nation was
complete: national interest, accordingly, had priority over law.
What finally showed the utter impracticality of the Minority
Treaties was, paradoxically, the fact that they did not go far
enough in protecting minority rights. The treaties covered language and cultural matters, which were important but quite
clearly secondary as compared with the right to work and to residence. The framers of the Minority Treaties did not anticipate
the possibility of wholesale transfers of people who had become
undeportable because they had no right to reside in any country
on earth.

The existence of stateless persons after the First World War
was a clear indication that the European national state was disintegrating. Stateless refugees had no right of asylum; unlike earlier fugitives, modern stateless people could find no sanctuary at
the shrines of deities to whom they appealed. Altars had been
replaced by internment camps and divine protection by the
whims of bureaucrats or of the police. Because stateless persons
came under no law, they constantly provoked breaches of inter-
nationally guaranteed treaties: every country sought (illegally) to
deport them. Indeed, lawlessness was the chief characteristic of
statelessness. Stateless persons were created by governmental
lawlessness; refugees gained no shelter from the law but were
subject simply to decrees: no law governed the operation of the
camps whether they were humane or not; governments would
break the law if they got rid of them.

After the Second World War, matters were even worse. So far
as the question of nationalities was concerned, the population

movements that attended the disruptions of war turned much of Europe into a belt of mixed populations. In Western Europe, stateless persons were called "displaced persons," a euphemism that hid what in fact they had lost, the legal protection of any state. In Eastern Europe the problem of minorities was, if not solved, at least dealt with temporarily, with the vast diminution of national self-determination consequent on Soviet hegemony. When the national question reemerged, in East Germany, in Hungary, in Czechoslovakia, in Poland, it was under completely different circumstances.

From the beginning of this process of disintegration, Jews were in a distinct position. In the nineteenth-century state, they were an identifiable group but not a class. Their status was defined by the state and not by their relationship to other classes. Whenever they were admitted to society it was as well-defined groups *within* one or another class. This meant that the fact of birth as a Jew had direct political consequences: either one was under special state protection by way of specific emancipation edicts, which frequently had to be reinforced against the hostility of society, or one lacked rights granted to citizens. After the First World War Jews were not covered by the Minority Treaties; their fate during the Second World War was as singular as the foundation of the new state of Israel. In Arendt's view, the rise and decline of the nation-state were directly tracked by the history of European Jewry.

Schematically the events unfolded in four stages. First, during the seventeenth and eighteenth centuries national states developed within the constitutional form of absolute monarchy. "Court Jews" handled princely finances; outside the courts, Jews and non-Jews alike were unaffected. Second, after the French Revolution, the modern nation-state needed more money than the court Jews could raise on their own. Capital and credit were provided by wealthy members of the Jewish community who entrusted their money to Jewish bankers. In return they were emancipated. Later their poorer coreligionists were emancipated as well, except in the comparatively backward non-nation-states of Eastern Europe. Third, since the direct relationship between the state and the Jews depended on the comparative indifference of the bourgeoisie to politics and on the European comity of nations, when these conditions changed the position of Jews changed as well. On the one hand, with late nineteenth-century competitive imperialism, and its accompanying modes of thought, chiefly race thinking, the economic role Jews had played was taken over by imperialist businessmen; on the other, the end of a concern for a balance of power, the end of European political solidarity, which was achieved by competitive imperialism, meant an end to the conditions under which a specifically "European" group could exist. Fourth, in the twenty years prior to the First World War, European Jewry disintegrated along with the legal order of the state. No longer were wealthy Jews an identifiable group who could provide a useful service; they were simply a collection of anomalous and wealthy individuals.

The last two phases, which coincided with the era of European imperialism, were crucial. Toward the close of the century, European businessmen changed their mind about the state. The attractiveness of expansion and the near-monopoly on efficient instruments of violence to achieve expansion made the state useful to businessmen rather than a threat to their wealth. This meant as well the automatic, if gradual, replacement of Jews at the center of state finance. At the same time, quasi-feudal princely wars gave way to national wars and to overseas national rivalries. This meant that Jews were no longer useful for financing wars (the Austro-Prussian War of 1866 was the last one financed by a Jew, and that occurred only because Bismarck had been refused the necessary credits by the Prussian assembly). They remained useful for peace negotiations until, with the slaughter of 1914–18, wars no longer aimed at peace and the restoration of a modus vivendi but at victory or death. The new style of war could be concluded only by an unconditional surrender, in which case there was a diminished need for intermediaries "above" the contending parties as the Jews had been (the last time the Jews played a role in international negotiations was at Versailles, which was virtually the last time treaties were used as instruments to conclude major hostilities). The collapse of the system of nation-states, and with it the "balance of power" in Europe, meant that Jews were politically as well as financially useless.

Imperialist operations made the scale of Jewish wealth insignificant; competitive expansion of overseas state rule diminished the sense of balance among the European nations; in this new context, the Jews were useless to the nation-state. There were still wealthy Jews, but they were powerless and so vulnerable. Moreover, useless wealth soon enough becomes an object of resentment and contempt. The Jews were no more exempt from this process than were the wealthy, powerless, and useless French aristocrats of 1788.[9] What proved fatal for the old regime in France was that the nobility retained its wealth but not its purpose, which had been taken over by the clerks of the Intendant's bureaux. Likewise, the downfall of European Jewry coincided with the ruin of a political order that had needed a strictly European and non-national element to exist. When the European balance dissolved, the first element to go was precisely its European one. When the nation-state became obsolete, Jews as a group became superfluous. Being superfluous is a much more dangerous condition than being a refugee or displaced person. To be a displaced person is to have no place in the world recognized by others; to be superfluous is to be excluded from the world.[10]

The same process that made the French aristocrats superfluous recurred first with the Jews and then with the masses themselves. There remained this difference, that the aristocrats and the Jews remained odious to others, whereas the masses were odious to themselves. A preview of their fate, however, like that of the Jews, was found in the Terror of 1794.

No doubt anti-Semitism is morally reprehensible, an affront to common sense, ugly, vulgar, and stupid; so is a prejudice against blue-blooded aristocrats. Even so, both attitudes are comprehensible. It makes sense to obey powerful people, because they do something purposive even if it is not necessarily to one's liking. But wealth without power and aloofness without purpose are felt simply to be parasitical. The sources for modern anti-Semitism, for the growth of an attitude equivalent to that held by the French *peuple* toward the French aristocracy in the late eighteenth century, and equivalent as well to that of the masses toward themselves, are to be found in the distinctive facts of Jewish history. Specifically, Jews were alone among European peoples in being stateless. Their leaders were almost uniformly apolitical, and as a consequence the Jews, politically speaking, were worldless. Isolation from society was obviously abstention from the world, but so was assimilation. It meant the destruction of Jewish communities, on the one hand, and the creation of lonely atomized individuals, "exceptions," on the other.

Anti-Semites, for their part, were also superfluous, though less immediately vulnerable. They owed their position not directly to the political consequences of the disintegration of the nation-state but to the accompanying economic and social changes. Why Jews became objects of hatred had less relation to their specific activities—the role of prominent Jews as middlemen in some colourful swindles, for example—than with what they symbolized to mob leaders. Such men and the mobs they led were the déclassés of all classes, as much outside class society as the Jews. By the end of the century as a consequence of political emancipation and the loosening of ties that had given Jews an inter-European purpose, increasing numbers of Jews found their way into intellectual and liberal professions, not banking and not business. This first generation of Jews who cared for social intercourse with non-Jews did not necessarily seek fame or social prominence but proximity to the famous, as critics, reviewers, and collectors. The desire for proximity was a way of trying to feel at home in a world that excluded you in principle. At the same time, publicity made Jews appear to the déclassés as symbols of Society as such, as the embodiment of everything hateful to those whom society had rejected. Increasingly the Jewish question had less and less significance for serious political individuals; increasingly as well, anti-Semitism grew into an ideology of social outcasts and crackpots seething with their own weird resentments. For such people, the population that came to constitute the masses, the entire human artifice was an odious thing. It excluded them, and they retreated to the darkness of nature—or rather, of race. Race was a difference and a particularity that no change in condition could alter; it was an absolute refuge against equality, law, and justice.

At the other end of the scale, high society developed a taste for the exotic and, indeed, for vice. Jews were exotic. At the top as at the bottom of the social heap, Jews were treated not in terms of what they did but in terms of what they were, namely Jews. Socially speaking, this was a group trait so that, when society turned against them, Jewishness was highly dangerous. There was no escape by conversion since Jewishness had nothing to do with religion; there was no possibility of punishment, since the exotic could not be normalized but only destroyed. Eventually, under the impact of further industrial and political crises and the consequent creation of additional déclassés, a significant number of superfluous individuals crystallized ideologically around the idea of exterminating Jews: worldless people committed unprecedented crimes against worldless people whose innocence was equally unprecedented.

The third constituent element of totalitarianism was the creation of expansive administrative apparatuses. Several competing theories have been advanced over the last century to account for the expansion of European civilization across the globe. Some have been general and gross, covering the centuries; others have linked the particularly striking expansion after 1884 to traditional questions of European balance and strategy in the Mediterranean. Arendt was not focally concerned with the history of imperialism, but with imperialist elements that became part of totalitarianism. Her account was neither the narrative of a four-hundred-year trend nor the minute examination of archival evidence pertaining to a single crisis—the British occupation of Egypt in 1882, for example—but ranged somewhere in the middle.

The most important political event of the generation prior to the First World War was the emancipation of the bourgeoisie, the first class in history to achieve economic preeminence without seeking to rule. When they did, the possibility of using state violence for administrative expansion and the capture of economic rents, which is the essence of imperialism, looked like a good business deal. "Imperialism," Arendt said, "is not empire-building, and expansion is not conquest."[11] The traditional actualization of imperial passions, whether its internal form be cosmological, ecumenic, and cosmopolitan or Germanic and sacred, has time and again spread culture and law. Empires based on large-scale looting generally have not survived the presence of the conqueror. If the conqueror had settled down, looting would be followed by creation of a new body politic and assimilation of the conquered population to the standards of the victor. European imperialism broke with this tradition, since it resulted neither in temporary looting nor in lasting assimilation.

Endless expansion, the driving force of imperialism, is not a political notion at all, properly speaking. Rather, it belongs to

the realm of economics and technology or, more precisely, to
the realm of business speculation. Economic and technological
growth are limited not by the capacity to produce—the productivity of animal laborans is essentially without limit—but by
political organizations, by legal instruments that establish boundaries and limit what is permitted. Imperialists deny the reality of
limits and forsake the stability of law in an endless search for further opportunities. Accordingly, imperialism was born when an
economically and technologically expansive population imposed
their views on the state. Almost by instinct, national political
leaders at first opposed the imperialists. They knew that comparison with the Roman Empire, so important to the classicist-
politicians of Victorian Britain, was a fraud. The Roman Empire
was thought to have been founded on homogeneous nations. Victorians could hardly adopt the Roman style when the law of the
state was conceived as growing from an unequal national spirit.[12]
The only option was tyranny, which can indeed rule foreigners
without their consent, but only on the condition that it first
destroy the national and legal institutions of its own people.
This was the lesson of Thucydides.[13] The solution was to separate
the colonial administration from the national political institutions. The imperialists sought and largely gained control over
political violence, which is essentially police power, without the
bother of founding a body politic.

Economically speaking, imperialism occurred when domestic
investment no longer seemed sufficiently profitable and capital
was in oversupply. Speculative capital export—large-scale gam-
bling—followed, along with great financial scandals and the ruin
of many small and greedy investors. Naturally enough, they
preferred not to lose their money and demanded that the state
protect their investments. The coincidence of technological industrialism and property holding, which we call capitalism, created excess capital, maldistribution, and scandal; from a domestic
economic perspective this new capital was superfluous, "needed
by nobody though owned by a growing class of somebodies" (OT,
148). As with other superfluities, something had to be done; expansion promised to put superfluous capital to work rather than
squander it in scandal and swindle. In addition, it would allow
the owners of useless capital to escape the odium of being para-
sites. Finally, it would finance the export of superfluous individ-

uals, another product of industrial productivity. And in southern Africa there occurred an amazing and poetic concentration of superfluities: superfluous money and superfluous men combined to produce the most superfluous of goods, gold and diamonds.

The political problem remained. The expansion of the economies of Europe overseas followed by the expansion of state power in the form of the police, armed functionaries of violence, was not followed by the founding of new bodies politic. All the new administrators could do was destroy. Just as nationalism served temporarily to bind individuals to the nation-state, the solution to the dilemma of national bodies' undertaking imperialist expansion was solved, again temporarily, by what Arendt variously identified as chauvinism, tribal nationalism, and racism. Under the pretext of empire building, European nations were drawn into the great expansive adventure, which precisely as national bodies politic they could not undertake. Socially, imperialism was an alliance between the homeless mob and superfluous capital. It promised national politicians that the political organizations they led would continue and that the ever-threatening social question, whether in the form of contradictions of class society or of problems associated with the growing capacity of people to produce, could be managed. The form was preserved and disaster postponed, but the political principle of the nation-state, namely its limited legal and constitutional structure, was under sharp attack.

A new political principle was required and found: bureaucracy. Civil servants, politically neutral servants of the entire nation-state, could hardly avoid being class functionaries at home. This famous criticism by Marx of Hegel's alleged "universal class" could, however, be circumvented overseas. There bureaucrats were in fact neither servants nor masters but representatives of a conquering race. Aloofness, so assiduously cultivated by the British, was the factual expression of their pseudomystical self-identification as "white men," men superbly endowed by nature or history or both to rule natives. It was more dangerous and more hopeless than old-style despotism and arbitrariness because it cut the last tie between the despot and the subjects, bribery. Integrity simply meant greater inaccessibility. In order to work properly, bureaucrats had to be separated both from the natives whom they ruled and also from interference by the nation they nominally served. The perfect bureaucrat was faceless, anonymous, the recipient neither of blame nor praise, "out there" and "on the spot" only to do a job, which was essentially technical, whether in the form of conquest, administration, or engineering. Unfortunately, when human beings withdraw from the public realm, morality withdraws as well. The meaning of morality is that it is fit to be seen. Accordingly, the great danger of faceless administrative despotism is not that bureaucrats are capable of nothing but evil, but that the conditions of their activity, whatever their intentions, hardly allow them to do anything else.

Of course, it did not seem that way to them. What made secrecy attractive was not personal whim, a base desire to escape political control or shame at doing evil. It was connected equally to the realization of the futility of glory. If expansion was endless, any particular victory was trivial. One is reminded of Kant's observation, in the admittedly different context of the eighteenth century, when progress remained yet an idea and not an ideological justification for brutality. Kant observed that, if progress were infinite, then any particular deed could contribute nothing to it because any finite quantity divided by infinity equals zero. Designed to baffle the credulous and cause the wise to smile, if his remark had been overheard a century later by an imperialist bureaucrat, it would have been taken very seriously indeed.

Precisely because neither praise nor blame could possibly touch the secretive and aloof functionary, he was able to identify himself with the process of history itself. As for the elite of the elite, the secret agent, it was all part of what one of them, William Thorburn, called "the great game." Kipling's *Kim*, a charming legend, told more of the story than all those pseudonymously published memoirs of intrepid men with boyhood ideals who lived briefly and dangerously along the Northwest frontier: "When everyone is dead, the Great Game is finished. Not before." Theirs was a kind of purified worldlessness, the ultimate purposelessness of which was close to the purposelessness of life, just as its secrecy was close to life's ultimate mystery. But politics is not an endless game; players who think it is can hardly avoid coming to a bad end themselves and laying catastrophe all about them.

Legally, bureaucracy is government by decree. In contrast to constitutional government, where rules, powers and, in the end, the police enforce the law, in a bureaucratic regime rule and the police are the direct source of all legislation. For bureaucracy, constitutional rule is inefficient because it separates the formation of law from its application; rule by decree, on the other hand does not exist unless it is applied and so appears without justification as the very incarnation of power. The administrator, correspondingly, appears as the accidental agent of rule, in no way responsible for anything. There are no principles by which rules can be debated, but only details, data, and information that can be processed only by experts. Efficiency is guaranteed by withholding information and ensuring thereby that expertise is restricted to those who use it properly, namely administrators.

Politically speaking, bureaucratic rule is virtually the opposite to the rule of law. Laws are like rules of the game, directives rather than imperatives, neither absolutely valid nor mere commands. Revolutionaries may wish to change the rules and criminals to make exceptions for themselves. Bureaucrats deny the existence of law on principle. Rules, which players in the great game enforce directly, are paradoxically without a real game going on inside them. They are imperatives, absolutely valid, mere commands that give no direction; they are so flexible or so arbitrary that they can never gain the worldly stability of laws.

Imperialism was the nineteenth-century consequence of the emancipation of the bourgeoisie and it was to be the cure for all the problems that emancipation brought with it. Foreign adventures have always been a way to divert domestic opinion from local problems. Imperialism, because it was unlimited, promised much more. Cecil Rhodes declared expansion to be everything and despaired because he could never annex the heavens, which to common sense or to prudential leaders seems an insane desire to repudiate the human condition itself. His contemporary successors would admit only that he had been born too soon. "Now," sing the choir of can-do NASA engineers and Air Force generals, "give us the budget and we shall annex the heavens too."

Another and more serious contradiction could not be resolved simply by the passage of time and an increase in technical cleverness. The ideas of progress, which earlier had puzzled Kant, had become the reality of bourgeois expansion against which critical analysis was useless. Just when what people had thought to be a principle of perpetual motion had been discovered, the sobering implications for political reality became clear: when the

globe had been domesticated and the heavens lay still out of
reach, the process continued, only now it was, from the point of
view of the world, obviously destructive. Even in the hour of triumph, the great imperialist poets grew melancholic. Like a modern Scipio's weeping bitterly as enemy Carthage burned, the
great emancipation was followed by the bitter words of a modern
Polybius: the West was going down almost before it had really
gotten going. Such fatal prophecies, however, simply gave voice
to the silent anonymous players of the Great Game, an elite
ready to sacrifice everything to the exhilarating greatness of the
event, to the mission, to the efficiency of system, to success as
such. How else could it all end but in extermination and suicide?
The threat of endless external war could apparently be met only
at the cost of endless internal war.

To summarize the argument so far: according to Arendt, the
three constituent elements of totalitarianism were (1) the disintegration of tradition and its institutional form, the nation-state;
(2) the creation of a superfluous population through capitalist
productivity and race thinking; and (3) the creation of expansive
but nihilist administrative regimes. Initially the particularity of
the nation eroded the universalist principles of the state. Then,
under the impact of imperialism, technology has completed the
task by destroying particularity as well. In an age of ecumenic
ideological empires and expansive high-tech multinational enterprises, though not, at present, of totalitarian regimes, the complex remains as firmly in place as it was in the last days of
Victoria.

*

Historically, totalitarian regimes have developed from one-
party systems. They have then proceeded to operate in a way all
their own so that traditional analytic concepts are not helpful in
understanding, predicting, or judging their course of action.
Arendt therefore raised the question, Is there "such a thing as
the *nature* of totalitarian government?" Does it have its own "essence" that can be compared and described as other forms of government can?[14] If totalitarianism is new, and if it makes sense to
inquire after its nature, then it must rest on an experience that
may be familiar enough, but nevertheless has never served as the
foundation of a body politic nor directed public affairs.

The experience that prepares people for totalitarianism, Arendt said, is loneliness. Loneliness used to be a borderline experience usually suffered in certain marginal social conditions such as old age; for the masses, it has become an everyday experience. Loneliness is more than isolation. Human beings are isolated when the common political sphere where they can act together is destroyed. But in isolation they are still in contact with the world; in fact, isolation is the condition for doing productive work, for contributing something of one's own to the human artifice. In a society where such activity is reduced to labor, isolation can become unbearable because the processes of labor are simply necessary and of no interest to anyone. Then indeed, as Marx might have said, the songs of Hank Williams or of Elizabeth Schwarzkopf are like the songs of cicadas or cuckoos.

Isolation affects only the political realm of life, whereas loneliness concerns human life as a whole. Tyrannies have traditionally sought to create isolated individuals; totalitarianism does more: it destroys private life as well. Loneliness is closely connected to superfluousness inasmuch as it is the experience of being abandoned by everything and everybody—and superfluousness has been described as the experience of not belonging to the world. Loneliness, finally, is not solitude. In solitude I am "by myself," which is to say, together with myself, whereas in loneliness I am deserted by everyone, including myself. Solitude is the condition for thinking, the silent-spoken dialogue between me and myself; it is cut off neither from the world nor from others because both are represented in the self with whom I carry on the dialogue. If I am deserted by my own self, solitude can turn into a loneliness that becomes gradually unbearable because I cease to trust others, myself, or the world. This radical and desperate experience is not sustained by confidence either in the world or in the self. It is a monad of grief.

Several times reference has been made to the masses. Masses are not mobs. The mob is a collection of selfish "individualists," unpredictable and incoherent, rootless, homeless, and without a common interest. All of which is shared by the mass, but in addition, masses lack self-interests or selfish interests. Masses are not necessarily brutal or backward or poor. They are isolated, lonely human beings lacking ordinary social relationships and prepared to substitute fanaticism for loyalty. Unlike mobs, masses can be organized, agitated, and directed by propaganda so that their behavior is fully predictable.

Before human beings become suitable material for totalitarian domination, all "spontaneous order," as Hayek called it, must be destroyed. In Germany, historical circumstances, namely war, unemployment, inflation, and migration, did a great deal to create the necessary conditions: large numbers of atomized humans, filled with bitterness and strange anxieties. In Russia, Stalin and the Bolsheviks had to devote a good deal of effort to creating these conditions "artificially." The result was essentially the same: social atoms ready to be stung into movement, people ready and willing to perform a ghastly dance of death, the steps of which were fully choreographed beforehand. The choreography typically took the form of scientific prediction and logic. In order for this propaganda to be effective, information must be acquired not by common sense or about the world but by imagination and about a universal, consistent nonexistent fiction. Propaganda provides a fictitious home for the homeless. Apparently it is easier to believe in ghosts and huge conspiracies than in nothing at all. Once the organization that created the fictitious world is destroyed, once the fiction is destroyed, then the masses cease to move and return to the quiet desperation of loneliness and superfluity, waiting to be galvanized into motion again. This is why, after the Nazi defeat, it was so difficult to find any Germans who really believed in nazism.

Like the imperial bureaucrats, totalitarian elite formations and organs put great emphasis on secrecy. The chief value of secrecy and conspiracy in totalitarian movements is that they ensure the capacity to establish and maintain the fictitious pseudoworld of consistent lying. The elite are trained for two tasks: first, to be unable to distinguish truth and falsehood, and second, to be able to interpret statements of fact, of alleged fact, as declarations of intent. This highly developed interpretive skill is precisely what makes them reliable members of the elite. For example, the allegedly factual statement "Jews are inferior" is correctly interpreted "We intend to destroy Jews." Or, "Moscow is the only city with a subway" means "We intend to destroy subways everywhere else."

The notion of comparing one's experience of the world with the fictitious pseudoworld of propaganda never enters the heads of well-trained members of the elite. Consequently, they never pay attention to what the leader's words may mean. What binds them together is not words but the presumed infallibility of the leader's actions sustained by faith in human omnipotence. "Their moral cynicism, their belief that everything is permitted, rests on the solid conviction that everything is possible." They are convinced "that everything can be done . . . that everything that exists is merely a temporary obstacle that superior organization will certainly destroy" (*OT*, 387). The technique of organization overcomes anything: it binds the masses into a predictable whole; it sets the mass firm in the belief that sufficient momentum will in the end prevail, even over stubborn factuality. Disregard of factuality is in one respect simple enough: facts can be changed by technique. In 1930 it was fact that you could not move between New York and London in six hours; technique has changed that fact. Politically, the same logic can be employed; if all subways other than Moscow's are destroyed, the statement that only Moscow has a subway becomes true. Since political facts depend for their reality on the testimony of others, on their bearing witness to reality, but since facts have no standing in a totalitarian fictional world, factuality itself depends for its existence on there being a nontotalitarian world.

The description of the nature of totalitarian government may be summarized as follows: it is founded on the experience of loneliness in the masses, who may be manipulated by propaganda deployed by an elite that believes-and-disbelieves in fiction. Totalitarian power is mobilized in a constant challenge to reality; it is an "experiment" that consists in the constant, unremitting effort to transform reality into fiction. Central to the effort is the systematic fiction of ideology, which no one believes in because all know it is just fiction, but which nevertheless moves real and not fictional mountains.

Considered by themselves, ideologies are curious nineteenth-century conceits, remarkable only for their bewildering variety. They are uncritical arbitrary opinions, harmless stupidities so long as nobody takes them seriously. Once the claim to total validity is actually believed and taken literally, they become the nuclei of logical systems. As with consistent paranoia, everything follows compulsorily from the first premise. The craziness of ideology lies not in the premise but in the logical train developed from it. Totalitarian ideologies have their own peculiarities: they "became strictly the *logic of an idea:* the idea was no longer applied to a given reality, but a logical process was developed from the chief 'idea,' which became a kind of logical premise."[15] The result of this operation was not a series of propositions about the world but a constantly changing logical process. Accordingly, what the idea actually happened to be was secondary to the necessity of logically deducing the correct implications from it.

Logic is powerless over beginnings or premises; it needs an "idea" to get started. Once under way, however, the movement of deduction is a tyrannical master dragging the mind along on a never-ending process. In this way the process of deduction overcomes the content of the idea (to the extent it had any factual reality in the first place, which is by no means necessary) and liberates the mind from all experienced reality. The indefinite extension of logic into the future makes ideology coherently and consistently contemptuous of reality. In this respect, ideology is the opposite to common sense, which is why it is impervious to objections based on utility. Utility never enters the picture; consistency does. The advantage of dialectical logic in this respect is that it can explain away factual contradictions as temporary stages of a single and consistent movement striving to supersede difference and end as identity. Because the world is inconsistent, the drive for consistency, whether tarted up with dialectical frills or not, ensures that action based on ideology will be aggressive. And the world, the real world, is inconsistent because new people, new beginnings, are born into it. The demand for logicality is thus a demand to end creativity, innovation, and the human condition of plurality. In commonsense terms ideologies are declarations of war against humankind's humanity insofar as they strive to make all human beings superfluous. Moreover, these things must end everywhere, which means that ideologies are recipes for world domination.

Fictional independence from the world, from reality, from common sense, and from the human condition does not inhibit the capacity to act. On the contrary, it may enhance it because, to the believer, it means that everything and anything is possible. The conviction that everything is possible is a more radical, because practical, version of the nineteenth-century nihilist declaration, Everything is permitted. Even if the attempt to turn reality into fiction were bound to fail, the opposite conviction, that lies can be turned into realities, has become a totalitarian commonplace, the outcome of consistent action guided by ideology. Initially, for example, no one outside Nazi Germany believed the lie that Jews were homeless beggars; when Jews were driven across the German frontier penniless, what had been a lie became a fact. In general, argument with a purveyor of totalitarian propaganda is as pointless as debate with someone holding a gun to your head whether you are still alive: if you think you are, your assailant can always prove you wrong.

Lies can be made real, facts can be destroyed, the world can be made consistent according to the ideologue, if sufficient violence is applied to remake it. If ideology is a recipe for destroying human beings in pursuit of a fiction, terror amounts to putting the recipe into practice. Simple or ordinary ideological violence is no more than homo faber loose in the political realm: you can't make an omelette without breaking eggs or a revolution without breaking heads. Violence in totalitarian regimes is something more and other than ordinary ideological violence. To begin with, it is not used to frighten opponents. Except at the initial stages, there is no political opposition. The destruction of real enemies must, therefore, be followed by the destruction of fictional ones, objective enemies, as they are called in ideological discourse. An objective enemy, Solzhenitsyn said, is a person guilty of committing a possible crime. Totalitarian terror is therefore both self-augmenting and without a goal. Instead it has a series of fictional pseudogoals: the continuation of the movement through the production of people incapable of forming convictions. The ideal citizen of a totalitarian regime is equally and indifferently prepared to be a victim or an executioner. Terror creates holes of oblivion darker even than death because memory is obliterated and mourning is impossible, a final proof of the complete unimportance and utter superfluousness of human beings as such. The final pseudogoal of the totalitarian movement is the fabrication of humankind, the organization of the infinite plurality of human beings into a single mass, as if every person were reduced to an interchangeable bundle of reactions.

When totalitarians set out to follow ideological recipes, the significance of those intellectual fictions was fully revealed. There could be no end to the process of killing because killing alone

kept the movement going. Objective enemies and possible crimes
are as boundless as human imagination. Totalitarian movements
need to create enemies, or rather, potential victims, in order to
have people to destroy. Destruction, an imaginary self-making
and an ultimate rebellion against the human condition, keeps the
movement rolling. Ideological faith in human omnipotence, the
conviction that everything can be done through organization, carries the ideologue into experiments that human imagination may
have outlined but, prior to the existence of totalitarian regimes,
human activity certainly never realized. The entire murderous
enterprise may be characterized as "experimental inquiry into
what is possible" (*OT*, 436). The central laboratories where the
experiments were carried on, the very liver of the regime, as
Solzhenitsyn said, were the camps.

*

Totalitarian terror reached its extremity in the concentration
camps; extermination camps were the extreme form of the concentration camp.[16] The senseless manufacture of corpses was preceded by a historically and politically intelligible preparation.
Acting on a population rendered rootless and superfluous by economic and political disintegration, preventive police measures
deprived individuals of the capacity to act and, in effect, destroyed their judicial persons. The administrative technique involved mixing genuine criminals with political opponents; later
the completely innocent were added. A second step destroyed
the moral person. Arrest meant instant oblivion, which for the
first time in history made martyrdom impossible. Destroying
memory made loyalty impossible as well. When victims were
made into accomplices, the ordinary human option, that it was
better to die a victim than to live as a murderer, was removed.
What is the meaning of a choice between betrayal of friends (and
their murder) and refusal that entails the murder of one's family?

A third stage destroyed individuality either by physical abuse
or by large-scale organization. This was the final stage in domination because destroying individuality also destroyed spontaneity
and initiative. The model citizen of a totalitarian state was an example of the animal species, human but reduced to the most elementary reactions, to a bundle of reactions that could always be
liquidated and replaced by other bundles of reactions that behave
in the same way. Convictions and opinions no longer mattered

since they were not needed; nothing spontaneous was required. The final result of the destruction of individuality was equality, an equality without fraternity or even humanity. After calculated neglect and starvation "came the death factories—and they all died together, the young and the old, the weak and the strong, and the sick and the healthy; not as people, not as men and women, children and adults, boys and girls, not as good and bad, beautiful and ugly—but brought down to the lowest common denominator of organic life itself, plunged into the darkest and deepest abyss of primal equality, like cattle, like matter, like things that had neither body nor soul, nor even a physignomy upon which death could stamp its seal."[17]

So far as the people who ran the operations went, a system of "consistent arbitrariness" apparently required completely normal people to make it work. Murder became an impersonal managerial technique required for the operation of the facility, nothing more. One of the startling points that Arendt observed at the Eichmann trial was that he was essentially a thoughtless administrator whose attention was directed almost entirely to the course of his own career and not to what he did in order to attain success. Like the proposal of the pseudonymous A. Carthill for the retention of India under British administration, Auschwitz was the scene of administrative massacres executed according to strict procedures and with no room for individual initiative. Everything was supposed to run like clockwork. In the event, however, human factors intervened, chiefly sadism and moodiness. So far as "desk murderers" such as Eichmann were concerned, this could only appear as regrettable weakness and inefficiency.

Many people besides Arendt have employed Kant's "radical evil" to describe the totalitarian regime. In such a regime all people were equally superfluous. The manipulators of the system believed they were as superfluous as the people they killed, which made them all the more dangerous because they did not care whether they themselves were alive or dead, whether they ever lived or never were born. Universal superfluousness enabled human beings to commit an entirely new category of crime. The scenes of those crimes, the concentration camps, are important for our purposes because they functioned as laboratories where the fundamental belief of totalitarianism, that everything is possible, was verified. The products of the camps were said to resemble bundles of reactions that behaved like Pavlov's dogs, which in turn had been conditioned by their laboratory surroundings. The verification of the belief that everything is possible is completely independent from any criteria of utility so that to ask, *Why* would anyone want to prove that something is possible? invites the reply: To prove that it is possible. This, Arendt several times said, was what made the camps so difficult to understand. And yet, one of the most astonishing aspects of totalitarianism is the extent to which its defining characteristics as brought to light by Arendt's phenomenology are shared by the phenomenon of technology.

# Conclusion

Evidence for modern worldlessness extends from the attitudes of citizens toward politicians, a mixture of contempt and distrust, to a wariness of facts that could always be something else. In Arendt's language, these are dark times, periods during which "the public realm has been obscured and the world become so dubious that people have ceased to ask any more of politics than that it show due consideration for their vital interests and personal liberty" (*MDT*, 11). Without a space of appearance, a public realm, trust in speech and in political action atrophies and with it the reality of one's own experience, which depends to some extent on the presence of others to witness and to hear one's story. Arendt's discussion of the genesis of modern worldlessness and of its regime has brought to light several external affinities between the technological society and totalitarianism.

Consider first, the "liver" of the regime. The camps were laboratories designed to test the belief that everything is possible. This is the principle of modern technology: one acts in order to see whether one can. Arendt realized the similarity herself, at least in the area of population management: promising social technologies "whose real field of experimentation lies in the totalitarian countries" have only to overcome a certain time lag to be applicable to human affairs in precisely the same way as technologies are applied to human artifacts (*PF*, 89). With recombinant DNA technologies an everyday practice, the time lag has largely been overcome. The laboratory image has another implication for the establishment of technology. All laboratories, including the camps, are, from the perspective of the "real" world, that is, the common world shared by all human beings, the anticipation of a changed environment. Arendt argued, in the first edition of her book, that the results of the totalitarian experiment would be conclusive only under conditions of a single, ecumenic totalitarian empire, which, she felt, made it unlikely that the conclusive experiment ever would be carried out. But considered from the perspective of the technological society and the pursuit of the one best way, the efforts of the totalitarians in the direction of this anticipated universal homogeneity appear to be crude: violence and terror are, from this perspective, inefficient and therefore technically irrational. For that reason, a technologist might say, they were abandoned.

One of the crises for which totalitarianism was the resolution was that of the nation-state. In the "belt of mixed populations" the nation-state had never been appropriate, had never existed, properly speaking, and it is there that the process of crisis and response has undergone its most significant development. Unification was achieved by military occupation, terror, and bureaucratic rule that was identified by the inhabitants of the region as Russian imperialism. But Soviet, as distinct from Russian, imperialism is first of all an administrative technique, not an ethnic hegemony. Moreover, it was successful largely because, unlike the imperialists of the West, the Soviet administrators were not handicapped by a division between domestic demands for legality and external bureaucratic tyranny. Soviet rule was uniformly administrative. In addition, Russia was never a nation-state in the Western sense but a multinational empire. Accordingly, the same methods of rule were and are applicable to the Soviet colonies in Eastern Europe as apply in Central Asia or the Caucasus: concessions on the level of folklore and dancing and imposition of a central, Moscow-directed policy. The problem of Soviet rule in Eastern Europe is just the opposite to Western rule over its former colonies. Whereas the Western nations could not undertake the administrative measures needed to retain their empires, the Soviets found it difficult to make political concessions to their satellites, despite their political and economic maturity as compared with Russia, because this would make the satellites privileged and so endanger the regime at home. Equalization in Eastern Europe initially meant equalization down to the level of Russia. The more recent changes can largely be understood in light of the grave technological backwardness that Soviet ideology and bureaucratic inertia have imposed on the empire. With or without Mikhail Gorbachev, some form of *perestroika* was necessary if the Soviet Union and Communist countries of Eastern Europe were going to survive as even second-rate technological societies. However that may be, the form of administrative population management has continued to be uniformly technological.

Negative evidence of the external affinity between the technological society and the totalitarian regime is found in one of the characteristics of those whom we may still call "dissidents," a characteristic that was also present in the Hungarian, Czechoslovak, and Polish interludes, namely the emphasis placed on learning the facts. After World War II, members of the Red army, who had seen for themselves that Europe was not the way Soviet lies had said it was, had to be shipped to concentration camps so as to be cured of the ability to form convictions. In his famous letter to the Politburo, Solzhenitsyn adopted the tone: Why bother keeping up the lies? We all know they are lies, why must this continue? The answer is clear: distrust of facts amounts to distrust of the world. Western political technology also requires that the distinction between truth and lies or fact and nonfact be undermined. The means, namely public relations and image making, are less crude, but in some respects are more effective.

The continuity between propaganda and public relations was noticed by Hitler (*Mein Kampf*, 1, 6). Advertisements and propaganda both emphasize "scientific" claims; the exaggeration inherent in the claims of advertisers betray an aggressive intent. Behind the message that people who do drink Miller's and Molson's have fun are the brewers' dreams that someday they may have the power to ensure that anyone who does not drink their beer will never have any fun. This is not to say that advertising is totalitarian propaganda. It is not. The difference is that totalitarian propaganda is guided by an ideology, whereas advertising and its political analogue, public relations, are guided by an image. More important is that neither is guided by facts, and therein lies a problem for political regimes influenced by public relations technologies. At the end of the Second World War, something like a massive advertising campaign was undertaken in West Germany in order to cover up the record of the preceding years. Chancellor Adenauer, for example, had to create the image of Hitler as a "madman" aided by a few "war criminals" rather than as a man who had the support of most Germans. General De Gaulle covered up the fact of a French defeat by sustaining the image that France remained always a "great power"; even Khruschev's Twentieth Party Congress speech and subsequent additions by Gorbachev can be understood as a post-totalitarian cover-up: Stalin's "excesses" were a consequence of an unfortunate cult of personality. Public relations and "image politics" are the staple of election campaigns in the technological society. The most successful campaigns are usually the most empty of facts and the most easily captured in a striking slogan.

Factual truth, Arendt said, "is political by nature" because it is the necessary condition for freedom of speech to be meaningful. If the facts are in dispute there is nothing to discuss and no possibility for divergent opinion (*PF*, 238). Facts are always contingent; they might have been otherwise because they are, politically speaking, the residue of action. In order to remain the ground for political debate, facts need testimony, remembrance, and trustworthy witnesses. This is why the transformation of reporters into "investigative journalists" with visualizations to defend or axes to grind is both dangerous to political discussion and typical of the technological society.

Ecumenic worldlessness has had the paradoxical result of creating a community of humankind in the sense that all human beings may be said to have a common concern. The modes by which this concern is expressed vary greatly, from fear of nuclear war to advocacy of animal rights, from armed resistance to totalitarian domination to advocacy of global affluence as a means to ensure disarmament. All such concerns gravitate around the phenomenon of technology. In this respect whether technology is the solution to humankind's problems or the source of the greatest danger is of secondary importance. The spiritual affinity of the technological phenomenon with totalitarianism is internal, not external: the meanings of the two phenomena may be said to overlap.

The chronological sequence of technological developments and the crystallization of the constituent elements of totalitarianism are roughly contiguous. The development of phenomenalism was followed by eighteenth-century anti-Semitism, nineteenth-century imperialism, and twentieth-century totalitarianism. Moreover, these events can all be intelligibly connected in light of the disintegration of the nation-state as the institutional shelter of Western societies. With the series of technological, economic, and political changes indicated earlier, increasing numbers of human beings have become superfluous. The modes of superfluity vary greatly, from the production of useless aristocrats by the *noblesse de la robe* to the production of refugees by the totalitarian bureaucrats. Whole societies can become expendable for totalitarians, and, as Ellul argued, society as a whole is expendable for the technological system. So far as concerns the institutional or external side of the process by which modern worldlessness has been actualized, it consists in the disintegration and destruction of national societies and their replacement with a congeries of classless, superfluous human beings. Both the totalitarian regime and the technological society are radically new forms of political organization with the difference that technology initiates radically new processes and totalitarian state-directed mass murder achieves a novel and absolute end: genocide. Moreover, neither technologists nor totalitarians think.[1]

Repeatedly reference has been made to the external or phenomenal aspect of the topics under discussion. The principle of relevance followed in part II of this study, which was that followed by Arendt, was to trace the disintegration of Western societies into masses ripe for organization and perhaps fit only for organization. Arendt has described the spirituality of such persons as follows: "Nothing perhaps distinguishes modern masses as radically from those of previous centuries as the loss of faith in a Last Judgement: the worst have lost their fear and the best have lost their hope. Unable as yet to live without fear and hope, these masses are attracted by every effort which seems to provide a man-made fabrication of the Paradise they had longed for and of the Hell they had feared" (*OT*, 446). As Voegelin observed of this spiritual disease, "agnosticism is the peculiar problem of the modern masses, and the man-made paradises and man-made hells are its symptoms; and the masses have the disease whether they are in their paradise or in their hell."[2] A common spiritual disorder has informed both the technological society and totalitarianism. In this sense the "origins of totalitarianism" and the "origins of the technological society" may be found primarily in process by which various late medieval heresies triumphed as secular immanentist creed movements. The phenomena of institutional disintegration express the substantive disease of the spirit. In part III the resulting disorientation is analyzed by means of three typical examples.

# PART III

# *Critical Disorientation*

# 7
# Scientism

Chapter 1 of this study considered Husserl's analysis of the crisis of the European sciences along with his solution to it. The solution proved to be in some respects defective, though the analysis, so far as it went, was unimpaired by that defect. According to Husserl, the exclusive reliance on "the positive sciences" for understanding reality along with the blinding effects of prosperity achieved by action based on those sciences have "meant an indifferent turning-away from the questions that are decisive for a genuine humanity."[1] Later in part I, reference was made to two distinctions, the first between noetic reason and calculative reason, the second between phenomenal and substantive being. In part II the significance of action was analyzed under modern conditions of worldlessness. Political action takes place within the world and into the web of human relationships. Technological action takes place under conditions of worldlessness and into nature. The political actor can be punished and forgiven for the consequences of his or her deed. No such redemption of technological action is possible. The technological society, which may be conceptualized as the social order consequent on action into nature, presupposes an imbalance with respect to the two distinctions just mentioned. Noetic reason has been effectively eclipsed by calculative reason, just as concern with questions of substance or meaning has been eclipsed by phenomenalism. The imbalance was referred to earlier as obsessive phenomenalism. The application of calculative rationality to phenomenal reality and the simultaneous neglect of noetic rationality and substantive reality did not take place all at once and without resistance.

The contrast may be seen at once if one compares two texts, one of Pascal (1623–62), and another of St. Thomas (1225–74),

about four centuries earlier. The *Summa contra Gentiles* was
written as a handbook for missionaries working in the field
against Islam. It expressed the height of imperial Christian spirituality, the military correlate of which was found in the Crusades.
Pascal's *Pensées* constituted an apology for Christianity directed
not against Islam but against infidels within the Christian civilizational area. Moreover, the order of the soul that was so beautifully described in Thomas's writings had been replaced by
Pascal's time with confusion. The atheists said, "But we do not
have any light," and Pascal could only agree: "That is what I see
and what confounds me."[2] God had hidden Himself. The experience of the *Deus absconditus*, so central to Pascal's apologetics,
was part of the crisis of Christianity, the institutional expressions
of which were the Reformation and religious wars of the sixteenth
and seventeenth centuries. The experiential and the institutional
aspects of the crisis reinforced each other with the consequence
that a socially significant spiritual disorientation occurred.

Two aspects of this disorientation may be distinguished. The
first arose from the atrophy of the experience of Christian faith.
Socially speaking, Christianity no longer provided a fundamental
meaning and orientation to human life by directing consciousness toward its world-transcendent divine ground. The second
was found in the inadequate, diminished complex of language
symbols and concepts used to express the orientation of existence. The loss of orientation or the refusal to orient human existence toward the divine world-transcendent reality prevented
the articulation of symbols adequate to express the full amplitude
of reality experienced. At the same time, the creation of inadequate symbols increased the difficulty for individuals who were
genuinely searching for the grounds of their own humanity. The
accretions of increasingly inadequate or opaque symbols made
recollection of the original and originary experiences of orientation toward the divine ground increasingly difficult to undertake. In consequence, the disorientation increased. Not only was
human existence cut off from experiences of the divine origin
of meaning but they increasingly lacked the symbolic and conceptual instruments to account critically for the resulting disorientation.

As an example one need refer only to Hobbes. In the *Leviathan*, book 1, chapter 11, Hobbes argued that the orientation of

existence was not toward the summum bonum "as is spoken of in the books of the old moral philosophers" but was the result of restless undirected desires arising from "the diversity of passions in divers men" and from differences in knowledge and opinion.[3] Hobbes's psychology of the passions was developed explicitly as a substitute for spiritual orientation toward the divine ground but also because he had experienced the overwhelming evidence that people were in fact driven by passionate and disordered souls.

However unsatisfactory Hobbes's abandonment of the beatific vision in favor of the Leviathan may have been as a solution to the crisis, his analysis of the spiritual disorder remains unsurpassed. Nevertheless, one must recall that there do exist alternatives to the creation of a "mortal god," as Hobbes called Leviathan, to become king of the children of pride. One, to be discussed in the following chapter, is utopianism. With this alternative, pride is assumed either not to exist or to be eventually or quickly extinguishable by means of institutional pressures. Either way, a change in the meaning of humanity, or of human existence, which is to say, a change in the nature of humankind, is anticipated. The implications of tampering with the image of humanity or with human nature are discussed further in the next chapter. The other alternative, given the atrophy of spiritual substance in community institutions such as the church, would be to look elsewhere. Under conditions of religious warfare, which constitutes evidence enough of a lack of spiritual direction in the community, if spiritual authority were to be found anywhere, it would be only in the soul of the individual mystic-philosopher, a Bruno or a Bodin, for example. In the event, something like the Hobbesian alternative was undertaken. In this chapter, two aspects of this alternative will be treated sequentially.

The first matter to be considered concerns the substitution of the system of mathematicized physics, as an ontologically real account of the external world, for a concern for the substance or meaning of the cosmos. The beginnings of this movement have already been discussed in chapter 3. The publication of Newton's *Philosophiae naturalis principia mathematica* in 1687 accelerated the process.[4] The second aspect involved the impact of Newton's *Principia* on his age and its significance for areas of human inquiry other than that of the external world. Made public at a time when Christian faith was weakening and spiritual awareness of the substance of nature all but lost, the notion that the universe was a huge dead mechanism that operated according to Newton's laws was persuasive. God having been squeezed out of His creation, the earth in turn was transformed from the home of human beings into an insignificant cog in the big machine. Human beings, now reduced to "selves," became even more insignificant. Both aspects of the problem will be discussed under the category of *scientism*.

The term exists in English as an ordinary adjective. It was developed as a technical term of analysis in French with the publication of Fiolle's *Science et scientisme* (1936) and was borrowed by Hayek in his series of articles in *Economica* a few years later. It was given a precise conceptual shape by Voegelin in 1948.[5] The creed indicated by the term *scientism* has three principle doctrines. First, mathematicized physics, understood as the science of natural phenomena, is the model science according to which the pretentions of all other sciences must be measured. Second, all realms of being, including that of meaning or substance, can be studied by means of the methods employed by the model science with no loss of information. Third, if nevertheless it is maintained that there are aspects of reality that are not amenable to treatment by the model science, those aspects are irrelevant to scientific knowledge or, more aggressively, can be reduced to scientific knowledge because, in their nonscientific form, they are illusions.

*

The origin of the intellectual movement of which scientism appears to be the culmination is found in the events discussed in chapter 3 in connection with the establishment of the doctrine of phenomenalism. Theologically, faith dissolved into a reverential attitude toward "tradition"; occasionally attention was focused on the utility of religion as a means to maintain civil peace, an attitude that Marx properly denounced as dishing opiates to the masses. Cosmologically, the end point was reached, as was just indicated, when God was expelled from His creation. Now, conceptions of the cosmos abhor a vacuum; in place of a cosmos from which the divine substance has been imaginatively removed, a new and ersatz reality had to be invented as a plausible substitute for God. The obvious source for the sought-for substance was the new cosmology. However, it has been shown that the new science was a science of phenomena, not of substance. In order for phe-

nomenal science to assume the task demanded of it, the new cosmologists were required to commit what Whitehead called "the
fallacy of misplaced concreteness."[6]

According to Whitehead, this fallacy occurs whenever abstrac-
tions are substituted for concrete realities. Whitehead's most important example was that of simple location. By the assumption of
simple location, a thing may be said to be *here* in space and *here*
in time without reference to other regions of space or time (or
space-time). Whatever is in space, by this assumption, is in some
specific and definite location in space; by implication, "space is
the location of simple locations."[7] This is a perfectly normal way
to think about things. "There is no doubt about this. The only
question is, How concretely are we thinking when we consider
nature under these conceptions? My point will be, that we are
presenting ourselves with simplified editions of immediate matters of fact." That is, the constituent elements of these "simplified
editions" make sense only in light of a prior commitment to the
validity of "elaborate logical constructions of a high degree of abstraction." The outcome of this "century of genius," as Whitehead
called the age that began with Bacon's *Advancement of Learning*
(1605) and ended with Leibniz's celebrated disputes with Newton, was the triumph of scientific abstraction. Its two chief pre-
cipitates were "on the one hand *matter*, with its *simple location* in
space and time, on the other hand *mind*, perceiving, suffering,
reasoning, but not interfering." The ultimate consequence was to
have "foisted onto philosophy the task of accepting them as the
most concrete rendering of fact" and "thereby modern philosophy
had been ruined."[8] It has been ruined by having been dissipated
into dualism or into one of two types of monism.[9] All three spring
from acceptance of the fallacy of misplaced concreteness.

Exposition of the fallacy does not require a taste for abstruse
and complex reasoning. It is a comparatively straightforward argument. One is therefore naturally led to wonder why physicists,
whether they belonged to the century of genius or not, had to
wait for Whitehead to explain matters to them. Voegelin has suggested that the answer to this puzzle lay in a notion that was built
into the foundations of modern physics, the notion of absolute
space.

The question of absolute space was not introduced with the
work of Newton but with Copernicus's assumption that the sun
was the ontologically real center of the solar system. The political

and theological implications were clarified with Campanella's "utopian" *City of the Sun.* The alternative account of reality was proposed by Bodin and Bruno and later by Leibniz in his dispute with Newton, carried on through the intermediary Samuel Clarke. The whole question was finally cleared up with Einstein's assumption that space was curved and unbounded so that it runs back into itself. As with Whitehead's fallacy of misplaced concreteness, the puzzle is why such a comparatively simple philosophical question as relativity took so long to gain acceptance among physicists.

One reason may be that, even though relativity is *philosophically* uncomplicated, it is anything but simple physics. The complexity of physics became a complicating factor because, as Voegelin has observed, three interconnected aspects of the problem were insufficiently distinguished. First was Whitehead's statement regarding the ruin of modern philosophy: the belief that scientific method establishes objectivity and truth was not seen as an untenable belief but as a fundamental fact. Second, practical or pragmatic success in applying the "scientific method" to the phenomena of the world was interpreted as evidence of the factual or concrete validity of the first belief. And third, the speculative interpretation of the first two questions led to the conclusion that the whole of human experience was adequately expressed as science.

Opposed to the first principle was the alternative, based on common sense, that methods are subordinate to theoretical relevance. If science or philosophy is the search for truth concerning the nature of various sorts of beings, then relevance of a method depends on the degree to which it contributes to success in the search for truth. Different objects, different sorts of beings, studied by scientific investigation will require different methods. "If," Voegelin wrote, "the adequacy of a method is not measured by its usefulness to the purpose of science, if on the contrary the use of a method is made the criterion of science, then the meaning of science as a truthful account of the structure of reality, as the theoretical orientation of man in his world, and as the great instrument for man's understanding of his own position in the universe is lost."[10] Opposed to the second principle is the argument made in part II, that the consequences of natural science and technology are not the result of brilliant insights by scientists and technicians but have resulted from the account of the structure of phenomena as objective, which permits the introduction of human agency into the natural causal chain. Opposed to the third is the observation that wisdom regarding the substantive concerns of human being is quite distinct from knowledge regarding the phenomenal structure of the world. On the basis of these three oppositions, an account of absolute space can now be given.

Regarding Newton's motivations, two distinct issues are involved. The first was religious. In chapter 3 of this study the topic of religious experience was introduced in connection with Bruno's speculations on the infinite. There it was noted that phenomenal nature was the accidental being of the substance of nature. The substance of nature, namely its identity with spirit, was the accidental being of God. The spirit that animated that substance was itself unknowable because it was infinite, whereas the knowing intellect of human being was finite. In Bruno's formular phrase, phenomenal nature was "the accident of the accident." It was, accordingly, knowable, as accidental and finite, to the scientific intellect. On the other hand, the finite intellect could contemplate but not know the infinite by an act of imaginative expansion. There could be no question, for Bruno, of an infinite phenomenal space but only of a substantive infinity that was itself a manifestation of the infinite first cause, namely God, and that was revealed to the intellect as a speculative idea.

Bruno's speculations constitute a synthesis not merely of spirit and nature but of two previously distinct aspects of infinity. The first can be traced back to Anaximander's apeiron, the unbounded; for Hellenic cosmology, what gave form and measure was bounded and finite. The second was derived from Christian spirituality and the distinction between the finite creature and divine infinity. In the seventeenth century the question of infinity was again prominent in philosophy, only now the speculative context was the new cosmology. In his dispute with Descartes, for example, Henry More developed a notion of extension that seemed to him to overcome the implication of Descartes's identification of space and matter. If, indeed, the universe were both infinite and filled with matter that operated according to knowable mechanisms, it seemed to More that there would exist neither mystery nor spirit. More therefore proposed that extension was an infinite attribute existing from eternity. Now, because attributes must be attributed to something, More was required to postulate an appropriate subject. He found it in God or rather in the divine substance or divine being. The theological doctrine, propounded by More, called Socinianism, was adhered to by Newton as well. In the *Optics* (1706), and in the general scholium to the *Principia* (1713), Newton argued that the divine being uses space "as it were, as its sensorium." By means of space, God sees all things everywhere.[11]

This ingenious response to Descartes's materialization of extension suffered from two serious defects. First, the God who was so massively present in phenomenal space as to be its spiritual substance could with difficulty retain His status as the cosmic-transcendent Creator. Second, the doctrinal form of the speculation would not appeal to those who were not already concerned, on other grounds, with the question of divine substance. As it happened, most intellectuals of the later eighteenth century were willing to accept Newton's notion of absolute space without much concern for its infinity nor Newton's religious reasons for postulating its infinity.

This last observation indicates the second aspect of Newton's motivation and the specific form that the fallacy of misplaced concreteness took in his work. The first law of motion in the *Principia* stated, "Every body perseveres in its state of resting, or of moving uniformly in a right line," unless it is acted on by external forces. In order for a body to be truly at rest, or at absolute rest, a notion of absolute space is required. If bodies are at rest, they "do rest in respect of one another," but this cannot be determined by observation. What to do? In the scholium to definition eight, Newton distinguished between absolute space, which exists "without relation to anything external, remains always similar and immovable," and relative space, "which our senses define by its position in respect of bodies; and which is vulgarly taken for immovable space." Newton admitted that relative motions were "without any inconvenience in common affairs" but that, if relative motions were all that could be *conceived* (he admits that relative motions are all that can be *sensed*), then no laws of motion would be possible. Accordingly, "in philosophical disquisitions [such as the *Principia*] we must abstract from the senses" so as to consider things themselves, distinct from what are only sensible measures of them. In Whitehead's language, we are obliged to commit the fallacy of misplaced concreteness in order to legislate the laws of motion.

In addition, Newton believed he could observe absolute motion in the effects of centrifugal force on the shape of the earth or any other rotating body. Samuel Clarke's fifth letter to Leibniz raised just this objection to the latter's criticism of Newton's concept. The argument remained unanswered for nearly two hundred years: if space is relative and not absolute, then the movability of one body would depend on the existence of other bodies; thus, a body that existed alone would be incapable of movement and a rotating body, deformed by centrifugal force from assuming a spherical shape, would, in the absence of other bodies, not rotate and would revert to a sphere. This, according to Clarke, was absurd.[12] Hence motion, and therefore space, must be absolute, not relative. It was not until Ernst Mach published *The Science of Mechanics* in 1883 that the argument was made that there was no point in making the fallacy of misplaced concreteness in order to avoid a contradiction.[13]

These observations, based on the work of Whitehead and Mach, may be generalized beyond the question of Newtonian absolute space. Relativity did not emerge as a serious alternative to Newtonian mechanics because the new understanding of nature that arose from the application of scientific method to phenomena was called true; it was in fact true, but only insofar as it remained a correlate or artifact of the methods used to describe its application. This simple and obvious argument was restated by Duhem, as was indicated in chapter 3. It had to be restated because it had been forgotten. The conclusion to be drawn, therefore, is that the question of the absoluteness of Copernican or of Newtonian space is not simply a physical question or a question of physics. To be properly understood it must be supplemented by metaphysical and theological arguments. In general, physics requires cosmological speculation even to appear in its own proper context as physics.

This understanding of the issue was provided by Cardinal Bellarmine when he pointed out to Galileo that *any* astronomical theory was acceptable so long as it did not pretend to remove the earth from the center of human religious and philosophical life. The earth remained at the center of the cosmos because that is where the spiritual drama of human nature and destiny takes place. If it took place on the moon, then the moon would be the center of the cosmos. But it does not. The spiritual drama takes place in the souls of human beings who dwell on earth. Any shift in the locale by which space is experienced therefore becomes an interpretation of the experience of this spiritual drama at variance, for example, with that expressed in Christianity and philosophy. In Hannah Arendt's language, Galileo sought the Archimedean point, but Bellarmine pointed out that it existed only as the void behind the universe where human beings could do nothing except become lost.

The distinction between the scientific truth of phenomena and the substantive experiential truth expressed through religious and philosophical symbols remained unclarified on the occasion of Galileo's difficulties with the Inquisition no less than on the occasion of Leibniz's arguments with Clarke. In the words that Voegelin used to reconstruct Leibniz's argument: "Relativity is not an appurtenance of objects which exist in themselves; it is part of the logical structure of a science of phenomena." Thus, as Mach said, it is senseless to isolate a rotating body and ask what its phenomenal properties might be in the absence of its actual relational field. It is one thing to abstract from concrete physical circumstances and quite another to abstract from the logic of phenomenal science while pretending to keep the object of phenomenal science in place. The latter act commits the fallacy of misplaced concreteness.

One further point remains to be made with respect to the question of absolute motion. The fallacy that has been discussed in connection with Newton's laws pertains to the pretense that absolute motion can be observed or, more cautiously, that observed motions can properly be conceptualized as instances expressing Newton's conceptual laws. The arguments of Leibniz, no less than the development of quantum mechanics, indicate that absolute motion cannot be observed. That does not mean, however, that such motion cannot be experienced. Jogging on a treadmill is *really* different from jogging on a trail; in the first, the belt of a treadmill moves and the runner stays in place; in the second, the runner moves and the woods and fields stay in place. There are, therefore, some bodies in the universe, namely human bodies, that know when they are in absolute motion and when they are at absolute rest.

Extrapolation from that concrete experience to the abstract assumption of absolute space, however, commits the extrapolator to the fallacy of misplaced concreteness. This was pointed out in the eighteenth century by Bishop Berkeley in *De Motu* (1721). Moreover, Berkeley explained how the fallacy was committed: we conceive of an idea of space without bodies but forget to subtract our own body.[14] Just as we forget about our own body as we jog through the woods, so do we forget about it in imagining an empty space while experiencing our own spatiality and motility. *That* experience may be unreflectively absolute: we really move through the woods. But its absoluteness depends on our tacit and prior commitment to the absoluteness of our bodies as the incarnation of our spatiality and motility. Reflection establishes the distance necessary to indicate the relative space that is defined by the lived body. The conclusion, which has also been confirmed by twentieth-century physics, is that we can only observe bodies moving relative to one another; the physicist, being embodied, is an observer of such moving bodies. Once again one concludes that it is a fallacy to hypothesize the immediate, unreflective experience of spatiality and motility into an objective quality of phenomenal space.

\*

The theoretical or philosophical inadequacy of Newton's concept of absolute space may be taken as having been established. It would only be a slight exaggeration, however, to say that the effectiveness of scientism, in a Newtonian or other form, is unconnected to the fallaciousness of the argument by which it is expressed. Indeed, given the experiential as well as intellectual demands of accounting for the relations of nature and spirit, the social and political success of simple but fallacious accounts should not come as a great surprise. One risks being charged with harboring antidemocratic tendencies in making such an observation. Even so, it appears to be true that the old distinction between the philosophic few and the nonphilosophic many is as close to being a permanent feature of human social existence as one is ever likely to find. It is also true, of course, that many contemporary intellectuals dispute such a contention, which may, however, merely indicate the social effectiveness of simple teachings.

The account of Newton's scientism had as its objective not merely to expose a theoretical error. Newton's fallacious postulate of an absolute is important not because it was a mistake that a Leibniz or a Mach might correct. Rather it was the expression of a new set of sentiments and attitudes, a will to establish a doctrine that ordered human existence by way of a specifiable class of intramundane experiences. Necessarily, therefore, it implied an unwillingness to order existence through openness to the experiences of world-transcendent reality. Scientism is important for the purposes of this study for two reasons. First, because it served as the ersatz religion or metaphysics on the basis of which the phenomenon of action into nature was justified. But second, the fallaciousness of its assumptions or their ersatz quality contributed to the existential disorders required to sustain the technological society.

Shortly after Newton's death an extraordinary memorial poem gave voice to the worst expectations of Cardinal Bellarmine. J. T. Desaguliers, a better physicist than poet, wrote of his friend:

> Newton the unparallel'd, whose Name
> No time will wear out of the Book of Fame,
> Coelestiall Science has promoted more,
> Than all the sages that have shone before.
> Nature compell'd his piercing Mind obeys,
> And gladly shows him all her secret Ways;
> 'Gainst Mathematics she has no Defence,
> And yields t' experimental Consequence;
> His Tow'ring Genius, from its certain Cause
> Ev'ry Appearance *a priori* draws,
> And shews th' Almighty Architect's unalter'd Laws.[15]

Discounting poetic hyperbole, it was Desaguliers's opinion that Newton's account of the mechanical order of phenomena constituted a splendid, and unsurpassed, spiritual insight. One need not even appreciate the mathematical elegance of the *Principia* to share, with Locke, in the feeling of having learned of a new absolute, of having shared in the sense of self-reliance and autonomy that comes from being part of the advancement of science. Indeed, the sentiment of having understood that one is part of a progressive age during which great things are done may well override any concern for exactly what is actually happening.

According to Isaiah Berlin, "The entire programme of Enlightenment, especially in France, was consciously founded on Newton's principles and methods, and derived its confidence and its vast influence from his spectacular achievements."[16] One might go further than this: without the remarkable success that Newton's celestial mechanics had in obscuring the fallacy of misplaced concreteness, subsequent ideological movements founded by encyclopedists, sociologists, Marxists, Darwinists, Freudians, and so on, would have quickly dissipated into intellectual bankruptcy.[17] A decisive ingredient to liberalism, progressivism, national socialism, international socialism, and any other mass political creed that has sought contemporary success is the belief that the "piercing Mind" of science compels Nature to reveal "all her secret ways." The fons et origo of this belief was Newton's doctrine of space.

More than the immodest praise of bad poets was required for Newtonian scientism to become a mass creed. His doctrine had to be simplified in a convincing way and expressed so that intellectuals could use it. Voltaire's *Elements of Newton's Philosophy* (1738) is in this respect an exemplary text.[18] Voltaire was of the opinion that the light of reason should fall on all corners and into all dark places. Mysteries should be dispelled because they were no more than superstitious excuses to persecute; if reason failed to dissolve them, then they must be crushed, for they were a scandal to his enlightened mind. It is undeniable that a streak of vulgarian activism animates much of Voltaire's writing, as does a somewhat antithetical esotericism.[19] More important for present purposes was his spiritual superficiality.

Consider, for example, the contrast between Voltaire's account of the relationship between the soul and God and the account of the spiritual process given by Thomas Aquinas in the *Summa contra Gentiles*.[20] According to Thomas, the Christian symbols of the soul and of God and the relations between the two are not dogmatic propositions regarding the relationship between entities or phenomena. Despite the form of presentation, Thomas was not providing his readers with a series of propositions that might be accepted or rejected on the basis of intellectual inspection. Rather he expressed a real movement in the soul of the believer responding to divine grace. In the soul's response, faith is "formed" by the experience of charity as a response to divine love or grace and is drawn toward God; moreover the soul is conscious of the process as an experience of reality for which the literary

text of Thomas is the trace. The concrete experience of this process in the soul of Thomas gave meaning to the theological and
anthropological terminology. When the focus was shifted from
the substantive experiences of human existence to phenomenal
knowledge of the external world, the essential point of the meditative exegesis, namely the expression or articulation of Christian
spiritual reality, is lost. Under such circumstances, either the ex-
egetical symbols will be abandoned because they have become
irrelevant or, if sentiments in support of tradition remain strong,
they will be simplified into psychological dispositions or justified
on the basis of social utility. In any event, the experiential meaning evaporates. As Voegelin said, "That last position, the combination of opaqueness of the symbols with traditional reverence for
them, is the position of Newton and Voltaire."[21]

Voltaire nowhere discussed the spiritual processes of the soul.
The following is the opening paragraph of his *Elements of Newton's Philosophy:* "Newton was deeply persuaded of the existence
of God, and he meant by this word not only an infinite, all-
powerful, eternal and creative Being, but a master who established a relation between himself and his creatures: for, without
this relation, knowledge of a God is but a sterile idea that would
seem to invite crime, by the hope of impunity, every thinker having been born perverse."[22] Newton happened to believe in God;
this biographical accident was Voltaire's starting point. There followed a conceptual specification of the meaning of the word *God*
and finally the reasoning that is meant to account for Newton's
having been persuaded to believe. The focus is not on spiritual
reality experienced but on externally described psychological
facts. The spirituality expressed by Voltaire's account reminds one
of the cri de coeur by Glaucon and Adeimantus in book 2 of the
*Republic,* with the difference, of course, that Plato's dramatic
characters sought deliverance. The consciousness typified by Voltaire is so far from being aware of a need for deliverance from the
climate of opinion that characterized his age that he could conceive of himself as the standard by which all others might be
judged. Moreover, he was untroubled by his own perverseness
because he considered it an occupational characteristic of "all
thinkers."

It is possible to cut through the spiritual fogginess of Voltaire's
account with the observation that the perversity of the thinker

exists only insofar as his existence is no longer ordered by the response of faith (formed by love) to divine grace. Because of this perversity, society was required to intervene to establish order; it did so by providing a content to the otherwise empty "idea" of God. The content was revenge and punishment for criminality, a somewhat more primitive conception of divine spirituality than is found in Thomas's exegesis of grace. According to Voltaire, belief in divine punishment deters crime; therefore, it is useful to believe in God. It is, perhaps, enough to observe that a Thrasymachus or a Callicles would not be persuaded as easily as Voltaire said Newton had been. On the basis of Voltaire's doctrinal approach to these questions, a person of Calliclean spiritedness would be more likely to take his chances later in order to enjoy a life of pleasurable perverseness now.

It is significant that Voltaire typically would avoid the genuine existential issue in order to present his convictions. Having, therefore, declared in favor of God, Voltaire adduced other evidence to prove the soundness of his decision. Gravity and planetary movements indicated that the hypothesis of a divine artificer was highly probable. The spiritual superficiality of the remark was evident from Newton's reservations on whether God followed the inverse-square rule when assigning the planets their positions.[23] The spiritual implications were fully exposed when Laplace explained to Napoleon that he had no need of such a hypothesis. In other words, the apparent reasonableness of Voltaire's assertion, that a divine artificer was required to construct the mechanical phenomenon so beautifully described by Newtonian mechanics, required for its plausibility a thoroughly unreasonable commitment to the fallacy of misplaced concreteness.

The direction of the disintegration of Christian spirituality is clear. It remains to indicate schematically the principle phases of the process. The enterprise of physics and, more broadly, of natural science was and is a particular occupation of human beings; it has its own conventions and standards, adherence to which is required if the resulting production of discourse is to count as the scientific knowledge of phenomena. Scientific truths, as was indicated earlier, are artifacts of scientific methods and independent of extraneous speculation. If the methodological preoccupations of physics or of the other sciences are transferred away from the particular occupation to the existence of the human being who undertakes it, certain distortions of reality experienced characteristically follow. When the transference is widely enough spread throughout a population, the result will be a kind of social pathology.

The first step in the transfer of the purposes of science and of its animating intentions to human existence is expressed in Voltairian or Newtonian sentiments that existence can be ordered by an absolute truth of science. If the fallacy of misplaced concreteness is committed on a sufficiently grand scale, then it is also believed that what is not science is not knowledge. Consequently it is unnecessary to pursue anything but scientific knowledge of phenomena. This argument amounts to a recipe for ignorance regarding all questions of substance. Whether or not the advances in the sciences of phenomena have necessarily been purchased at the cost of understanding the existentially important questions, that is, questions of substance, it is certainly true that scientific knowledge and existential ignorance have kept pace with one another.

The second step in the advance of scientism consists in the capture of the educational institutions of society, which was certainly part of Newton's program.[24] The Royal Society was quite properly the model for Laputa. More to the point, deficiencies in substantive understanding cannot be made up by increased knowledge of phenomena. Obliviousness to questions of existential order is not mere ignorance that can be repaired by taking a few refresher courses at night school. Bruno's characterization of those incapable of spiritual insight as being akin to pigs and cattle was, perhaps, too severe. Nevertheless, it seems true that human beings are not equally endowed with this capacity or gift. Accordingly, the spread of scientism will have the social consequence of favoring those who are deficient in terms of human substance. Voegelin has used "spiritual eunuch" to describe the type of personality likely to subscribe to scientism.[25] It would apply equally to a society where persons of the scientistic temperament have become politically or socially dominant. The principle of analysis here is essentially that employed by Plato to characterize the defective regimes in books 8 and 9 of the *Republic*.

A third stage has arrived when the standards of the spiritual eunuch are imposed on everyone. Voltaire's fantasies regarding priests and kings were still only aggressive epigrams. Moreover, the combination of vulgarity and sublime ignorance of spiritual matters was no more than his personal misfortune. What turned Voltaire's ignorance into a political problem and, indeed, into a civilizational disaster, was its social success. Newton's opinions on absolute space would simply be a mark of his philosophical illiteracy and a matter of curiosity for political science had they not become the paradigm for any number of additional scientistic dogmas.

In the eighteenth century, for example, the notion of a chronological succession of forms of life was conceived as a replacement for divine creation, but this interpretation was balanced by the awareness that knowledge of the mechanics of evolution said nothing about the substance that evolved.[26] Accordingly, one again encountered the Leibnizian questions: Why is there something and not nothing? Why is it as it is and not some other way? The triumph of Darwinianism, both in its nineteenth-century form and with the addition of twentieth-century molecular biology, constitutes as well an instance of the triumph of scientism. The distinction between substance and phenomena has been so far suppressed that it is nowadays taken to be an obvious truth that a theory that provides an account of the mechanics of evolution is accepted as a revelation about the nature of life. Moreover, it is said to contain implications for our understanding of the nature of human, society, and the place of human beings in the cosmos. Voegelin's term "spiritual eunuch" was no exaggeration. There is no need to trace the course of the successful assault on the remnants of Western spirituality during the nineteenth century. The monographic literature is vast. The problem with understanding what Roger Martin du Gard called the century of rubbish is not a lack of information but an inability to discern rubbish.

The triumph of the spiritual eunuchs of the nineteenth century was followed by the spiritual anarchy of the twentieth. The most impressive symptom of that anarchy to date has been the establishment of totalitarian regimes. In light of the eclipse of experiences of Christian and philosophic spirituality, the inner connection of totalitarianism and the technological society seems clear enough. The totalitarian murderers undertook the physical extermination of those who continued to bear within themselves the experiences that are identified with Western spirituality; the

technological society achieves the same result by less lethal
means. This is not to say that the archipelago of the gulags is in
any sense equivalent to the archipelago of McDonald'ses: one of
the consequences of the current crop of spiritual eunuchs is an
apparent inability to distinguish the two in light of a doctrine of
"moral equivalence" between communist socialism and liberal
capitalism. There are, in fact, great differences in various parts of
the world with respect to the possibility of personal escape from
the deformations of the age into the freedom of the spirit. Nevertheless, to the extent that the inner form of the technological
society is that of scientistic civilization, it is quite unrealistic to
expect that the tradition of Western spirituality will find expression anywhere in the contemporary world. It remains to point out
what can be expected.

# 8

# Utopianism

Political philosophy has voiced great respect for nomothetes, lawgivers and "founding fathers," because of the ability of such individuals to understand what Solon called the "unseen measure" and to establish the "right boundaries of all things." The best regime, or rather, the best practical regime, was best because its institutions achieved a stable equilibrium of equality with inequality, which, to paraphrase Aristotle, is what most people mean by justice. Durability did not guarantee that the regime was just, but it was a reliable indicator because the criteria of good order or justice do not change. They do not change, by this understanding, because human nature does not change. The nomothete was praised, therefore, for understanding of human nature and skill in fashioning a regime that expressed that insight as good law, *eunomia*. All cities, including the city in speech of Plato's *Republic*, are threatened by change for the worse or disintegration. This is why political philosophers have argued that the nomothetic founder's work must be continued not by another founding but by statecraft that preserves the eunomia of the founding under different circumstances. Socrates' criticism of Pericles' policies was not that his grandiose schemes spelled the eventual ruin of Athens but that he had corrupted the political virtue of the Athenians: corruption meant change for the worse, and then disintegration, because first Pericles then the rest of the Athenians rejected the unseen measure first explicated by Solon. For classical political philosophy, the more or less adequate imitation of what is always and everywhere just ensured the endurance of the regime. In this way, the subsequent acts of the politicians prolonged the initial act of the nomothete.

Let us begin by overlooking the experiences of the divine source of justice, the Solonic *dike,* and consider political action as pragmatic Periclean greatness. In his famous Funeral Oration (Thucydides 2:34) Pericles told his fellow Athenians that their great deeds would be remembered without the mediation of the poets because the citizen body of the polis itself supplied witnesses to their own deeds. The glory of the Athenians, he told them, would be remembered "on every occasion when deed or story shall fall for its commemoration." Poets were not needed so long as the city recalled and commemorated its heroes and in so doing afforded them the immortality of remembrance. Such a conception of immortality and of politics, which was reintroduced to political philosophy with the Renaissance notions of fame and fortune, is both anti-Solonic and anti-Christian.

Periclean greatness is not, however, a recipe for thoughtless brutality. Here one must distinguish between the purpose of political action, undertaken "in order to do . . . something," and the meaning of political action, undertaken "for the sake of . . . something." Pericles' point, if that distinction is borne in mind, was that the Athenian polis was founded not in order to achieve certain purposes, such as administering an empire, but to immortalize the Athenians. Political action is undertaken for the sake of glory, whatever its immediate purpose might be. By such an understanding, politics is precarious. The meaning of deeds may easily pass away as memory fades with the passing of generations; it may pass more abruptly as well when cities fall. This sense of perishing animates the opening pages of both great historical texts that have been preserved from Greek antiquity. No one who reads Herodotus and Thucydides with even a modest amount of sensitivity can fail to be moved by the pathos of the impermanence of human deeds and the urgency of the task of the historical narrative, namely the preservation of meaning.

A great contrast can be seen when the attitudes of homo faber are applied to political action. The unseen measure becomes imaginatively visible in the mind of the founder who laid the foundations on which the just regime eventually would be built. Initially the symbolism to express this activity was taken from biblical texts. Activist mystics claimed to be building a new Jerusalem and embodied their claim in a self-vindicating ethic of success. By the same logic their focus remained on the present: the

Kingdom of God and the rule of saints was present from the moment it was acknowledged but ordained from the beginning. This kind of disorientation has been termed by Voegelin *metastatic faith*. In order to flower as the modern notion of progress, of which technology is the greatest contemporary exemplar, metastatic faith was blended with the symbolism of utopia.

*Utopia*, the book, was published in Latin in 1515 and has been translated into nearly all modern languages. The word has become a common noun, and the author, Thomas More, has been honored by two ecumenic but opposed organizations, the Communist movement and the Roman Catholic church. This latter fact attests to the complexity and subtlety of the work to which More owes his fame. The central element in the meaning of utopia is that of a nonexistent but imaginative perfect society or state. The form in which the conception of such a state of affairs is cast is fiction. When fictions are taken as blueprints that are considered impractical, the term has a pejorative connotation. More peripherally, the term has been expanded to mean a genus of political speculation of which More's *Utopia* was simply the example that endowed the entire category with a name. When the word is used in this ahistorical sense it is possible to include the Gilgamesh "epic" from the third millennium. By the same token, Mannheim could write *Ideology and Utopia* without mentioning More.

The limitations of anachronistic conceptualization are clear with a little reflection on the opinion that Plato's *Republic* is a utopia. The polis of speech is not perfect; inherent in its genesis is its decline. Neither is it a blueprint for action, nor a fiction; it is rather a concrete and realistic exploration of the soul seeking the same unseen measure introduced by Plato's great ancestor, Solon, with the difference that Plato was able to draw on the noetically more differentiated vocabulary of philosophy and tragedy to express that search.

The act of founding a political order on the basis of principles is about all the *Republic* and *Utopia* have in common. But even here, the reasons why this form of political writing was plausible were quite different. In antiquity, the foundation of a colony required the work of a nomothete; thus Socrates' proposal in book 2 that the two young men join him in founding a city in speech was a dramatically realistic appeal to their aristocratic pride. In

More's day, the voyages of discovery provided a background of verisimilitude to the claims of Raphael Hythlodaeus that he had accompanied Amerigo Vespucci. Moreover, if we consider "utopias" to be the literary form of political speculation characteristic of periods of actual political foundation, as with the Greek colonies or the empires of the western hemisphere, then St. Thomas Aquinas's *De regimine principum* deserves inclusion as well, the corresponding political events being the establishment of the new Latin kingdoms in the eastern Mediterranean after the Crusades. In other words, though a case can be made for a restricted use of the term prior to More's *Utopia*, based on the real experience of founding new regimes, the substantive variations in the actual evocations are much greater than the formal similarities of type.

After the publication of *Utopia*, a general history of utopian thought exists. A century later Campanella's *City of the Sun* was set in the Indian Ocean, as More's *Utopia* was in the South Atlantic. Bacon's *New Atlantis* was in the South Sea; Swift, Defoe, Stevenson, Melville, Conrad, Maugham, and Mead all depended on the evocation of the notional South Seas as a place of escape. Locke's famous "in the beginning all the world was America" indicated both his rejection of the Biblical "In the beginning" and the possibility of finding an "ideal state of nature" in the land to which Vespucci gave his name. The motif of noble savagery, which is still felt in Rousseau, depended for its persuasiveness on a combination of ignorance and geographic remoteness. Even before Rousseau, however, the agency of utopian speculation was science, not geography. After him, the utopian (and eventually dystopian) form was filled with a varigated socialist and technological content. This latter development is what concerns us here.

Galileo had "seen" a new heavenly world through his telescope. In 1610, his *Sidereus Nuncius* announced its existence to the old mundane world using imagery that anyone could understand. The dark shadows on the moon looked like spots on a peacock's tail; its surface seemed to resemble a vase, hot from a kiln, plunged into water. The rhetoric of his book indicated it was a kind of popularization. Moreover, the later utopians, such as Bacon and Campanella, started from such works as Galileo's and extended its doctrine but by interpreting its meaning and effects on human society. Not scientists themselves, they nevertheless were capable of understanding the science of others. More to the point, they were ready to receive and develop the new ideas. They stood in relation to seventeenth-century science much in the way that Voltaire stood with respect to Newton.

The direction of utopian speculations was increasingly technological. Bacon's arguments against alchemists and astrologers such as Campanella were arguments for the conceptual and then actual overcoming of the otherness of nature. The *New Atlantis* was sufficient testimony that Bacon found scientific knowledge to be productive knowledge. The College of the Six Days' Works was devoted to understanding the secrets God employed during His creation of the cosmos. There was, moreover, an anti-Christian implication in its very title. Action that sought to reproduce and reform God's work by cooperative division of labor and not contemplation of the divine activity was the purpose of the college; organization, not individual philosophic reflection, was the way to truth.

Bacon's "inductive method" also indicated the direction of change. For the most part it meant collecting examples in the search for new knowledge. Since the search was for *new* knowledge and the *eventual* but actual conquest of nature, the focus shifted from a care for justice in the present and existing society to one of making it in the future. More's playfulness was replaced with a mood of earnestness. Bacon gave himself the serious task of persuading the reader that the fictional image could be realized. The Baconian utopians were reformers rather than ironic critics. The result of his inductive method, however, was inherently unstable. If the goal was *new* knowledge rather than apprehension of the unseen and uncreated measure, then true "ideas" would be the latest ideas or at best the successful ones. What began as a static "ideal state" slid easily into the process of progress. In More can be found the beginnings of this deformation of consciousness.

More's spirituality was displaced from the Christian orientation toward the summum bonum to the problem of the joint rule by prince and intellectual of a secular commonwealth. His fictional answer was Raphael ("God heals") Hythlodaeus ("huckster of chatter"), a man whose very name expressed the tentativeness or contradictoriness of More's attitude. Raphael is a wandering secular monk, a fictional symbol of More's refusal fully to capitulate to the demands of his demanding prince. Raphael's counsel is precisely the kind that princes ignore; having divested himself of his property in favor of his family, having left his country to sail with Amerigo, he remains a homeless, nearly a worldless, chaser of "ideals." More's great insight was that he finds them in *Utopia*, that is, no-place. As Voegelin observed, this is More's great strength. "He indulges in an 'ideal'; but at least he knows that the ideal is nowhere, and has no place in the somewhere of a commonwealth."[1] In place of a noetic connection between the somewhere of life in a political commonwealth and the unseen measure, he has substituted an "ideal" that exists in imaginative or fictional suspension above the actual course of politics.

The purpose of this twilight "ideal," halfway between the Christian eschatalogical fulfillment through grace in death and activist mysticism of the later revolutionary killers, was to offer criticism, not to serve as a basis for reform. The ambiguity, not to say the irresponsibility, of More's position is doubtless the reason for his double canonization. The communists can look to his condemnation of private property, ignoring the indications that More considers property an effect, not a cause. The Catholics look to the cause, pride, *superbia*, but overlook More's fiction that in Utopia pride has been removed through the institutional rearrangement of society.

More's socialism was a fiction designed to present an image of society deprived of the chief means of satisfying pride. His theological knowledge and his Christian faith both indicated that pride cannot be abolished merely by abolishing property, which only raises a further question. It exists as well with Kant's expectation that a proper constitution could tame a race of demons, to say nothing of the fancies of progressive intellectuals who anticipate "political development" to take place as a result of imposing liberal constitutions on a congeries of tribes or introducing more ruthless plans for change. T. S. Eliot has summarized the consciousness of this mode of rebellion against reality as one of trying constantly to escape from the darkness of human existence by "dreaming of systems so perfect / that no one will need to be good." In the example of More, the darkness outside was his own society, a "conspiracy of the rich" who act on the basis of unrestrained pride. He was sufficiently aware that the attempt to banish pride, which is part of the reality of human being, was evidence of the darkness within that he removed the operation to his fictional noplace. But if More knew that, why did he indulge in the fiction at all? If the darkness outside was pride on the rampage, nothing would be changed by seeking refuge in a darkness within.

Voegelin identified the problem as an "impasse of sentiment."[2] It is an impasse of analysis as well because further examination of the text will not reveal More's motives. It is for that reason that we used the metaphor of twilight to characterize his "ideals."

In this context a recovery of the light would have meant a Christian answer, namely the restoration of spiritual order through church reform. When the mood of playfulness that proclaimed an unobtainable ideal had dissipated, More's twilight turned into darkness. Characteristically, there were three ways to disturb the balance of More's dream. First, one might begin a campaign to eradicate pride (or property) in order to clear the field so that the utopian institutions could arise. Second, the utopian ideal could be taken at face value, with the implication that "really" the human being is good and without pride; a little effort, a little persuasion, is all that is needed to realize the ideal. The result of the intellectual confusion spread by the second response is to make the work of the activists easier. The third response, which we may identify with liberalism, has been to accept as given the unlimited pride of human beings. The task then is to devise institutions to suppress it, as with Hobbes, or to channel pride into a productive equilibrium, as with Locke and Publius. The condition for the liberal solution to work, in practice, is an abundance of human and material resources. As long as there is enough to go around, as long as a regime of mutual exploitation can increase the size of the pie, one can anticipate if not stability at least the contentment of well-stuffed consumers.

Whether the response is one of activist mysticism, gentle exhortation, or liberal productivity, the truth of the utopian ideal remains unquestioned. The consequence for political discourse when even one side enlists the support of an infallible ideal is to introduce and sustain a tone of vituperative moralism. Once the ideal is accepted the convert loses any residual sense of personal pride: pursuit of the ideal is guiltless because of its (imaginary) status as a moral absolute. Second, since the ideal sanctifies actions taken to achieve it, the actor is under an impression of bearing no responsibility for the consequences of action. Third, since the ideal is considered a moral absolute, anyone who opposes it is

automatically immoral; More's fictional Utopians fight only just
wars. Modern Utopians fight only wars of national liberation
against criminal regimes. In consequence, fourth, the ideal eliminates from history the tragedy and precariousness of particularist
conflict since only one side has any moral substance. Practical
defeats are moral victories, and in the end it becomes impossible
to mind one's own business since anything less than commitment
to the ideal is criminal. The idealists have an obligation to reed-
ucate the criminals, which means they are not really criminal but
misguided or ill-informed. Opponents of the idealists cannot be
afforded the dignity of recognition, which turns them into objects
suitable only for therapy.

More's *Utopia* is a more evocative symbol of demonic power
than even Machiavelli's *Prince,* insofar as it indicates that spiritual disintegration has spread from the prince to the entire body
politic. In More's work one finds the first evocation of a fictional
people's erecting itself into a standard for everyone else. The political style followed by the Utopians, namely to proclaim their
ideal as the standard of justice and to prosecute wars as technical
or efficient means of serving the ideal, has become a decisive
component of modern politics and of social administration. The
efficient pursuit of an ideal that is found nowhere is, however, of
questionable rationality. To the extent, therefore, that modern
technology is utopian, it displays the same characteristics of unbounded pride masking itself with moralism so as to avoid responsibility. At the same time, actions undertaken on the basis of
utopian technological ideals have had real consequences.

*

In part I, the novelty of technology was described in terms of
an enhanced human capability for action. Part II included a description of the alteration in the human condition achieved by
this new capacity. Now, ethics has traditionally been the discourse and practice concerned with the direction of action. More
particularly, the concept of responsibility has been central to our
understanding of the significance of action. Because human beings are responsible for the consequences of their initiatives, the
capacities to forgive and to punish have been central to ethical
reflections. But as indicated in part II, punishment and forgiveness presuppose that action takes place into the web of human
relationships, not into nature, which is constrained to react ac-

cording to the consequential chain of cause and effect. The changed context of action does not, however, alter the relationship of responsibility to it. That is, responsibility is to some extent a formal attribute of the capacity to act.

There is an additional meaning of responsibility evident in the judgment that someone acted responsibly: that is, in a manner appropriate to a situation. The second sense of responsibility, which Hans Jonas has called substantive responsibility, may be accompanied by feelings of responsibility.[3] More importantly, substantive responsibility implies a nonreciprocal relationship of care, the violation of which calls forth the judgment of irresponsibility. For example, reckless drivers are merely careless for themselves but are irresponsible if they endanger their passengers or others who share the road. Because drivers have been entrusted with care for the well-being of others, their irresponsibility exists independent of whether reckless driving results in a mishap. Likewise are parents responsible for children and, more tenuously, siblings for one another. By the same token, irresponsibility is not confined to positive acts of abrogation, such as reckless driving, but may arise from mere inattentiveness.

The natural responsibility of parents for children, which originates in the direct causation of the latter by the procreative act of the former, is to be contrasted with the spontaneous assumption of responsibility by rulers for those over whom they have power. Despite differences in origin, both kinds of responsibility are continuous and comprehensive. Moreover, the continuity extends into the future because the greatest responsibility for the individual or collective life involved is concerned with its spontaneity. To be precise, the intent of both parental and political responsibility "must be not so much to determine as to enable," that is, to prepare and keep intact the capacity for action, and so for responsibility as well, in those to come, and never to foreclose the future exercise of responsibility by them.[4]

The end of parental responsibility comes with the maturity of children, who repeat the process. There is no analogy in the political community because history does not "mature." The pseudomaturing of history would mean the end of sponteneity, which is the essential characteristic of totalitarianism. In this respect the responsibility of political leaders indicates that they act so as to ensure the possibility of future leaders. The advent of the

mass technological society has given this imperative a new significance because of the realistic potential of extinguishing future
spontaneity by establishing self-perpetuating and ecumenic administrative organs.

Prior to the existence of mass technological society, it made no
sense to discuss human responsibility for the preservation of
spontaneity. Under present conditions, the danger arises not from
any shortcomings of the Baconian program but from its success.
Economic success, which certainly owes much to the Lockean
liberation of pride and to its subsequent satisfaction through ac-
quisitiveness, has been accompanied by biological success. Together they have so vastly increased the metabolism of society
with nature that Jonas seriously suggested, "Only a maximum of
politically imposed social discipline can ensure the subordination
of present advantages to the long-term exigencies of the future."[5]
Since current economic and biological productivity can be understood as the consequence of action taken to fulfill Baconian and
Lockean principles, the suggestion has been made that communism might supply the sought-for social discipline.[6] Likewise Ellul has indicated that "a world-wide totalitarian dictatorship" may
be the inevitable way to "resolve" current difficulties.[7] On the
other hand, there are demographic indications that economic
productivity is negatively associated with biological productivity.
The long-term viability of technological society would, on these
grounds, seem questionable, notwithstanding the obvious technological answer: the importation and training of human resources
from pools of low economic productivity. All this solution ignores
is politics.

There can be no doubt that Communist regimes are coercive,
if not disciplined, but there are several reasons not to expect
communism to counter whatever danger is posed by technological success. Leaving aside the observation that Marxism intensi-
fies the spiritual disorder outlined in More's *Utopia*, the "ideal"
of a classless society presupposes the truth of the Baconian ideal.
Second, considered in the context of technology, the Marxist criticism of capitalism is that the latter is inefficient, which flies in
the face of all evidence to date. And third, Marxism would have
to reinterpret itself from being the consummation of capitalism to
being the means of preventing disaster, which means renouncing
its central doctrines. The renunciation is pragmatically required

because it is at least questionable whether resource and environmental tolerance is sufficient to permit a global increase in material abundance.

Any commonsensical proposal for greater equality in the global distribution of resources and wealth leads to the conclusion that the result is likely to be closer to the lower than to the upper end of any scale that measures material abundance. Why it is reasonable to expect majorities in the powerful countries, who will have to foot the bill, to acquiesce in a drastic reduction in their prosperity is not at all clear. It may be true that the virtues associated with entrepreneurial activity in a mass technological society have the consequence of diminishing the goodness of the souls of those who undertake it, but it is certainly true that despotism, which is what is implied by "a maximum of politically imposed social discipline," positively encourages vice: arbitrariness and cruelty among the rulers; cowardice, fatalism, hypocrisy, and betrayal among the ruled.

Under these conditions and faced with these alternatives, utopian fantasies make their appeal to the bewildered. Unlike More's, modern utopias are not understood to be fictions and instruments of criticism only. They are also to be realized by historical action. Of these modern revolutionary utopias, the most important is Marxism. As Jonas observed, "In Marxist utopianism technology is put to its most ambitious test. A critique of the one is thus a critique of the other in surrealist magnification."[8] Consider, then, the meaning of revolution for Marx.

Marx was an activist mystic; his awareness of the crisis of his age was expressed in his consciousness of epoch. The old world was passing away and the new about to arrive. Because "life is not determined by consciousness, but consciousness by life," a radical change in "life" will produce the sought-for *metanoia*.[9] The catalyst of change for Marx, as for Hegel, was the experience of revolution: "Both for the mass creation of communist consciousness, and for the achievement of the object itself, a change of man on a mass scale is necessary, which can occur only during a practical movement, a *revolution*." The revolution is therefore necessary not only to get rid of the ruling class but to transform the consciousness of the revolutionaries: "Only by the experience of revolution can the *overthrowing* class reach the point where it gets rid of the old filth [*Dreck*] and becomes capable of founding a new society."[10] The revolution is conceived not so much as an institutional upheaval as an agent of purification.

The change in program from More's fictional evocation to Marx's activism was accompanied by a change in the depth of the spiritual disorder. Marx created not a playful critique but a recipe for ever-increasing misery. In its commonsensical form, if a revolution does take place, human consciousness will not change. The new world will be filled with at least as much Dreck as the old.

The Marxist reply to common sense accounts for the far-reaching consequences of the doctrine. Previous messianic revolutionaries first undertook the task of creating the new human beings. What made them "new" was precisely that their consciousness had been changed. That change made them fit to lead the revolution. Marx reversed the order. The revolution made sense only if it was a catalyst for the metanoia. Should any great political upheaval take place, it would be recognized as the long-awaited revolution because new individuals, whose consciousness had been changed, would have sprung forth during the course of events. If no such persons erupted, it was evidence that this particular upheaval was not *the* revolution. As Eric Voegelin remarked, "The pneumopathological nonsense of the idea could not break on the rock of reality before the damage had been done."[11] Since no revolution can produce the metanoia, which is why the fictional expectation that it can is "pneumopathological nonsense," Marx's recipe could ensure only the following consequences: first, the creation of pneumopathological heroes and second, a great deal of destruction and disorder. Moreover, the two results were linked; every revolution, no matter how bloody, must be a prelude to even bloodier destruction next time.

Unlike those of his revolutionary contemporaries, Marx's "ideal" has inspired several generations of pneumopaths. If nothing else, this fact is testimony to Marx's intellectual shrewdness. From his observation that the industrial system was the source of great misery he did not make the eschatological leap to the fictional world he criticized as "utopian socialism." Nor did he indulge in any "romantic" hopes of returning to a preindustrial economy. The achievements of the bourgeoisie, the *Communist Manifesto* declared, were revolutionary. History moved in one direction; the new world would be even more industrial than the old. Nor did Marx countenance a new priesthood of positivist intellectuals sharing power with technological managers along the lines evoked by Comte. His new world would be one of "true democracy," namely a society where the spirit of "socialist man" would be realized in every individual. Marx's ideal, his "utopia," was one where industrialism satisfied human wants and human beings had been galvanized by the experience of revolution to what in his late work Marx called a "realm of freedom."

Our concern, however, is not with the pneumopathology of Marx's vision. That may be taken as given. Within this closed imaginative world, intellectual operations of great vitality can still occur. The first requirement of high-tech "true democracy" *after* the metanoia is material plenty. The second requirement is that it be easily obtained. To satisfy these two conditions, an enhancement by several orders of magnitude of both technology and resource appropriation is required. Both nature and technology must be imagined limitless. The briefest reflection on the question of planetary energy consumption indicates that if the industrial average of energy use were more widely distributed the consequences for the biosphere, decreed by the laws of thermodynamics, would be catastrophic. Or rather, they would seem that way to human beings, for nature knows no catastrophes. Common sense, therefore, would indicate the prudence of abandoning the ideal of ecumenic material plenty. The technological response to this particular threat is population management, a response that might range from state-directed mass murder, to compulsory abortion, to milder forms of birth control and euthanasia.

The conclusion we would draw is this: belief in the utopian ideals that putatively justify mass technological society effectively eclipses any sense of responsibility for action taken with the objective of actualizing the ideal. We have seen that human beings can be responsible only for contingent beings or perishable things, not necessary or eternal ones. The threat posed by technology is to something nonexistent, namely the future. In principle, therefore, it is something for which present human beings may be responsible. The intervention of utopian ideals makes this next to impossible. To begin with, the future is not represented in the present; it cannot have rights and therefore its rights cannot be violated. Even if, following Burke, we conceive of society as embracing the dead and the unborn as well as the living, it is hard to see the force of any claims the future may have against living utopians. To state the obvious, the living cannot be held accountable when future human beings complain that their ideals have entailed catastrophe.

The example of energy use under conditions of ecumenic affluence indicates the empirical impossibility of the ideal. If, nevertheless, the belief in the ideal is maintained, we may conclude that utopian fantasies encourage irresponsibility by encouraging thoughtlessness. Gadamer has expressed the sobering thought that the promise of technological science to relieve those on whom it operates of any responsibility is the source of its widespread support, at least in terms of expectations.[12] The end point in the process occurs when utopian ideals are introduced not with respect to transforming without limit the nature of things around us but to transforming the nature of humankind.

*

There is a vast and recent literature on the topic of biomedical ethics, much of it intended for the guidance of physicians for whom healing technologies have apparently made the oath of Hippocrates useless as a guide to proper behavior. Whatever else may be said of those who write on the topic and of those who use their teachings, the novelty of this genre of ethical reflection is eloquent testimony to the speed and extent of technological intrusion into the practice of medicine. One branch of medical technology is especially dramatic insofar as it reveals not the utopian idealism of contemporary medicine but the capacity to realize utopian dreams in action. The reference is to recombinant DNA technologies, the practice of biogenetic art.

It is a platitude to observe that all technologies can take on a life of their own. Not that the objects produced or organized are alive but that the process of creation, production, and utilization is more or less autonomous in its ability to integrate humans, and the human capacity for action, into the smooth operation of the system. So long as we are concerned only with the production of inanimate objects or with human organizations, it is still possible to conceive of undoing the system. In practice, however, the imperatives of "progress" push the development of technology in one direction so that it is more accurate to speak with Ellul of the self-augmentation of technology. The story of the sorcerer's apprentice is often invoked to indicate the characteristics of auton omy and self-augmentation, with the intention of having us experience the apprentice's position just prior to the intervention of the old wizard who commands the broom to return to the closet.

It is questionable whether the old wizard can be found today. Even if he were available to deal with normal hardware technologies, he would be powerless to control his creation when it was itself a living creature and not, figuratively speaking, a broom. As Aristotle observed, living creatures contain the origin of their own movement, which means not merely their motility but a capacity to propagate. With biogenesis, the product truly and not metaphorically has a life of its own. The ethical implications of new life-forms, not begotten but made (and so capable of being protected by patent), are far from clear.

The comparative innocence of genetically altered bacteria or plants slips away when the prospect involves composing creatures from the hereditary material of different species. In principle, what can be done to unicellular organisms can be done to multicellular ones because the latter begins as the former. One must conclude that there exist only technical hurdles to be overcome before the production of what used to be thought of as chimeras (*Iliad*, 6, 181) may be undertaken. The archaic motive for such a creation, as Eliade has indicated, is to supersede the telluric matrix, to replace cosmic time and its rhythm of gestation with will.[13] In the eighteenth century, for example, Maupertuis considered experimenting with animals to breed "curiosities" that had been collected previously. He proposed, for instance, mating a bull and a female donkey, as, he said, sometimes occurs in nature if the water hole is crowded.[14] And what of human beings? Why not crossbreed humans?

On the sixth day of Creation, God "created man in his own image, in the image of God created He him, man and woman created He them" (Gen. 1:27). *Whatever* the image that guides the hand of biogenetic homo faber it must be a contrast to the person made in the image of God. That such a creature would be an abomination before the Lord is not likely to move contemporary biotechnicians to desist in response to the recollection of ancient pieties. For the practitioner of biogenetic art, human being is a combination of accident and necessity ontologically indistinguishable from other kinds of being. Human being is more like the being of the unbroken prairie in the eyes of a dryland farmer: a kind of free "no-man's-land" available to grow a number of alternative crops. The unity of the species "human" may be split without ethical reflection, though we, who are yet human, will have the curious political task of deciding what rights to accord creatures that theretofore would have been called freaks. Perhaps the advocacy of the "animal rights" movement will be our guide. But what if the relationship were reversed? What rights would humans be granted by the products of biogenetic art? What is to be done with the inevitable number of flawed products? If they are to be scrapped, how is this act to be distinguished from murder? And once the utilitarian habit of disposing of the useless products becomes normal, what is to prevent it from being made the norm of human relations? Certainly no one could argue that merely natural being was superior to artificial being when the only difference between them is that the genesis of the former was haphazard and of the latter deliberate and, indeed, scientific.

With the prospect of producing homunculi we have surely passed the boundary of current research projects. But the purpose of utopian speculation is to do just that. Moreover, the example of biogenetic technologies is in no way otiose inasmuch as it brings to light as clearly as possible the phenomenalist assumptions regarding action into nature.

Phenomenalist assumptions govern the technological understanding of the "person" in light of which, for example, it is permitted to experiment on human embryos and fetal tissue. The question of fetal tissue (or of unborn humans) is, of course, highly contentious. Consider, then, the matter of experiments with the products of in vitro fertilization. Such beings are not considered persons and they are treated as materials disposable in service to knowledge or art.

As all readers of Hobbes know, the term *person* is derived from the Greek for mask, which was used in dramatic performances.[15] The dramatis personae are not, however, mere masks or faces, but characters that put in an appearance, enact a story by revealing their character, and disappear. A person, even in a drama, is unique; a person has a history, and, insofar as the same person reappears throughout the story or history, persons possess an identity. As Oliver O'Donovan has pointed out, this understanding of personhood is biblical rather than philosophical.[16] In

Patristic usage, for example, the Latin *persona* was interchange-able with the Greek *hypostasis*, substance. This made for certain difficulties and misunderstandings inasmuch as the one empha-sized appearance and the other a reality that underlay appear-ance. Even so, both terms also contained the connotation of historically unique continuity.

In contrast to the Patristic usage of person, whether in Latin or Greek, were the qualitative attributes psyche, intellect (*nous*), spiritedness (*thymos*), and so on, used by classical philosophers to think about human attributes. The two usages came into conflict most spectacularly over the great Christological debates that ended with the definition of Chalcedon, that Christ was one per-son with two natures.[17] The distinction between person and na-ture may be indicated by the observation that a person is a substance whereas a nature is the property of a substance. Ac-cordingly, what is distinctive or substantive about the Christian account of human beings can be attributed to their persons. This carries with it the implication that to every nature there does not correspond a person and that personhood cannot be attributed to the presence or absence or specific natures or qualities.

When one undertakes to speculate on anthropological as well as theological topics using not the qualitative or "natures" lan-guage of classical philosophy but rather the substantive and his-torical language of the Bible, then the question of beginning and of action becomes central. It is no accident that the political phi-losopher most concerned with action, namely Arendt, began her scholarship with the study of Augustine, who was the first to write not "on the soul," *de anima,* but "on the beginnings of the soul," *de origine animae.* Moreover, the Arendtian notion of na-tality is central to the Biblical stories of the birth, the new begin-ning, of Jesus.[18] It accounts as well for her concern for the human condition rather than human nature and her critical ap-proach to dogmatic formulae declaring that "man is" a rational animal, a political animal, and so on. All of these attributes pre-suppose for their intelligibility the subordination of the identity of the person enacting his or her own story to the contingent con-figuration of specific qualities. Such a language, Arendt might have said, eliminates the meaningfulness of the individual's story.

These theological matters may seem remote from the topic of phenomenalism as it relates to biomedical technologies. They are

not. First of all, the discussion is rather more anthropological
than theological. Second, the point is to isolate the specifically
human question regarding the beginnings of individual identity
or of personal history. Regarding the product of in vitro fertilization in particular, one would have to say that, despite the fact that
we do not regard these things as persons, it is difficult to know
how else to understand their short existences.

If one can say without ambiguity that a new personal history
begins with conception, however conception may be observed genetically, one would also have to say that the same is true with
respect to the products of in vitro fertilization. The difference
between the two kinds of personal history, of course, is that the
second is usually much shorter than the first. Moreover, it is designed deliberately to be a very short story.

So there is no misunderstanding, we should recall that what is
at issue is the question of a person, which is not a biological or
genetic matter. Biology can, of course, account for genetic phenomena but genes are not persons. Behind the phenomena lies
the substance, the hypostasis, of the person.

This way of looking at the topic contrasts with the perspective
of modern biomedical technology in more or less the same way
that Bodinian and Newtonian cosmologies were contrasted with
one another. Consider the famous Kantian practical imperative,
"Act so you treat humanity, whether in your own person or in
another, always as an end and never only as a means." Why? Because, Kant said, what is worth respecting in humanity is "rational nature," and such a "nature" must always respect itself, no
matter whether that nature is in one's own person or in another
person. The point to notice is that the nature, in this instance a
rational one, is "in" the person. That nature is what forms the
"objective purpose" of the Kantian moral law. In contrast to the
presence of an admirable nature in a person, the Chalcedonian
definition of Christ is that he is one person in two natures, human and divine. Here the person is primary and the attributes
secondary; in the modern understanding, of which Kant's formula
is a particularly incisive example, nature or attribute is primary
and the person is secondary.

Now, natures can be specified. Kant, for example, had a clear
understanding of what he meant by reason. Let us agree that we

respect the humanity of others as a result of having discerned
their, and our, rational nature. Supposing, however, that one of
us, let us say the other, had no discernable rational nature, what
then? Or, more to the point, since most of the people who undertake the acts in question are unconcerned with Kantian formulae,
what is it about human persons that morally requires that they be
respected?

The Christian or at least the Chalcedonian answer is simply
that they are persons, new beginnings. That is the substance behind the notion of the sanctity of life. The modern answer is to
create a personality test: a score of more than 20 on the Stanford-
Binet test, for example.[19] That is what lies behind the modern
notion quality of life. What such operationalizations of Kant's
teaching mean is that phenomenal attributes experimentally measured are taken to constitute if not a person, then the phenomena
of a personality. But attributes in general, like genetic phenomena in particular, do not constitute a person. Phenomenal de-
scriptions may indicate a personality but only as a composite of
the phenomena and not as the substance, the person. As
O'Donovan remarked, "We discern persons only by love, by discovering through interaction and commitment that this human
being is irreplaceable."[20] It is on the basis of that direct experience of personhood that we are able to discern a similar or equivalent significance in others whom we do not love and to whom we
are not so committed. In contrast, to discern attributes, to determine experimentally the characteristics or phenomenal knowledge of an individual, to discover a personality, one must keep an
appropriate distance and devote all one's commitment to the
truth that appears by way of the instrument that records the vari-
able quantities of an attribute.

The actual criteria used to specify variables are not particularly
important as compared to the prior commitment to phenomenalism by which attributes can be ascertained in the first place.
Modern conservatives, for instance, are concerned to attribute
personality, and so "value," to the presence of fetal brain activity,
which can be measured by appropriate meters. Disputes between
conservatives and liberals regarding the "value" of brain-damaged
fetuses would center on the appropriate level of activity, which
means a specific reading on a meter. Or, in the example of in

vitro fertilization of human embryos, by the modern account, they are human phenomena but they are, in anything but an experimental sense, valueless because they have no measurable personality.

These remarks on in vitro fertilization indicate that once we start making human embryos it becomes impossible to encounter them as persons. In simple language we cannot love such things because they are mere creatures of our will and so at our disposal. This is not to say that embryo experiments constitute murder of babies but that the more we understand our actions as a kind of making the less there is to love. Our products are not our fellow beings when they owe their being to our agency. The stories attached to such beings have qualitatively different beginnings.

It remains to bring to light the sentiments motivating research whose object is to make possible such actions. The usual answer that is supplied in response to the question, Why bother? is a variation on the theme of meliorism. Research will enable "humankind" to improve the human race. Let us ignore the question already answered of whether an "improved" human race is still human; let us also avoid raising the question of *who* the agents of "humankind" are and *who* the representative instances will be that are about to be "improved." Let us treat the question as a kind of enhanced Baconian desideratum: "the relief of man's estate" has merely been replaced with the improvement of it.

The examples adduced in support of such an apparently innocuous shift would be such processes as the creation of artificial insulin to control diabetes. What is usually forgotten with such examples is that heretofore technologies have been directed at disabilities and afflictions, the removal or control of which improves the life of a patient by restoring it to what we usually call normal, which obviously has a great range of types. Improvement in a patient's life may be understood on a grand scale as Baconian relief, but it does not constitute an improvement in normal human being.

But what is meant by improving what is already normal in the sense of not being disabled or afflicted? What is "better," Jonas asked, "a cool head or a warm heart, high sensitivity or robustness, a placid or a rebellious temperament, and in what proportion of distribution rather than another: who is to determine that, and based on what knowledge?"[21] If such knowledge of an "improved human being" were available, then it would be knowledge of what is above humankind. If such knowledge were available, it would be known by somebody so that the superman would already be here. But if that were true, then the species that brought forth that knowledge, that created the superman, is obviously adequate and so stands in no need of improvement. But in fact, all evidence indicates that the credentials of those who claim such knowledge are forgeries, which suggests again that such persons are the last to be entrusted with the fate of human existence. The sentiment of meliorism is, one may safely conclude, spurious.

A clue to what is actually involved arises from the reflection that if human being does not stand in need of improvement, that is, if there is no emergency to be met, then only a combination of curiosity and will remains. From Galileo, technology learned that curiosity is rewarded, but will, in this context, is identical with the *superbia* that More's Utopians were said to lack.

# 9
# Vulgarity

The initial promises of technology were distinctively utopian. Bacon's *New Atlantis* (1627) is conventionally grouped with More's *Utopia* (1515). The institutions of the later work are explicitly directed to the "mastery of nature" and to the increase in the production of commodities that such mastery promises.[1] The unreality characteristic of utopian consciousness means that actions considered rational with respect to the process of actualizing the utopian dream will, in reality, increase the disorder that the utopia is imagined to overcome. That is, the same activity that is rational with respect to the dream is irrational with respect to reality. The real irrationality of technology has been diagnosed for at least a century and a half in these or similar terms.

The focus of this chapter is on literary and aesthetic judgment of some of the products of technology. The gravamen of the analysis is that technology contributes to, or even produces, vulgarity. As a first approximation, vulgarity means the inability or the unwillingness to tell the difference between the beautiful and the ugly, the high and the low. It is a defect in the faculty of judgment, resulting from an absence of cultivation and taste. Since all human beings are born more or less uncultivated, vulgarity also indicates a lack of what used to be called a liberal education and has recently been termed "cultural literacy." One can trace a concern with vulgarity to Horace or even to Homer's "rank Thersites."[2] It is more accurate, however, to consider someone such as Matthew Arnold as being near the origin of the contemporary concern with vulgarity. His essay "Equality" or *Culture and Anarchy* can almost serve as a model for all subsequent "cultural criticism," including the somewhat bizarre variety penned by Marxists.[3]

The vulgar are members of both mobs and masses. In the first instance they can see nothing beyond their own immediate interest; in the second they lack even self-interest. The vulgar tolerate no standard transcending the immediacy of experience that might be apprehended in reflection. They are indiscriminate enough so that one might say they have no taste. They do not, on their own self-understanding, have bad taste. Bad taste appears only in light of good taste, which presupposes the legitimacy of standards of taste, which is what the vulgar deny. The affinity of vulgarity with democratic equality, with love of opinion, with sensationalism and movement, is obvious enough. The affinity with technology, to the extent that technology homogenizes, is also clear.

It has often been observed that modern communication technologies open the possibility for inexpensive, universal, high-quality journalism, for comprehensive analytical reports. But, as Ellul observed with respect to similar remarks about "quality newspapers," if such products were ever produced, no one would watch them, no one would read them. The mass media are, accordingly, inherently vulgar, a branch of the entertainment industry.[4] When he first listened to Thomas Edison's "talking machine," in 1888, Arthur Sullivan's response was prophetic: he said he was astounded at the wonderful machine "and terrified at the thought that so much hideous and bad music may be put on record forever."[5] Technology democratizes and vulgarizes because it gives everyone access to art on the same terms. What once required leisure and the use of leisure to cultivate refinement and a sense capable of appreciating art is now immediately available. Only now what is available is no longer art but its vulgarian transformation into antiart, a consumer good. As such, it contributes to the expression of modern worldlessness.

This chapter is concerned to analyze the particular kind of disorientation that results from devotion to technology and is indicated by the term *vulgarity*. Second, consideration is given to a historicized account of the genesis of this disorientation; the incoherence of historicism, however, ensures that any projected remedies will be abstracted from reality. These remarks on the suitability of applying Hegel's master/slave dialectic to the question of technology may be expanded to cover a vast range of Marxist and quasi-Marxist or *marxisant* speculation. Two examples indicate the connection between technology and vulgarity: C. P. Snow's opinion regarding the "two cultures" and rock music.

*

In 1829 Carlyle published a short essay, "Signs of the Times," in the *Edinburgh Review*.[6] The chief characteristic of the age, he said, is that it is mechanical. "It is the Age of Machinery, in every outward and inward sense of that word." The outward sense was obvious from all the equipment and from all that had been achieved by means of it. There existed "mechanic furtherances for mincing our cabbages; for casting us into magnetic sleep." The same art of adapting means to ends, which was the essence of mechanism, had altered the internal and spiritual as well. "Thus we have machines for Education," but also religious machines of all imaginable varieties, philosophical and literary machines, called Royal Academies and Institutes, that adorn capital cities "like so many well finished hives, to which it is expected the stray agencies of Wisdom will swarm of their own accord, and hive and make honey." Should religion or education or art be thought in decline, the response is to appropriate money for bricks, and bricks for institutes.

A balance had been lost, but the mechanical consciousness was such as to be unaware of it. All that counted as science was physical; what used to be called metaphysical and moral sciences were in decay. What was analyzed in a previous chapter as scientism was partially indicated by Carlyle's "mechanism." "In most of the European nations there is no such thing as a Science of Mind." The methodological dogma that insulated mechanical consciousness from an awareness of its own imbalance and, more immediately, from pursuit of the old metaphysical questions was that "what cannot be investigated and understood mechanically, cannot be investigated and understood at all." This remains the fundamental doctrine of scientism. Accordingly, it was no longer the moral, religious, or spiritual condition of human existence that concerned the best minds but economics and the production of commodities.

To the mechanical vulgarian with the brutal question, So what? Carlyle replied that such matters as concern the "domain of Machanism" did not embrace more than "a limited portion of man's interests, and by no means the higher portion." The highest and unlimited things, in Carlyle's language, concerned the "domain of Dynamism." If one ignored what he called the "dynamic nature" of humankind, expressed in the human concern for justice, beauty, and truth, in a concern for the old metaphysical questions, and pursued only what expressed humanity's "mechanical nature," one followed a recipe for disaster and unhappiness. His was a plea for balance. Too great a concern for "the inward or Dynamic province" resulted in impracticality, superstition, and fanaticism, whereas "undue civilization of the outward," which produced so many immediate benefits, in the longer term destroyed "moral force." The latter danger constituted "the grand characteristic of our age." The age may well have surpassed all others in the management of externalities, but "in whatever respects the pure moral nature, in true dignity of soul and character, we are perhaps inferior to most civilised ages." Such internal activities of the intellect as were admitted took the form of logic and argument, not meditation.

The signs of Carlyle's times were not far different from those of any technological society. Piety was experienced not as reverence but, as Voltaire had indicated, as a "vulgar Hope and Fear"; literature was untouched with wisdom and beauty and so was praised for its strength, not its truth; morality took the form of ambition and popularity. These things were symptomatic not of vigorous refinement but of luxurious corruption, of vulgarity. With corruption came servility, which was simply another expression of the unself-consciousness of mechanism. Civil liberty was secure, but "our moral liberty is all but lost. Practically considered, our creed is Fatalism; and, free in hand and foot, we are shackled in heart and soul with far straiter than feudal chains." The creed of Carlyle's day was fatalism, but he did not believe in it. His answer, or rather his interpretation of the signs of the times, like all interpretations that increase our understanding, was encouraging.

The metaphors of shackles and chains, he said, referred only to opinion and so were "of our own forging." Accordingly, it is up to us to break them. "This deep, paralysed subjection to physical objects comes not from nature, but from our own unwise mode of *viewing* nature." And for Carlyle, wise people begin to overcome their subjection by reforming themselves, not society at large. His successors, who also have described the broken promises of technological dreaming in terms of the increasing servitude of human beings, are usually less encouraging. One of the reasons for their change in sentiment arises from the historicization of Carlyle's understanding of human nature. The source of this reinterpretation is Hegel's dialectic of master and slave understood in the context of Goethe's (or Disney's) story of the sorcerer's apprentice. For example, Langdon Winner, who has written an entire book on the theme of "technics-out-of-control," concluded: "To be commanded, technology must first be obeyed. But the opportunity to command seems forever to escape modern man."[7] The reason why technology always escapes human command was a variation on the old theme of fear of the Golem: "The artificial slave gradually subverts the rule of its master."[8] Norbert Wiener, the "father of cybernetics," also found the imagery useful. "We are," he said, "the slaves of our technical improvement. . . . We have modified our environment so radically that we must now modify ourselves in order to exist in this new environment."[9] William Leiss has likewise made the master/slave dialectic the central image of his interpretation of the technological society.[10] Even so unlikely a person as the Soviet physicist Kapitza has complained that science has become enslaved.[11] The theme, in short, is common.

Let us consider more closely the master/slave tableau. In the account provided by Hegel in the *Phenomenology*, the consciousness that developed as slave was initially terrorized in a serious, life-threatening fight by the consciousness that emerged from this primordial encounter as master. Thereafter, the master lived a life of ease, consuming commodities served up by the slave. The slave meanwhile created commodities by changing given-being (*Sein*) or nature. By changing nature, the slave created history and a world. Eventually he changed the world in both its material and spiritual dimensions in such a way that the need for masters was overcome. They were thereby extinguished. But a slave required a master in order to exist as slave; a world without masters would also be a world without slaves. A world without slaves would be a world without history. Accordingly, history, the story of the slaves' (self-)liberation from mastery, came to an end. Following the (self-)liberation of slaves, achieved by the transformation of nature that eventually made mastery superfluous, existence would properly be described as posthistorical. Several interesting implications follow, none of which need presently be dealt with.[12] The terms *master, slave, nature, history,* and so on, take their meaning from the fictional second reality of Hegel's system. They are used uncritically here in order to indicate the inappropriateness of the notion "mastery of nature."[13]

The essential feature of the master/slave dialectic, so far as concerns the present essay, was that it consisted in the domination by one consciousness of another. By analogy with chemistry, the master was catalyst; the slave and nature were the elements that changed in response to the catalytic presence of the master's terror. The slave changed by changing what had been given, namely nature. Naturally consciousness wished to live; in the anthropogenic fight that resulted in the creation of master and slave, the slave desired to live whereas the master was willing to risk death. History consisted in the slave's laboring to overcome nature, including the slave's own nature as slave. In the absence of catalytic terror, the slave would exist as an unconscious part of primordial nature rather than in opposition to it. By this reading, the slave eventually (at the end of history) succeeded in overcoming nature, including his or her own. By this reading, technology mediated the slave's consciousness to nature, just as the slave mediated nature to the master.

According to Hegel, several somewhat unexpected things took place when history ended. While laboring, the slave sought to create a world after his or her own image. The image or "ideology" was other than what the world actually was at any given historical moment. One might say, then, that the slave's existence was inherently alienated and that history was the story of the slave's overcoming that alienation. Ideology, another of the slave's products and so essentially servile, gave the slave reasons to labor: namely to change the world, to abolish its otherness, to overcome alienation. But it could do so only so long as there was history. But according to Hegel, history was over with the self-liberation of the slaves. Moreover, it was not just "theoretically" completed and at an end. The end of history was a fact. Proof of the fact that history was ended is found in the transformation of ideology (including philosophy) into wisdom. Hegel, or more exactly, Hegelian consciousness, was and is not philosophical but wise. Hegel was the first self-conscious wise man.

This, of course, is a great scandal. It is scandalous, moreover, in different ways to different audiences. The objections of the

philosophers and of the people of common sense are more persuasive than are those of intellectuals. They have interpreted the
master/slave dialectic in the context of technological domination;
they would retain the moments of the dialectic but ignore, or
perhaps deny, the facts that brought it to a successful conclusion,
namely that history was over and that the proof of its conclusion
is that Hegel was wise. Instead, they would discourse on the artificiality of technological domination. In contrast, domination
that was not artificial, that was, so to speak, natural, must have
been the historical domination of master over slave. Perhaps this
was an insight; more likely it was a piece of moralizing typical of
intellectuals, denizens of what Hegel called the spiritual bestiary.
In any case, it expressed a bad or fractured dialectic.

The importation of the master/slave dialectic into the context of
the relationship of the slave to nature changed a great deal, not
least of all the terminology used to describe the moments of the
dialectic. The original slave, created from the primordial fight,
must now be called the historical slave. The lazy, commodity-
consuming source of catalytic terror is now called the historical
master. By Hegel's account, both historical masters and historical
slaves had been overcome. By the account of the intellectuals,
technology is now master and "we" are slaves. What can this possibly mean?

Formally or abstractly, this argument has a certain plausibility.
Nature was mediated to the historical master by the historical
slave. But eventually, by taking the whole course of history to do
it, the mediating slave abolished both mastery and the otherness
of nature. By analogy, technology mediates human beings to nature and ultimately abolishes both. We are meant to think of
technology as slave and "human beings" as masters.

The analogy is misleading. If one thinks the way it leads us to
think, one makes a grave error. The analogy implied that technology was slave and the "human beings" were masters. Where do
these "human beings" come from? If they were historical, then
nothing more is implied than historical masters and slaves. If they
were posthistorical, they were not masters or slaves; accordingly,
technology cannot be a slave since there exist neither masters nor
slaves posthistorically. Moreover, if technology was initially a
slave, it was only temporarily servile because it soon became
master and "we" became slaves. How did this happen? If "we"

were truly masters, we would not change but rather would die fighting; happily will the true master destroy the enemy, even if that act of destruction also destroys the master. And in any event, whatever moves technology to rise up against "us," its master?

One could move through other moments of the dialectic and show other incoherencies. Rather than ring the changes on the same theme, which would do no more than indicate a kind of playful intellectual virtuosity, let us return to nature. What makes the dialectic of master and slave incoherent in the hands of intellectuals is that they share with Hegel the opinion that nature is given-being, dead matter. The dialectic of master and slave is a dialectic of consciousness. Historically speaking, nature has long ceased to be conceived as being conscious or in any sense infused with spirituality. No one, and especially not the intellectuals who are concerned with the domination of humanity by technology, thinks that nature is conscious. If there were a genuine example of the master/slave dialectic at work in the story of the sorcerer's apprentice, then nature would not only have to become conscious; its consciousness would have to change in response to the actions of the historical slave who has temporarily become the technological master, namely the apprentice. It is precisely because there is no consciousness in the forces the apprentice sets into motion that the master/slave dialectic is inappropriate, except insofar as it describes the relationship of the apprentice to the master, the genuine (fictional) wizard.

The fictional character of images such as the sorcerer's apprentice or the servility that technology has introduced has often been forgotten. Such images are immediate and captivating and for that reason require the mediation of interpretation. We are, moreover, compelled to interpret this particular image of master and slave because it makes no sense under the abusive interpretation of moralizing intellectuals. What is gained by such interpretations is an apparent independence from individual responsibility. Historical changes have brought about technological domination; historical changes will end it. Accordingly, there is nothing to judge. The starkness of this consequence has inspired several attempts to soften it by introducing subtle distinctions between base and superstructure or vanguard and mass. But as was indicated in chapter 8, such attempts must end in failure and thus in the expression of the difficulty they hope to resolve.

Carlyle was closer to reality when he discussed the permanent aspects of human being in terms of our dynamical and mechanical natures. An imbalance was evident to him and he issued a warning. For him nature was not given-being but an order to which individuals strove to attune themselves. As the century wore on and the imbalance grew, the warnings grew more shrill. Dr. Frankenstein was killed by the monster he created; Dr. Jekyll was destroyed by Mr. Hyde. The mythic structure displayed by these later fictions is that "the transgression of a certain norm of knowledge and power . . . necessarily leads to punishment and destruction."[14] Every violation of a taboo required punishment; every sense that limits had been transgressed generated more and vaguer fears. Like Kurtz and Marlow a half-century later, the narrator of Poe's "MS: Found in a Bottle" had also penetrated the heart of darkness. Before his final going down he reflected: "It is evident that we are hurrying onward to some exciting knowledge—some never-to-be-imparted secret, whose attainment is destruction."[15] These literary meanings can also be expressed discursively.

In 1897, Paul Valéry published "Une conquête méthodique" in the London magazine the *New Review*.[16] The immediate subject was Germany; the larger one was technological modernity. Like Carlyle's, Valéry's common sense freed him from the historicizing distortions of fractured Hegelianism. Moreover, he could account commonsensically for the going down of Poe's narrator as well as for the myths of transgression expressed elsewhere in European literature.

Germany was in the process of becoming an industrial and commercial power by the same system of deliberate action that had gained it victory in the wars of unification. Careful planning, precise knowledge, and exact execution proved capable of successful coordination by the state. The secret of German success was method, applied not to the activity of a single person but to a whole nation; disciplined intelligence stood ready for deployment against the great enemy, accident. Common sense, however, expects, and usually finds, the cost. In the example of German success, the cost of method was the necessity of "genuine mediocrity in the individual, or rather for greatness only in the most elementary gifts, such as patience or the ability to disperse one's attention on everything, without preference and without enthusiasm. And finally, the will to labour."[17] With those talents, victory of the mediocre and of the (non)aesthetic of vulgarity was assured.

The German triumphs were but a prelude. "I believe," Valéry wrote, "that we are presently witnessing only the beginning of method." As a result of the German activities, "we should doubtless see the final triumph of mediocrity over the whole earth." Superior individuals would no longer be needed. Moreover, because superiority was at least in part the result of the pain of individual effort, the absence of such pain would no doubt increase the amount of pleasure in the world. Valéry's gentle irony recapitulated Carlyle's rejection of mechanism. Both saw organization of society by way of military and economic bureaucracies as entailing a vast increase in commodities and consumption along with an exaggeration of the pleasures connected to the life process. For people of sensitivity and superiority such as they, for individuals of civilization and culture, the result was the triumph of the inferior and the base elements of human existence, the triumph of vulgarity, of the human type identified by Toynbee as *homo occidentalis mechanicus neobarbarus*.

The literary expression of the process is captured in a common theme of literary criticism, from utopia to dystopia. The promises of technological liberation and abundance gave way to the promises of technological tyranny, the extinction of civilized culture, and eventually the extinction of human being. We have seen from the beginning, however, that the utopian genre moved in a peculiar twilight of unreality. Shifts of mood are therefore to be expected when the initial dreams approached realization.

The utopian/dystopian genre is a kind of fictional speculation that bears some resemblance both to philosophical writing and to the novel. Certainly contemporary dystopias such as *1984* or *We* bear more than a family resemblance to the novel, so that it is not an obvious solecism to speak of a utopian or dystopian novel. Indeed, the two literary forms bear elective affinities to one another. Considered from the perspective of the world or, rather, from the perspective of modern worldlessness, the novel is the literary form appropriate to society. By portraying destinies and fates (rather than, say, willed action, as is expressed in drama) characters become victims of an overriding necessity or the favorite of an unintelligible luck. Society as such is accepted as given and human beings submit to whatever turns up. Great destinies beyond human virtue and vice appear in a world not governed by laws. Considered in this light, the master of the genre was Kafka, who has occasionally been seen as a dystopian writer as well. His sober analyses of the dissolution of society appear contemporary because his characters, like so many real members of modern society, are simply jobholders without any other quality. One must eat, and that means one must have a job. In Kafka's fiction one sees the precariousness or instability of a society of jobholders brought into clear focus. Consider how much easier it is to be deprived of a job than it is to be expropriated, especially in a regime where job permits, or work permits, or membership in a union, are required. Kafka and contemporary authors of dystopian fiction have provided the spiritual aroma to the most social and most worldless form of rule, bureaucracy.

The great advantage of fiction, whether in the form of utopia, dystopia, or novel, is its immediacy. To read fiction is to participate imaginatively in the milieu of its characters. By the same token, the requirement of imaginative participation means that disagreement about the meaning of any particular work is assured. Disagreement is as central to criticism as it is to political philosophy. The latter discourses, however, aim at analytic coherence so that in principle one can reach a judgment that is verbally more demonstrable than the connoisseurship of literary criticism.[18] The specious charge of "subjectivity," which is in no way to be confused with taste or connoisseurship, has become the infallible sign that the first assault by the vulgar, or, rather, by the intellectual spokesman for vulgarity, has commenced. For example, two years after Carlyle's essay appeared, Timothy Walker wrote "Defence of Mechanical Philosophy" for the *North American Review*. The dispute of Carlyle and Walker was repeated more recently in the controversy between C. P. Snow and F. R. Leavis. Both controversies were connected to literature but took the form of an argument, not fiction. It should be possible, therefore, to come to a conclusion in which some confidence can be placed.

\*

Just as Walker's vulgarian defense of mechanical philosophy may easily be summarized by the observation that mechanical

consciousness has provided large numbers of people with the
commodities they desire, so does the thesis of C. P. Snow admit
of a quick summary.[19] The premise was contained in the title;
there are two cultures, one literary, one scientific: "Between the
two, a gulf of mutual incomprehension." This state is much to be
deplored. "The feelings of one pole become the anti-feelings of
the other. If the scientists have the future in their bones, then
the traditional culture responds by wishing the future did not exist." Such an attitude is dangerous because the traditional culture
"manages the western world." The traditional culture indulged its
own vanities when it pretended to be the whole of culture, "as
though the natural order didn't exist." For their part, young scientists (with the future in their bones) "feel that they are part of
a culture on the rise while the other is in retreat." What is to be
done? "There is only one way out of all this: it is, of course, by
rethinking our education." What was wrong with British education, "nearly everyone will agree," was that it is "too specialized."
The Americans taught their children "far more wisely, but nothing like so rigorously. They know that; they are hoping to take the
problem in hand within ten years, though they may not have all
that time to spare." The Soviets taught their children "far more
widely . . . but much too rigorously. They know that—and they
are beating about to get it right." The Swedes, who could be
counted on to do things right in combining rigor, breadth, and
wisdom, were unfortunately handicapped by having to master
foreign tongues.

There were several reasons for the division and animosity between the "two cultures," Snow said. Some were personal; some
reflected the "inner dynamic" of the mental processes involved.
The main one, however was more a "correlative" than a reason.
"It can be said simply and it is this: if we forget the scientific
culture, then the rest of western intellectuals have never tried,
wanted, or been able to understand the industrial revolution,
much less accept it. Intellectuals, in particular literary intellectuals, are natural Luddites." Members of the literary culture, according to Snow, thought very little about industry. Only in
Germany was it possible "to get a good university education" in
applied science. Almost to a person, members of the literary culture voiced "screams of horror" at the industrial revolution. "The

only writer of world class who seems to have had an understanding of the industrial revolution was Ibsen in his old age, and
there wasn't much that old man didn't understand."

In addition to being noisy, the horrified literati were insensi-
tive to the plight of their fellows. "For, of course, one truth is
straightforward. Industrialization is the only hope of the poor."
This was why, he said, "in any country where they have had the
chance, the poor have walked off the land into the factories as fast
as the factories could take them." The content of the hope of the
poor, the reason for walking off the land and into the factories,
was, in Snow's striking metaphor, for "jam." More specifically, it
was for "jam tomorrow." "Jam today, and men aren't at their most
exciting; jam tomorrow, and one often sees them at their no-
blest." Human beings alive today are heirs of the noble pursuit of
"jam tomorrow" by our forefathers. The gains have been great.
The industrial revolution, Snow said, brought with it an increase
in population, resulting from medical science, and "enough to eat
for a similar reason. Everyone able to read and write, because an
industrial society can't work without." Health, food, and "education" have been diffused to all; "those are the primary gains."
And the losses are confined to the ease of organizing for war.

Snow's position in this scheme was clearly but silently presented. He had bridged the frightening gap between the two cultures. "By training, I was a scientist; by vocation I was a writer."
Who better to harmonize science and literature than he? The
question invites one to make explicit the answer. If the world has
come to such a dangerous pass by trusting to the political naviga-
tion of the traditional culture, should not the people with the future in their bones be called to the command of the ship of state?
And who better than C. P. Snow to provide the transition? He is
a man of two cultures; he knows "the corridors of power"; he
knows about educational reform, the first thing to be done.

Leavis began his commentary by remarking on Snow's
rhetoric.[20] His was "a tone of which one could say that, while
only genius could justify it, one cannot readily think of genius
adopting it." Snow's remarks on Ibsen, "There wasn't much that
old man didn't understand," clearly implied, "There is still less
that Sir Charles Snow doesn't understand; he pays the tribute
with authority." The tone was present in his analysis of British,
American, Soviet, and Swedish education; of the reasons for the

alleged division among them; of the significance of the history and consequences of the industrial revolution.

And yet, Leavis showed with more than enough evidence that "Snow is in fact portentously ignorant." It was not Snow's ignorance that was Leavis's chief concern, though it was necessary to point it out. More important was his status as a "portent." Snow had good reason to think that he was a literary writer or even a novelist; his fiction sold widely and it was considered by authoritative bodies such as the British Council to be an example to the world of splendid English prose. What sort of "portent" was indicated by Leavis's observation that Snow was unable to do the things that novelists ordinarily do, such as show characters falling in love, or even to show character at all, through the use of dialogue. Instead, Snow told you that hero and heroine "fall in love" or "grow tired of one another." Since it is a ready means of identifying the novelistic form, there exists dialogue in Snow's fiction, but no humanly recognizable person ever would speak it. Leavis therefore concluded: "As a novelist he doesn't exist; he doesn't begin to exist. He can't be said to know what a novel is." In the language used in chapter 7, Snow was one of Voegelin's spiritual eunuchs as well as a non-novelist.

On the evidence of his fiction and of *The Two Cultures and the Scientific Revolution*, there was no reason to think that science mattered to Snow: "The only presence science has is as a matter of external reference, entailed in a show of knowledgeableness." Thus, for example, Snow mentioned "an experiment of the greatest beauty and originality," one of "the most astonishing experiments in the history of science" that had been "brought off" at Columbia by persons called Yang and Lee. Snow told us nothing more than that "it makes us think again about some of the fundamentals of the physical world. Intuition, common sense—they are neatly stood on their heads." The point of this show of knowledgeableness was made in the next sentence: "If there were any serious communication between the two cultures, this experiment would have been talked about at every High Table in Cambridge. Was it? I wasn't here [in Cambridge], but I should like to ask the question."

Lacking the capacity of a novelist but enjoying great repute as a master of the form, showing no interest in science beyond the show of knowledgeableness that transpires at Cambridge High

Tables, it seemed clear what sort of portent Snow was. The "significance of C. P. Snow" was that he was a fraud. Snow was in
reality "intellectually as undistinguished as it is possible to be,"
and yet "he has become for a vast public on both sides of the
Atlantic a master-mind and a sage." Snow was more than a fraud;
he was a successful fraud. Properly to understand Snow's significance as a portent, one must look at his teaching, but one must
do so having learned that it is the teaching of a successful
fraud. That is, one must strive to appreciate both his fraudulence
and the secret of his success because the two are intimately
connected.

The "literary culture," which Snow considered himself especially well qualified to discuss, was identified with the "literary
intellectual." Literary intellectuals were identified as the people
who write reviews of various kinds for British newspapers and
magazines. There are analogous institutions in North America:
the *New York Review of Books*, the book review sections of the
*New York Times*, or perhaps the *Globe and Mail*, the *New Republic*, perhaps *Harper's*, the CBC, and PBS. Many people, of
whom Snow was an example, take the "culture" expressed
through such media of communications "as representing the age's
finer consciousness so far as a culture ignorant of science can."
For Leavis, however, *that* "literary culture" was "something that
those genuinely interested in literature can only regard with contempt and resolute hostility. Snow's 'literary intellectual' is the
enemy of art and life." For Leavis, that is, the institutions to
which Snow referred expressed the debasement of literary culture, not its height. In a word, they were debased successors to
Voltaire, the bearers, perpetrators, agents, of vulgarity.

Accordingly, the ease with which Snow identified this literary
culture with the "traditional culture" indicated two things: first,
that Snow had no knowledge of what culture was; and second,
that he had no knowledge of the historical changes that spawned
his particular literary culture. His use of the term *culture* was
especially revealing in this respect. The "scientific culture," Snow
said, comprised people who share "common attitudes, common
standards, and patterns of behaviour, common approaches and assumptions." These people, with the future in their bones, "may
or may not like it but they have it." As evidence, Snow asserted,
"Without thinking about it, they respond alike. That is what a

culture means." This was a "hint," Leavis said, "worth taking up." The hint referred not to the people of science and their alleged culture but to Snow, and to his interpretation of scientific "culture" as a thoughtless collective response. Snow's "definition" of culture in fact expressed his own understanding of what culture is. "Snow's habits as an intellectual and a sage were formed in such a milieu." The correct term to describe the habit of expression of this milieu is cliché.

Cliché was first of all evident in the "embarrassing vulgarity of style" that was made plain on every page of *The Two Cultures*. Stock (and meaningless) phrases about the future in the bones of the scientists, or about Ibsen, or about experiments being brought off, or about jam, or about the Soviet Union's beating about to get it right were not thought by Snow to be clichés but, Leavis said, "an idiosyncratic speech-raciness that gives his wisdom a genial authority." This too was "portentous" because it indicated the quality of Snow's thought and of the "cultural" world he inhabited, where cliché emerged uncritically and was taken for inspired and authoritative wisdom.

Cliché extended beyond the ugly insensitivity of his style to the substance of Snow's understanding of the significance of the technological society and his opinion of its worth. Members of the "traditional culture," whose contemporary members constituted the "literary culture" of the mass media, were the "natural Luddites" who had never come to terms with the industrial revolution. Anyone whose concern about the future was expressed otherwise than in terms of productivity, hygiene, and material productivity was a "natural Luddite." Like those who called attention to what the poor lost when they entered the factories, the natural Luddite was devoid of what Snow called "social hope." The content of that hope was expressed in Snow's symbol, "jam." The ultimate aim of the technological society and what, therefore, justified it in his eyes, was the promise of more commodities.

Leavis rejected the charge of Luddism along with the mental processes governed by cliché that allowed Snow to make it. There was no question of "reversing" technology. "What I *am* saying is that such a concern [with more commodities] is not enough— disastrously not enough. Snow himself is proof of that," being a product of the initial consequences of technological "culture"—or rather, of the deculturation that has accompanied technological productivity. The felicity represented by a "social hope" for "more jam" cannot, Leavis said, "be regarded by a fully human mind as a matter for happy contemplation." Just as with animal laborans's having no further labor to do, the beneficiaries would be unable to find the results satisfying.

Leavis's lecture prompted a great deal of controversy after it was published. The reason, anticipated in his identification of Snow as a portent, was that he described the "literary culture," that is, the contemporary milieu of intellectual deculturation, with cogency, sharpness, and clarity. The "literary world" that defended Snow and attacked Leavis claimed to be coherent and comprehensive, the guardian of culture, not its enemy. In fact the "literary world" is no more than one of the "cultural consequences" of the technological society. From early in his scholarly life Leavis had been concerned with the usually unacknowledged results of widespread literacy, namely that it was impossible to characterize the reading material of ever-larger numbers of people as excellent. The fraudulence of C. P. Snow, novelist, scientist, and sage, represented for him the end of the process.

That Snow was a fraud *and* a portent of technological society was significant. What apparently gave Snow the confidence to say the things he did, what apparently covered his blank ignorance sufficiently to allow him to opine on matters far beyond the range of his spiritual and even intellectual horizon, was that he knew what he knew from within the corridors of power (to use the title of one of his books). Those who constituted the "literary culture" in Snow's sense were the same ones who maintained with such thoughtless confidence the fraud that he was a mastermind. That they achieved this fraud by publicity rather than intellectual and spiritual argument, analysis, or demonstration was, Leavis said, "a concomitant of the technological revolution." Leavis could judge that Snow expressed the end point of the process of deculturation because Leavis was, in fact, connected to what he called the great tradition, a tradition to which Snow at least paid some respect by writing books. The most one can say on his behalf, therefore, was that his vulgarity was not self-conscious.

*

Carlyle indicated that a disproportionate concern for the mechanical was purchased at the cost of neglect of the spiritual and

moral realities of human life. The hopeless hope of a Hegelian
reversal, of "mastering technology" or of taking (taking back?)
control of technology, was based on several misconceptions. Technology was presumed to be neutral, which it is not; the dialectic
of master and slave was presumed to be applicable to the liberation of human beings from technological domination, which it is
not. Valéry has indicated, more accurately, that the technological
order entailed the triumph of mediocrity, an insight expressed
splendidly by Nietzsche's terrible symbol: the last man. One
way of dealing with the darker aspects of technology is to consider "progress" and "degeneration" to be two sides of the same
coin. Teddy Chamberlin, for example, proposed a sophisticated
distinction whereby both sides might be acknowledged, but only
according to distinct "logics": a "logic of changes in form, or a
morphologic; and a logic of changes in purpose, or a teleologic. It
was quite possible that progress in morphological terms would be
looked upon as degeneration from a teleological perspective, and
vice versa."[21] One is reminded here of the attempt by Schutz to
remain neutral as between Socrates and Athens.

Leavis, however, like Voegelin before him, indicated by the
concrete example of C. P. Snow that neutrality, whether but-
tressed by sophisticated distinctions or not, amounts to a kind of
complicity with baseness and vulgarity insofar as it leaves unquestioned the ties binding the portentous intellectual to the corridors of power. Better the undiluted and undialectical common
sense of Valéry: this is mediocre. Better the frankness of a Leavis:
this acclaimed literary intellectual is a vulgarian, an enemy of art
and of life. A final example, written very much out of a concern
for the questions raised by Carlyle, by Valéry and by Leavis, is
Allan Bloom's now famous book, *The Closing of the American
Mind*.[22] One of the more controversial chapters in a controversial
book is concerned with music, specifically the music favored by
contemporary university students in technological societies.

Music has always been connected to human activity in light of
its amazing power to justify emotionally the activity it accompanies. Military music, sacred music, music to skate or ski with, all
have the ability to still reason and transport the soul someplace
else. This power is found in music, according to Plato, because it
is *alogon*, without reason or logos. This is why, in his discussion
of musical education, beginning with book 3 of the *Republic*,

Plato subordinated rhythm and harmony to lyrics. By so doing,
by mediating music by words, he interrupted the direct contact
between music and the soul and thereby countered the tendency
of what is *alogon* to turn barbaric. A barbarian is not an animal
but a human being who hates *logos*: hence the popular meaning
of *barbarikos*, a foreigner who was unable to speak the Greek
*logos*. The educational intentions of the *Republic* carry with them
the implication that younger human beings are, to an extent, barbaric even if they are Greek. The barbarian, properly speaking,
is hostile to *logos* and expresses that hostility in an eager desire
to destroy it. Plato's musical education had as its purpose the
taming or civilizing of the raw desires of the soul. Desires should
be formed by music not excited by it; music, in turn, should not
be suppressed, which would simply destroy eros, but be measured by higher harmonies apprehended by *logos*.

In *The Merchant of Venice*, Lorenzo's "Platonic speech" in act
5, scene 1 indicates what the higher harmonies are. Whereas
Venice was filled with dark plots and sordid struggle, Belmont,
the beautiful mountain, is above that: at Belmont Jessica can love
her Christian lover. Stephano is sent away to bring forth music
and Lorenzo reminds Jessica of the cosmic harmonies made visible in the heavens above them.

> Sit Jessica,—look how the floor of heaven
> Is thick inlaid with patterns of bright gold,
> There's not the smallest orb which thou behold'st
> But in his motion like an angel sings,
> Still quiring to the young-ey'd cherubins;
> Such harmony is in immortal souls,
> But whilst this muddy vesture of decay
> Doth grossly close it in, we cannot hear it.

The ultimate harmony comes not from our daily lives because
"this muddy vesture of decay," our bodies, prevents the soul from
hearing. Only when we transcend our daily concerns, when our
souls are transported someplace else, when we are no longer particular individuals, Christian and Jew, Venetians and strangers, is
it possible to attain that higher harmony. Music, Shakespeare indicated, has the power to transport the soul up, to a beautiful
mountain, and so relieve the squalor of Venice. It does not overcome the problems of daily life or, in general, of natality and

mortality. Music does, however, soothe the anxieties that arise from our generated condition by presenting us with sensible imitations of the immortal music of the heavens.

Lorenzo indicates as well the results of a lack of musical education along the lines Socrates indicated. Jessica says she is "never merry" when she hears sweet music, to which Lorenzo replies that the reason is that "your spirits are attentive." If she would open her soul, "the sweet power of music" could work its wonder without the intervention of the mind.

> . . . therefore the poet
> Did feign that Orpheus drew trees, stones, and floods,
> Since naught so stockish, hard, and full of rage,
> But music for the time doth change his nature,—
> The man that hath no music in himself,
> Nor is not moved with concord of sweet sounds,
> Is fit for treasons, stratagems, and spoils,
> The motions of his spirit are dull as night,
> And his affections dark as Erebus:
> Let no such man be trusted:—mark the music.[23]

The unmusical person, the person of unsoothed anxieties, simply employs "spirit," calculative intellect. He is a plotter and untrustworthy. Neither Shakespeare nor Plato considered the possibility that music might enhance chaotic rage and unmeasured anxieties. The Ramones' "Teenage Lobotomy" expressed the new doctrine:

> All the girls are after me,
> Now I guess I'll have to tell 'em
> That I've got no cerebellum.

In order for such teachings to be persuasive, an intervening step, which has already been discussed in a different context, was taken. Instead of attempting to persuade the poets, instead of attempting to give form and measure to music, to "mark the music," as Lorenzo said, this antique approach to the dialectic of reason and eros was replaced by a new one. Passion (not eros) would be managed by being transformed into interest and directed by calculative reason. All the evidence, from Rousseau to Nietzsche to the Ramones, indicates that this enlightened solution to the musical problem is ineffective. Like the alleged non-lover in Plato's *Phaedrus*, the followers of Hobbes, Locke, and Smith turn out not to be devoid of desire but to have base desires centered chiefly on the production of more commodities. By attempting to overcome music, calculative enlightened reason has made it more primitive. Incapable of forming music into art, enlightened reason has enabled the primitive and barbaric emotions to flourish without measure.

Bloom's analysis of rock music stressed this aspect. It has, he said, "one appeal only, a barbaric appeal, to sexual desire—not love, not *eros*, but sexual desire undeveloped and untutored."[24] Against those who would tutor such desire resentment grows, and with it the sweet flower of moralism. "Sexual liberation," an elevated name for a common adolescent problem, turns into the self-righteous desire to overcome all repressive forces. The tragic Hegelianism of the universal and homogeneous state parades as the smarmy farce: "We Are the World." The vivid imagery of modern barbarism increases the temptation to rhetorical excess. One should, therefore, be precise: the barbaric meaning of such music is expressed not by the notion that "progress" culminates in the image of an adolescent doing homework wearing Walkman headphones, "a pubescent child whose body throbs with orgasmic rhythms; whose feelings are made articulate in hymns to the joys of onanism or the killing of parents; whose ambition is to win fame and wealth in imitating the drag-queen who makes the music."[25] Impressive as this description by Bloom is, such a result, one may safely say, was present from the start. The real barbarism, the technological barbarism that is expressed on the consumer side by the ubiquitous Walkman and on the production side by enormous mountains of expensive hardware, appears not just as the creation of ugliness but also in its artificiality. "Without effort, without talent, without virtue, without the exercise of the faculties, anyone and everyone is accorded the equal right to the enjoyment" of "the greatest endeavours—victory in a just war, consummated love, artistic creation, religious devotion and discovery of the truth." In response, the cool economist replies: "There is no free lunch." In short, the opposition of the quick fix and plodding calculation is false. There is no dialectic, no overcoming, no transformation. They are two sides of the same coin. Less metaphorically, the opposition articulates an internal conflict.

The connection between technical reason and romantic irrationality has long been observed. Romanticism and technology came into existence about the same time. Walter Ong established approximately the internal connection between the two. They were "mirror images of each other," both being products of the self-interpretation of human and society as dominating nature. In addition, Ong emphasized the importance of literacy for creating a new commodity, "Knowledge." New "chirographic and typographic techniques of storing and retrieving knowledge . . . had made this dominance over nature possible."[26] The incoherence of the metaphor of "mastery" has already been indicated. One effect of print, however, has been to help hide that incoherence.

Until the use of print was widespread, humans (in this case, almost exclusively male human beings) carried a great number of details in their memory. "Memory systems flourished," wrote Ong, "until typography had its full effect—until romanticism. When print locked information into exactly the same place upon the page in thousands of copies of the same book in type far more legible than almost any handwriting, knowledge came suddenly to the fingertips." Knowledge expressed through print was spatially fixed: "Man acquired an intellectual security never known before."[27] Considered in that light, the Romantics appear almost Socratic in reminding people how little they "really" knew; "the heart has its reasons that reason does not know," as Pascal wrote in opposition to Descartes. More generally, the more knowledge is technicized into a fixed space and frame, the more appealing become the adventures of violation. Technology used the new commodity of knowledge for practical and productive purposes. The attitude of the Romantics was more ambivalent and for that reason more interesting.

On the other hand, they rejected the new typographically grounded knowledge and technological rationality in favor of the "law of the heart." But on the other hand romanticism "covertly relied on rationalism."[28] It did so in two distinct ways. First, as *opposition*, it did not create what it opposed. Without the new commodity, without the new incoherencies of "technological domination," without the new surveillances of nature, the Romantics would have nothing to oppose. In addition, however, the Romantic poets wrote and published their poetry; they did not sing it, nor did they return to a tradition of formular repertoire characteristic of rhapsodic epic singers. Their skills were directed toward novelty, originality, and contrast—to be sure, the contrast was with technology; they were not, however, concerned with the pretechnological skill of virtuosity.

Consider what is probably the most famous Romantic document, the preface to the *Lyrical Ballads*, by Wordsworth and Coleridge (1802). They indicated initially that the object of poetry "is truth, not individual and local, but general and operative; not standing upon external testimony, but carried alive into the heart by passion; truth which is its own testimony, which gives strength and divinity to the tribunal to which it appeals, and receives them from the same tribunal. Poetry is the image of man and nature." But nature is not a given. Should the labors of people of science "create any material revolution, direct or indirect in our condition," the poets "will be ready to follow the steps of the Man of Science, not only in those general indirect effects, but he will be at his side, carrying sensation into the midst of the objects of the Science itself." Indeed, the poet would follow Science anywhere: "If the time should ever come when what is now called Science, thus familiarized to men, shall be ready to put on, as it were, a form of flesh and blood, the Poet will lend his divine spirit to aid the transfiguration and will welcome the Being thus produced, as a dear and genuine inmate of the household of man."[29] Romantic poetry is no less promethean than biotechnology.

Thirty years later Wordsworth praised "Steamboats, Viaducts, and Railways" as expressing the Romantic spirit.

> Nor shall your presence, howso'er it mar
> The loveliness of nature, prove a bar
> To the Mind's gaining that prophetic sense
> Of future change.

Ten years after Wordsworth's poem, in 1843, Turner painted his great masterpiece "Rain, Steam and Speed," a picture of a Great Western Railway locomotive crossing a trestle in a storm.

If Romantic artists could easily embrace the new technologies, it is only fair that engineers should prize their craft by invoking the images of Romantic change. The pamphlets of T. C. Keefer, who did so much to make engineering a respectable profession in Canada, who worked on the Erie and Welland canals, who supervised the construction of Montreal's municipal waterworks, read

like Romantic manifestoes. "The civilizing tendency of the locomotive," he wrote, "is one of the modern anomalies, which however inexplicable it may appear to some, is yet so fortunately
patent to all, that it is admitted as readily as the action of steam,
though the substance be invisible and its secret ways unknown to
man." Poverty, prejudice, indifference are all overcome by the
locomotive; no tyrants have the right to oppose it. "It calls for no
cooperation, it wants for no convenient season, but with a restless, rushing, roaring assiduity, it keeps up a constant and unavoidable spirit of enquiry or comparison." It both ministers to
material want and civilizes through commercial intercourse.[30]

The alliance of romanticism and technology, so improbable on
the surface, may be taken as established. To see its significance in
connection with rock music, and thereby its barbarism, two further points must be made. The first is that refinement, taste,
"cultural literacy," or civilization has been by nature restricted to
a minority. The conventional reasons for this are related to power,
whether courtly and autocratic or bourgeois and bureaucratic.
But as has been indicated earlier, there are reasons connected to
the variety with which human nature is actualized that also limit
the appeal of civilization to a few. The distinction being made is a
dilute version of the severe distinction between the philosopher
and the nonphilosopher. It is usually cast in a form that empha-
sizes how restricted, in reality, is the practice of a liberal education, notwithstanding the universality of its aim.

The second point was made by the great economic historian of
the Roman world Michael Rostovtzeff. "Is not every civilization,"
he asked, "bound to decay as it begins to penetrate the masses?"
Rostovtzeff believed the answer was affirmative but also that our
contemporary civilization could not endure "unless it be a civilization not of one class, but of the masses."[31] If, by joining civilization, the uncivil many destroy it, and if our civilization cannot
survive unless the uncivil many do just that, the prospects for
civil decency seemed to him to be dim. Accordingly, one may
anticipate the triumph of barbarism. Likewise George Steiner observed "The democratization of high culture—brought on by a
crisis of nerve within culture itself and by social revolution—has
engendered an absurd hybrid. Dumped on the mass market, the
products of classic literacy will be thinned and adulterated."[32]

The space filled by refinement and culture, by reasoned civilization, has been emptied by energetic romantics in order to cele-
brate what Hegel called the "freedom of the void."

The democratic expression of this romantic freedom, or rather,
to retain the aesthetic focus, its vulgar expression, is most perfectly expressed in rock music.[33] As Steiner also observed, the
social dynamism of technology coupled to economic productivity
has enabled increasingly large numbers of unrefined and uncul-
tured persons to express their vulgarity unimpeded and unaware
that vulgarity is what they are expressing. This is not to say that
barbarian hordes now slake the thirst of their rough ponies in the
Tuileries fountains, but only that what once was the elite culture,
or culture simply, has been reinterpreted in a popular mode.
More specifically, "Vulgarity is nothing but a mirror image of
what now passes for elite culture."[34] It is impossible, therefore,
for a C. P. Snow to criticize KISS on the basis of any coherent
principle. Despite their public personae, spiritual eunuchs really
are impotent. For those who are genuinely cultured, such as Arnold or Valéry, Leavis or Bloom, neither Snow nor KISS would
have the faintest notion of what they were talking about. That
such a situation does not make for productive discussion reinforces the significance of the title of Pattison's book.

His argument is indicated by the subtitle: rock music has vul-
garized romanticism. The political rather than aesthetic version
would be that it has radicalized romanticism. Radicalization has
also meant depoliticization.

Rock has appropriated romantic or "romantic-pantheist" versions of the self, of sex, of technology, and of social organization.
Where the Romantics invented the myth of the noble savage,
rockers have invented the myth that their music has its roots in
the blues, in the pain of black slavery in America, and ultimately
in the heart of darkness itself. But just as romanticism made forgeries of genuine folk traditions, so rock has made over the blues
in a vulgar key. The conventions of rock are all derived from romanticism: the glorification of noisy and uncontemplative youth
over maturity, wisdom, and moderation; the hatred of boredom
and ennui as evidence of a lack of energy, from which comes a
hatred of what Marx called "the idiocy of rural life"; and, especially important, the hatred of education. As Bruce Springsteen
tells it:

We learned more from a three minute record, baby,
Than we ever learned in school.

The result, which Pattison called "musical barbarism," has been
to reinforce the Romantic emphasis on feeling and to increase the
distrust of speech. The end of the road may be glimpsed in the
1958 hit by the Silhouettes, "Get a Job":

Sha da da da
Sha da da da da
Yip yip yip yip
Yip yip yip yip
Mum mum mum mum
Mum mum mum mum
Get a job

Nonsense and disconnected syllables may well be the appropriate
discourse for vulgar romanticism. On the one hand rock elevates
freedom, individuality, and authenticity; on the other it promotes
collective experiences of frenzy. On the one hand it claims to be
the oldest music with roots deep in primordial Africa; on the
other it relies on the latest technologies to be produced, transmitted, and consumed. These contradictions have found the correct form for articulation both in the babble of the Silhouettes
and in their instruction: get a job. If there is no difference between good taste and bad taste, if all is a matter of opinion, what
difference does it make whether one aims at giving a coherent
account or not? What difference does it make whether one speaks
or keeps silent? Only this: that the inability to make such distinctions is the emblem of nihilism. True to his vocation, the rocker
would reply: so what? Moreover, he would be right if he were
content to live on pogey.

*

The account of the aesthetic criticism of vulgarity began with
Carlyle's observation on the imbalance of mechanical consciousness, a notion taken up later by Valéry. The escape for the bewildered that marked historicism remains firmly barred; or rather,
those who take it end up in the same incoherence they tried to
avoid. Leavis indicated that there was only one culture, the culture that he identified with the great tradition and that once was
transmitted by a liberal education. He analyzed a famous contemporary intellectual and exposed the reasons for his eminence,

namely his having been supported by powerful administrative agencies that declared him a great novelist as well as a great scientist. Under such conditions it hardly mattered that he could not write. Oddities such as C. P. Snow have not, of course, been confined to the technological society. One recalls again Plato's description of the Sophists and of the city of Athens as the greatest Sophist of all. But it is also true that the particular configuration of administrative power in the technological society gives Snow a specific set of attributes. They may be summarized by the same term used to describe rock music: vulgarity.

The aesthetic that accompanied the technological society from its beginnings was romanticism. On its own terms, romanticism would soften the harshness of liberal productivity.[35] The transformation of a regime dedicated to the defense of property into one dedicated to having fun indicates a peculiar reversal. Since the beginning of the industrial revolution, which is the beginning of the technological era, Western nations have postponed their enjoyment of leisure in favor of increased prosperity. Now that prosperity has been attained by nearly the whole population, any serious notion of the purpose of leisure has evaporated. "Fun culture" is the soft barbarism of self-conscious vulgarity.

# Conclusion:
# Paying for It

Take what you want, said God.
Take what you want—and pay for it.
　　　　　—Spanish proverb

"We are impelled," wrote Leo Strauss, "to turn with passionate interest, with unqualified willingness to learn, toward the political thought of classical antiquity." What impels us is "the crisis
of our time, the crisis of the West."[1] That crisis "consists in the
West's having become unsure of its purpose," and its "core" is
the replacement of modern political philosophy by ideology.
Modern political philosophy itself replaced classical political philosophy. The obvious means by which the crisis could be overcome would seem to be the restoration of classical political
philosophy to its proper place. On closer inspection, the initial
attractiveness of this notion appears somewhat misplaced. To the
extent that modern political philosophy has proved successful it
has helped to generate a kind of society to which classical political
philosophy appears as a stranger, and for which its principles do
not seem immediately applicable. But perhaps that, too, is part
of the crisis.

To say that the West has become uncertain of its purpose implies that once it was certain of its purpose. And, indeed, much
of the evidence reproduced in this essay indicates how that purpose was construed. It is surely part of the modern project or the
project of modernity to raise the active life over the contemplative. Political philosophy, in its modern guise, to say nothing of
ideology, has in several different and conflicting ways aimed at
justifying that reversal. It has sought to provide a meaning to the
enterprise, which has been identified in a general way as "action

251

into nature," so that it is accurate to say that modern political philosophy, fully as much as modern technological science, has aimed at the compassionate relief of humanity's estate.

By this understanding, the purpose of the West consisted in the conquest of nature and the progress of humankind toward affluent self-preservation, freedom, and justice, which has come to mean the development of one's individual capacities as far as possible in a manner consistent with everyone else's doing so. Moreover, "everyone" meant everyone: the freedom, justice, and prosperity of one class or of one country could not last, it was believed, if it was gained at the expense of others. In Kojève's formula, the purpose of the West was to actualize the universal and homogeneous state.[2]

The crisis of the West, therefore, consists in uncertainty regarding the desirability of the universal and homogeneous state, the incarnation, as it were, of modern political philosophy. What gave the goal its plausibility as a worthy objective for human action was the belief that it was both universally desired and being increasingly actualized by a large majority of human beings. Several events contributed to commonsense or popular as well as to reflective or philosophical misgivings about the desirability of such a regime. One such event stemmed from the fact that the purpose of the West had been embraced by Communists as well as liberals. Even before the horrors of the National Socialist regime were known, the international socialists had revealed themselves as Stalinists, that is, as totalitarian killers. And Stalinism, as Merleau-Ponty once observed, is a doctrine subtle enough or twisted enough to encompass de-Stalinization.[3]

Thoughtful people saw in communism the gorgon's face of the purpose of the West. Stalinism was more than an embarrassment for which apologies were in order. Yet many apologies were made. Indeed, one of the articles of faith among contemporary Western intellectuals consists in the doctrine of "moral equivalence" between Stalinist totalitarian killers and their adversaries who, paradoxically, are identified with the West. The premise of this doctrine consists in the hope or expectation that Stalinism can "mature" into something like liberal democracy. Apologetic intellectuals, it seems, still retain their faith in the purpose of the West but prudently avoid looking at the gorgon's face. One suspects they retain their faith in order not to be forced to look at it.

Unfortunately, there is no evidence to indicate that a transformation of Stalinism into liberal democracy, or something like it, is likely; there is, however, an overwhelming amount of evidence to indicate that the Stalinists believed that Stalinism is a more "advanced stage" of the actualization of the purpose of the West than was achieved by Western liberal democracy. This assertion has not contributed to Western self-confidence, but to several doctrines of "revisionism," including the current version propagated by M. Gorbachev as "new thinking."

A sophisticated version of the apology holds that the purposes of the West and of the Stalinists are identical and that the quarrel between them concerns the appropriate means to actualize it. The grain of truth in this opinion consists in the view that Stalinist measures to promote rapid industrialization aimed at replicating the technological society. This same approach would consider Peter the Great a "Westernizer." What is forgotten in such simplicities is that neither Tsar Peter nor Generalissimo Stalin nor, indeed, President Gorbachev has much concern for freedom of inquiry, personal liberty, or personal initiative. A commonsensical understanding of recent events in the Soviet empire would focus more on the technological imperatives of industrial and administrative order, or, rather, on the degree to which those imperatives have been undermined by ideological fidelity to Marxism and the unobtrusive inefficiencies of terror, than on the Heideggerian meditations of President Havel. Likewise it is important to recall that the heartland of the European imperial core is occupied by the same German-speaking people who constitute the dynamic center of European technological activity.

However that may be, it remains true that the sophisticated doctrine of equivalence between liberal-technological regimes and Stalinist (or Leninist, Marxist, communist-socialist) ones cannot survive close examination of the difference in "means" characteristically used as instruments of rule. In this context, means constitutes the substance of politics. Whereas Communist states sanction murder of enemies of the people, no state functionary accused of murder in a non-Communist regime is likely to use such an argument in a court of law. From the side of the state functionary, no Communist policeman needs to concern himself with "Mirandizing" persons whom he arrests. All the evidence indicates that this is especially true for the secret police, a category of functionary for which there is no equivalent in the West. In short, "there is not only a difference of degree but of kind between the Western movement and Communism, and this difference was seen to concern morality, the choice of means."[4] If state-sanctioned murder is an unacceptable or immoral means of actualizing political purpose, then the regimes that use it, as Arendt said, are to be resisted. So far as Stalinist leaders are concerned, one can expect that their use of systematic murder will be mitigated only by fear of popular or palace revolutions and by fear of Western military capabilities. The latter, of course, depend on technology.

The sinister comedy of Western intellectuals' apologizing for Stalinists is not the only evidence available to common sense that indicates the West is unsure of its purpose. It has become a platitude among contemporary intellectuals in the social sciences to proclaim an inability to validate or evaluate what are called value judgments. As has been indicated, the principal doctrine of modern political philosophy was that the universal and homogeneous state was both universally desired and increasingly actualized. The progressive achievement of that state was, loosely speaking, as historically inevitable as anything can be. That it has resulted in Stalinism is, of course, regrettable, say the Western intellectuals, but modern social science remains untroubled by such regrets. Because it aims to be "value-free" the entirely acceptable doctrine of "moral equivalence" has for social science the implication that modern political philosophy is an ideology, a more or less systematically elaborated opinion in no way superior to any other. Distinct from modern political philosophy, modern social science does not flinch from judging the efficiency of state-sanctioned murder though it is unable to comment on the goodness of it. Besides, say modern social scientists, Stalinism has given way to new thinking, to openness, and to restructuring. The circle of value-free social science in this way is closed on historicism. If President Gorbachev should be succeeded by a Stalinist nothing would be changed except the "means."

Such an argument confirms the fundamental assumption of modern social science, namely that it has detached reason from any affiliation with goodness. The eclipse of noetic reason by technical reason has meant that it is equally impossible to assert the goodness of reason as it is to assert the reasonableness of the good. The consequence, as Stanley Rosen has indicated, is nihilism.[5] Rosen followed Nietzsche in his understanding of what nihilism meant, namely "Everything is permitted." As has been indicated, this understanding is but a prelude to the technological variant, "Everything is possible." The difference between the two formulas, like the difference between Napoleon and Stalin, is one of intensification. The proof that everything is possible is in doing what had been thought to be, by nature, impossible. Thus humans can fly and boys can become girls, more or less. Corresponding to the increased actualization of the universal and homogeneous state, the response to it from intellectuals has grown less energetic. Whereas nineteenth-century prophets anxiously foretold a coming silence, their contemporary successors have accommodated themselves to it.

As with Strauss's remarks on classical political philosophy, the obvious implication is that the remedy would be to restore the connection between reason and goodness. But, again as with Strauss's remark, the premise of modern, mass technological society seems to make this obvious remedy obviously impossible. "In an older terminology," Rosen wrote, "one must show that nature, not history, is the link between or the source of the significance of, reason and the good."[6] But the whole course of modern philosophy, to say nothing of the action of modern technology, has proceeded on the assumption that nature is without moral significance. It is for this reason that one can speak of progress.

The argument is straightforward and the implications are ominous. When nature is "dead" or morally insignificant, human beings look longingly to history for meaning. There, however, they encounter the paradoxes of progress according to which it makes sense to dispose of, or sacrifice, a real present for an ever-receding future. The phenomenalist and Averroist assumptions are clear: humanity is conceived as world-immanent species evolving toward a final generic perfection. When the center of meaning is conceived as an intramundane collective existence, the individual becomes an instrument, subordinated "to the technical means with which the organization of the collectivity incorporates him."[7] Kant expressed his astonishment at the fact that this implied that human beings existing in the present would necessarily be treated as the means by which the advances of future were assured. By the same logic, presently existing human beings had turned their forebears into the posthumous means by which they were able to enjoy whatever fruits of progress were currently available. Kant recognized that this implication violated his categorical imperative but also that progress cannot resolve the individual's desire for spiritual fulfillment, whatever the consequences for the intramundane collectivity. Despite the fact that, for Kant, the individual and the generic human being have the same rational structure, only the generic collectivity could attain its rational perfection: the individual must die.[8] But serving as the "manure for future harmony," Dostoevsky said, is no substitute for the meaning of existence because it makes no sense of the individual's death.

Many modern individuals, especially in the technological society, seem to have come to terms with this absence at the heart of the doctrine of progress. Perhaps they are compensated by an implication that progress shares with the Enlightenment, namely that freedom is the highest good and that scientific technology is the most adequate means to actualize that good. This means that the coherent conclusion to progress or the fulfillment of the Enlightenment is the universal and homogeneous state. In such a state, error and superstition are suppressed, along with many other things. What is left has been accurately described by Nietzsche as the last man.

Maurice Blanchot observed that Nietzsche saw "that from now on all the world's seriousness would be confined to science, to the scientist, and to the prodigious power of technology."[9] It is important here to note the word *seriousness*. Nietzsche's word for serious is *stupid*. "A 'scientific' interpretation of the world," he wrote in *The Gay Science*, section 373, "might therefore still be one of the *most stupid* of all possible interpretations of the world, meaning that it would be one of the poorest in meaning." What we make of this depends on whether we think *The Gay Science* is a serious book. To Zarathustra's question, "Who shall be masters of the earth?" the answer seems to have turned out to be, the stupid. Speaking historically, the nineteenth-century bourgeois known to Nietzsche was a person of small ambition and low sights. The portrait drawn in Zarathustra's prologue was repeated later in the book.[10] They are the types of human beings who "will gradually come to be the majority in any realized technological society."[11] Both Strauss and Rosen are of the opinion that the citizen of the universal and homogeneous state is precisely Nietzsche's last man.[12] But who or what is the last man?

The prologue tells of Zarathustra's going down, like Socrates in the *Republic*, from the high place to the low town. Zarathustra went alone, first meeting a saintly silvan hermit who had not heard the news that God had died. He then proceeded to the town at the edge of the woods. Like the madman in the *Gay Science* (section 125) who announced that God had been murdered, Zarathustra was not well received. The people were awaiting some entertainment, a tightrope walker. Zarathustra preached a sermon proclaiming the overman, but the people laughed at him and said they wanted to see the tightrope walker. Zarathustra then preached a sermon that began, "Man is a rope, tied between beast and Overman—a rope over an abyss." But that concession to stupidity was lost on them. "I am not the mouth for these ears," he said. "Must one smash their ears before they learn to listen with their eyes?" Zarathustra then proceeded to smash their ears.

What are they proud of? he asked. Their education: "It distinguished them from goatherds." They do not like to hear the word *contempt* applied to them because it offends their pride. Zarathustra smashed their ears with a speech of contempt that engaged their pride. Man is running out of steam he announced; soon he will have no goal beyond himself. Soon the last man will be here. Such a one asks himself big questions: "What is love? What is creation? What is longing? What is a star?" And then he blinks. The last man seems to be very stupid. He is a small man on a small planet whose small ambition is to live long, whose joy is to rub bodies together for warmth, whose aversion is illness (but he can relieve it with a little poison for agreeable dreams). "And much poison at the end for an agreeable death." There is plenty of entertainment, but none of it strenuous; for the same reason, no one is poor or rich, no one rules or obeys.

> No shepherd and one herd! Everybody wants the same, everybody is the same: whoever feels different goes voluntarily into a madhouse.
>
> "Formerly, all the world was mad," say the most refined, and they blink.

One is ever clever and knows everything that has ever happened: so there is no end of derision. One still quarrels, but one is
soon reconciled—else it might spoil the digestion.

One has one's little pleasure for the day and one's little pleasure
for the night: but one has regard for health.

"We have invented happiness," say the last men, and they
blink.

The crowd clapped and were delighted and called on Zarathustra
to turn them into last men. The trick has been performed, but
not by Zarathustra. "The last men," wrote Lampert, "are the
men of technological mastery, not ruled but managed by one another, living comfortably with their neighbours, serviced by the
line and race of inventions springing from their science of
nature."[13] Nietzsche's joke was plain enough, though one risks
spoiling it by an explanation: these vulgar intellectuals, snobs
who look down on goatherds and up to no one and nothing, have
had their ears smashed with Zarathustra's contempt. But they are
too stupid to notice; they are beneath contempt.          ·

Nietzsche's own account is found in a passage in part 4 entitled
"On the Higher Man." There Zarathustra recalled his first encounter with human beings. "I committed the folly of hermits,
the grand folly: I stood in the market place." He learned from
that experience that he had no concern with the mob and no
need to speak into "long mob ears." What was the point in
smashing asinine ears? To the higher men to whom he spoke in
part 4, Zarathustra explained again God's death and their own
resurrection, which followed from it. Of the stupid he recalled
that they believed in equality: "Before god we are all equal. Before god! but now this god has died. And before the mob we do
not want to be equal. You higher men, go away from the market
place!" The resurrection of the higher men, Nietzsche said,
would be followed by the overman; the contempt that the higher
men felt for the last men allowed Zarathustra to hope that humanity would not be preserved. "The most concerned ask today:
'How is man to be preserved?' But Zarathustra is the first and
only one to ask 'How is man to be overcome?' " The small people
who wish only for a long life and a pleasant death "preach surrender and resignation and prudence and industry and consideration
and the long etcetera of the small virtues." These "womanish,"
servile, nauseating preachers of smallness "are the overman's

greatest danger." More particularly, Nietzsche indicated that, lacking a common goal, humankind cannot be said to exist.[14] The Hegelian or Kojèvian end of history in the universal and homogeneous state also implies the end of our humanity, which is conceptually proper.[15]

Yet the danger remained. If ever the small ones created a humankind infused with democratic-socialist mediocrity, its destruction would be that much more to be desired.[16] Nietzsche's answer to the problem of the technological society, and to the fulfillment of the Enlightenment in the universal and homogeneous state, to the fulfillment of the dreams of progress that still puzzled Kant, was to counsel large-scale murder. The conceptual propriety of ending history, and our humanity all at once had bloody implications whether it was successfully actualized along Hegelian lines or not. That the twentieth century has enacted much of this hard political teaching is evidence both that Hegel, as modified by Nietzsche, was right concerning the threefold end and that this truth is evidence of a deepening of the crisis it was meant to overcome.

*

In the course of this essay we have often relied on German thinkers. One reason for this is that German speakers have been unsurpassed in their ability to articulate the spiritual disorders of modern technological consciousness. And one reason for that is that the German heartland of Europe has borne the material and political consequences of technological modernity so extensively. This does not mean, however, that we are dealing with simply a German problem.

The previous section, for example, began with an allusion to Oswald Spengler's great study of the going down of the West, a late expression of the uncertainty of the purpose of the West. Commonsensical evidence was found not simply in national socialist policies but in the apologies by Western intellectuals for the equally criminal acts of the international socialists. Moreover, the view of noncriminal social scientists regarding the irrationality of value judgments expressed both their defenselessness and their complicity in what the great thinkers of the modern world have diagnosed as an ecumenic crisis.

To the extent that the spectacular actions of the totalitarian killers were based on assumptions regarding reality that are shared with contemporary technological consciousness, it seems fair to say that the defeat or the disintegration of the totalitarian political regimes has not resolved the spiritual disorders they expressed. We saw, for example, that, in spite of being puzzled at the paradox of progress, Kant was of the view that the individual and the state, "the city and man," were eventually reconcilable. Hegel's teaching may be said to constitute the blueprint for reconciliation. Two conditions were necessary, that history be rational and that it be complete; Hegel taught that those conditions had been met. Nietzsche, however, denied that they had and advanced the opinion that history was not rational, though it might appear that way from any particular standpoint or within any given horizon. The particular horizon that Nietzsche found so especially repulsive was constituted by progressive intellectuals and scientists, or rather by the social type, the last man, who was exalted, justified, and explained by their words and deeds. The difficulty with the triumph of the stupid, Nietzsche would say, is that one cannot say anything to them about it. Or as Schiller did say, "With stupidity, even the gods struggle in vain."

If Nietzsche and Schiller were right, it would be pointless to argue with the stupid. Since they could not be educated, they must be killed, either by one another or by the overmen. But large-scale killing appears to have been one of the things adduced by common sense as evidence for the uncertainty of purpose of the West. More killing will not, therefore, restore a sense of purpose. One would like to know, therefore, what Nietzsche's solution to the problem of modern stupidity shares with the stupidity he wished to extirpate. To put the matter bluntly: What is wrong with killing off the stupid?

If there is an answer, we may begin to see it by reflecting on the fact that both Nietzsche and the progressive intellectuals and scientists share a commitment to history as the fundamental reality for human being, the fundamental constituent of human experience. History, Nietzsche said, was really created by the great individuals who pierced any given horizon and thereby created them for others. These immoderate few were laws unto themselves. As regards the stupid, the overmen will revolutionize them by smashing what is given, which means nature and the final historical product, the last men themselves. The central doctrine of Nietzsche's teaching, which may be said to "justify" all this smashing and killing, was the will to power. However, the doctrine of will to power was based as much on the rejection of nature as standard as any of the several doctrines of the stupid that the overman chose to overcome. Will to power, in Rosen's language, was self-conscious nihilism, but nihilism still.

Concerning will to power Strauss has observed:

> The difficulty inherent in the philosophy of the will to power led after Nietzsche to the explicit renunciation of the very notion of eternity. Modern thought reaches its culmination, its highest self-consciousness, in the most radical historicism, i.e., in explicitly condemning to oblivion the notion of eternity. For oblivion of eternity, or, in other words, estrangement from man's deepest desire and therewith from the primary issues, is the price which modern man had to pay, from the very beginning, for attempting to be absolutely sovereign, to become the master and owner of nature, to conquer chance.[17]

The act of renunciation of eternity or of a consciousness of oblivion of eternity was a large renunciation, and it has not been confined to German philosophy, or to Heidegger, the thinker to whom Strauss was alluding.

Eternity does not mean a long time but may perhaps be visualized as a vertical dimension for which time is the horizontal. "It is," said Kohak, "the confrontation with the full moon through the trees dark with the day's rain. It is the goodness of an act or the truth of a witness which avail nothing in the order of time, yet are still irreducibly good. It is the awareness of the intensity of the blue sky on a summer day." There is no romanticism here, but only an epistemological insight: "Humans are beings capable of perceiving all that." In the language used earlier, they are capable not only of perceptual experience of phenomena but of meditative apprehension of substance. Kohak's point was twofold: that such experience is an achievement, and that what it achieves is an awareness of the elevation "of time's passage into eternity in the eternal validity of truth, goodness, and beauty of their joy and sorrow."[18] To the extent, therefore, that an immersion in the things of the moment is evidence of barbarism and vulgarity, oblivion of eternity is characteristic of the barbaric and the vulgar human types. Such persons typically substitute the question, Do I like it? for Is it beautiful?

If both Nietzsche and the stupid are oblivious of eternity, with the difference being that Nietzsche is aware of his own obliviousness and the stupid are not; if Strauss is nevertheless correct in his assertion that such obliviousness, whether deliberate and self-conscious or not, can only lead to alienation from reality or "estrangement from man's deepest desire and therewith from the primary issues," then perhaps it is legitimate to consider the question, How does one avoid oblivion of eternity? With respect to the question of technology two clear answers have been advanced by contemporary thinkers.

The first was folly. Let us assume it is true that "there is no way out, no alternative to technology. There is no mediation, no logical compromise with the contemporary world. The technological world is a world of total seriousness, of the earnest itself. When the world takes itself seriously, the fool must step in."[19] Verene's analysis relied on Vico and Hegel, not Aristophanes or his comic successors. To the extent that the technicians are serious-minded, laughter is something they cannot accept. More generally, it is also true that laughter is a threat to technology because "there can be no technique for folly, for madness, for the laugh."[20] One would like to know, however, what is so funny.

It is true that Socrates laughed, and that philosophers must have a sense of humor, and that there is a large element of comedy in the achievement of the technological society. Zarathustra made many jokes about the serious ones. But it is also true that philosophers would like to know not what makes any particular joke funny but what are the grounds for laughter. Merely laughing at the serious fools is not enough, even though laughter challenges seriousness. The insufficiency is indicated by the observation that the serious people can normalize the laughing fool by employing the correct therapeutic technologies. Verene's remedy, attractive as it may appear, is defective insofar as it is a practical version of the master/slave dialectic, the insufficiencies of which have already been discussed.

A second alternative has occasionally been suggested by Jacques Ellul: God may intervene directly in history. About that possibility nothing can be said by way of analysis. Perhaps one might rephrase Ellul's response with reference to a genre of literature that bears witness against evil in its technological form. Here one thinks of Solzhenitsyn, Timerman, Zorn, Mandelstam.

Such literature, it seems to me, is a restatement of the famous phrase from the *Agamemnon* of Aeschylus, *pathei mathos*, learning through suffering (lines 177–78). In the present context, the experience of learning that oblivion of eternity is a deprival will be undertaken, I suspect, "in the heat of life where many sparrows fall."[21] That is, private anguish and public catastrophes may be the means by which human beings renew their vision of nobility and excellence. On the other hand, there may be no transfiguration of suffering into the preparation for wisdom. But even then we will forcibly be reminded of the unavoidable truths of the cosmos. From the Bible we learn:

> To everything there is a season,
> And a time to every purpose under the heaven;
> A time to be born and a time to die.

The Kohelet goes on to indicate that the human mind cannot comprehend "the work that God maketh from the beginning to the end" (Eccles. 3:1–2, 11). Likewise the great philosopher Anaximander: "The origin of all things is the Boundless [*apeiron*]. . . . It is necessary that things should perish into that from which they were born; for they pay one another penalty [*dike*] for their injustice [*adikia*] according to the decree [*taxis*] of Time."[22] If the West has grown uncertain of its purpose in the midst of the triumphs of the technological society the reason, it seems to me, lies in having expunged from modern consciousness the experience of the mystery of being that once lived in these two ancient texts. Whether we can recover the truth they expressed is not a matter about which it makes much sense to speculate.

# Notes

### Introduction: Technology and Consciousness

1. Maurice Merleau-Ponty, *Phénoménologie de la perception* (Paris: Gallimard, 1945), pp. i–xvi.

2. Paul Ricoeur, *Freud and Philosophy: An Essay on Interpretation*, trans. Denis Savage (New Haven: Yale University Press, 1970).

3. Michael Polanyi, *Personal Knowledge* (New York: Harper Torchbooks, 1964).

4. Edmund Husserl, *The Crisis of European Sciences and Transcendental Phenomenology: An Introduction to Phenomenological Philosophy*, trans. David Carr (Evanston: Northwestern University Press, 1970), part 2.

5. Reproduced in English in Claire H. Schiller, ed. and trans., *Instinctive Behavior* (New York: International Universities Press, 1957), 5–80.

6. Erazim Kohak, *The Embers and the Stars: A Philosophical Inquiry into the Moral Sense of Nature* (Chicago: University of Chicago Press, 1984), 199.

7. Kohak, *Embers and the Stars*, 203.

8. G. W. F. Hegel, *Phänomenologie des Geistes,* ed. J. Hoffmeister (Hamburg: Meiner, 1952), 165–66, 196.

9. Eric Voegelin, *Anamnesis: Zur Theorie der Geschichte und Politik* (Munich: Piper, 1966), 19; cited as *Anamnesis* (German).

10. For details see Barry Cooper, *Merleau-Ponty and Marxism: From Terror to Reform* (Toronto: University of Toronto Press, 1979). See also David Levy, *Political Order* (Baton Rouge: Louisiana State University Press, 1987).

11. Quoted in Helmut Wagner, "Agreement in Discord: Alfred Schutz and Eric Voegelin," in Peter J. Opitz and Greggor Sebba, eds., *The Philosophy of Order: Essays on History Consciousness and Politics for Eric Voegelin on his 80th Birthday* (Stuttgart: Klett-Cotta, 1981), 85.

12. Eric Voegelin, "Reason: The Classic Experience," *Southern Review* n.s. 10 (1974): 237.

13. Wagner, "Agreement in Discord," 74–90. See also his book, *Alfred Schutz: An Intellectual Biography* (Chicago: University of Chicago Press, 1983), chap. 12.

14. Schutz to Voegelin, November 1952; reprinted in Opitz and Sebba, eds., *Philosophy of Order*, 445.

15. Voegelin to Schutz, 10 Jan. 1953, in ibid., 461.

16. Eric Voegelin, *Science, Politics and Gnosticism*, trans. William J. Fitzpatrick (Chicago: Regnery, 1968), 45.

17. Voegelin, *Anamnesis* (German), 21–36. This essay was also a letter to Schutz, dated 17 September 1943, as was "On the Theory of Consciousness," in *Anamnesis*, trans. and ed. Gerhart Niemeyer (Notre Dame, Ind.: University of Notre Dame Press, 1978), 14–35; cited as *Anamnesis* (English). We cite the English edition where possible.

18. Husserl, *Crisis*, 17, 71.

19. Voegelin, *Anamnesis* (German), 36.

20. The locus classicus was, of course, Hegel. See Barry Cooper, *The End of History: An Essay on Modern Hegelianism* (Toronto: University of Toronto Press, 1984). See also Helmut R. Wagner, "Husserl and Historicism," *Social Research* 39 (1972): 696–719.

21. Voegelin, *Anamnesis* (English), 10.

22. Ibid.

23. Ibid., 11.

24. *Anamnesis* (German), 31.

25. John Burnet, "Ignorance," in his *Essays and Addresses* (London: Chatto and Windus, 1929), 240.

26. *Anamnesis* (English), 4.

27. Aníbal A. Bueno, "Consciousness, Time and Transcendence in Eric Voegelin's Philosophy," in Opitz and Sebba, eds., *Philosophy of Order*, 100.

28. *Anamnesis* (English), 33.

29. For details, see Marjorie Grene, *Approaches to Philosophical Biology* (New York: Basic Books, 1965); Barry Cooper, "Hegelian Elements in Merleau-Ponty's *La Structure du comportement*," *International Philosophical Quarterly* 15 (1975): 411–25. The following remarks rely chiefly on K. Goldstein, *The Organism* (New York: American Books, 1938), and Hans Jonas, *The Phenomenon of Life* (New York: Delta, 1966).

30. See Bernard Lonergan, *Insight* (New York: Longmans, 1957).

31. Coleridge used the term polemically in a different context. See, however, Neil Evernden, *The Natural Alien: Humankind and Environment* (Toronto: University of Toronto Press, 1985).

32. Voegelin, "Reason: The Classic Experience," 240.

33. Husserl, *Crisis of European Sciences*, 5–6.

34. In the words of an old children's paradox, The moon is more important than the sun because we need it to see at night.

35. See, for example, J. Agassi, "The Confusion between Science and Technology in the Standard Philosophies of Science," in F. Rapp, ed., *Contributions to a Philosophy of Technology: Studies in the Structure of Thinking in the Technological Sciences* (Dordrecht: Reidel, 1974), 40–59.

36. Leo Strauss, *What Is Political Philosophy? And Other Studies*, (Glencoe, Ill.: Free Press, 1959), 11.

37. Strauss, *Natural Right and History* (Chicago: University of Chicago Press, 1953), 122.

38. See Alexandre Koyré, "Galileo and Plato," *Journal of the History of Ideas* 4 (1943): 400–428.

39. See Jacob Klein, "Phenomenology and the History of Science," in Klein, *Lectures and Essays*, ed. Robert B. Wilhamson, and Elliott Zuckerman (Annapolis, Md.: St. John's College Press, 1985), 65–85.

40. An alternative way of formulating the problem, which Husserl also used by calling phenomenology a "strict science," is to say that the premodern understanding of science as *episteme* is to be recovered. This means a shift in the meaning of science from its contemporary concern with abstract quantity to the antique meaning, which was connected to concrete quality.

## Part I
## 1. Novelty

1. Langdon Winner, "Techne and Politeia: The Technical Constitution of Society," in Paul T. Durbin and Friedrich Rapp, eds., *Philosophy and Technology* (Dordrecht: Reidel, 1983), 109.

2. Eric Voegelin, *The New Science of Politics* (Chicago: University of Chicago Press, 1952), 27.

3. Hans Jonas, *The Imperative of Responsibility: In Search of an Ethics for the Technological Age* (Chicago: University of Chicago Press, 1984), 6.

4. William Barrett, *The Illusion of Technique: A Search for Meaning in a Technological Civilization* (New York: Anchor, 1978), 179.

5. Carl Mitcham, "Philosophy and the History of Technology," in George Bugliarello and Dean B. Toner, eds., *The History and Philosophy of Technology* (Urbana: University of Illinois Press, 1979), 182.

6. George Grant, *Technology and Justice* (Toronto: Anansi, 1987), 12.

7. See Friedrich Rapp, *Analytical Philosophy of Technology*, trans. S. R. Carpenter and T. Langenbruch (Dordrecht: Reidel, 1981), chap.

1, and L. Tondl, "On the Concepts of 'Technology' and 'Technological Sciences,' " in F. Rapp, ed., *Contributions to a Philosophy of Technology*, 1–18.

8. Martin Heidegger, "Die Frage nach der Technik," in *Vorträge und Aufsätze*, (Pfullingen: Neske, 1954), 13ff.; William Lovitt, trans., "The Question Concerning Technology," in *The Question Concerning Technology, and Other Essays* (New York: Harper, 1977), 3ff. On the meaning of *das Gestell* see David Kolb, *The Critique of Pure Modernity: Hegel, Heidegger and After* (Chicago: University of Chicago Press, 1986), 144–50.

9. Laslett, *The World We Have Lost: England before the Industrial Age* (New York: Scribner's, 1965).

10. Hannah Arendt, *The Human Condition* (Chicago: University of Chicago Press, 1958), 256.

11. Don Ihde, *Technics and Praxis* (Dordrecht: Reidel, 1979), 21.

12. See John Burnet, "Ignorance: The Romanes Lecture, 1923," in his *Essays and Addresses* (London: Chatto and Windus, 1929), 237–38.

13. "Vita contemplativa simpliciter melior est quam vita activa," St. Thomas, *Summa theologica* 2.2.182.1, 2. That contemplation was "simply better" than action seemed to be self-evident.

14. Hans Blumenberg, *The Legitimacy of the Modern Age*, trans. Robert M. Wallace (Cambridge: MIT Press, 1983), 373; see also Marjorie Nicholson, "The Telescope and Imagination," *Modern Philology* 32 (1934–35): 233–60.

15. The four observable natural forces are (1) gravity, which keeps your feet on the ground and holds the universe together; (2) electromagnetic force, which governs the interactions of electrically charged particles and accounts for ordinary chemical changes and the everyday properties of solids, liquids, and gases; (3) strong nuclear force, which holds the atomic nucleus, protons and neutrons, together; (4) weak nuclear force, which does not seem to hold anything together but is responsible for the decay of radioactive atomic nuclei. See Steven Weinberg, "Unified Theories of Elementary Particle Interaction," *Scientific American* 231, no. 7 (July 1974): 50–59. A more recent and experimentally confirmed theory, called electroweak theory, states that forces 2 and 4 are different manifestations of the same underlying force. See David B. Cline, Carlo Rubbia, and Simon van der Meer, "The Search for Intermediate Vector Bosons," *Scientific American* 247, no. 3 (March 1982): 48–59.

16. Hannah Arendt, *Between Past and Future* (New York: Viking, 1968), 49.

17. *The Cloud of Unknowing*, ed. Phyllis Hodgson (Oxford: Oxford University Press, 1958), chaps. 5, 26.

18. Voegelin, *Anamnesis*, 34.

19. Hans Jonas, *Philosophical Essays: From Ancient Creed to Technological Man* (Englewood Cliffs, N.J.: Prentice-Hall, 1974), 48.

## 2. The Technological Society

1. Eric Voegelin, *The New Science of Politics* (Chicago: University of Chicago Press, 1952), 61.

2. See Jacques Ellul, "Mirror of These Ten Years: How My Mind Has Changed," *Christian Century,* 18 Feb. 1970, 201–4.

3. The Hegelian argument, which is not without controversy, is developed at length in Barry Cooper, *The End of History* (Toronto: University of Toronto Press, 1984).

4. Jacques Ellul, *The Technological Society,* trans. John Wilkinson (New York: Vintage, 1964), xxix.

5. Ellul, *Perspectives on Our Age,* trans. J. Neugroschel (Toronto: CBC, 1981), 59–60.

6. Ellul, *Perspectives on Our Age,* 62.

7. *Republic* 358e–59b.

8. Voegelin, *Order and History,* vol. 3, *Plato and Aristotle* (Baton Rouge: Louisiana State University Press, 1957), 75–76.

9. For details see Darrell J. Fasching, *The Thought of Jacques Ellul: A Systematic Exposition* (New York and Toronto: Edwin Mellen Press, 1981).

10. Ellul, *Perspectives on Our Age,* 101–2.

11. Hans Jonas, *Philosophical Essays,* 75–80.

12. For details see Sherry Turkle, *The Second Self: Computers and the Human Spirit* (New York: Simon and Schuster, 1984).

13. J. David Bolter, *Turing's Man: Western Culture in the Computer Age* (Chapel Hill: University of North Carolina Press, 1984).

14. The Turing test consists of deciding which responses from two computer terminals come from a human and which from a computer. The computer is programmed to respond as a human would, by taking its time doing sums or by making errors. If you cannot decide which is which, Turing said you must conclude that the machine is "intelligent." Alan Turing, "Computing Machines and Intelligence," in Edward Feigenbaum and Julian Feldman, eds., *Computers and Thought* (New York: McGraw-Hill, 1963). For an account of some obvious objections, see John Searle, "Mind, Brains, and Programs," *Behavioral and Brain Sciences* 3 (1980): 417–24, and "The Myth of the Computer," *New York Review of Books,* 29 Apr. 1982.

15. For what it is worth, it seems to be obvious that the very name, *artificial* intelligence, indicates an ontological difference from intelligence that is begotten. What is begotten is alike in being (though not in will) with its begetter; what is made is unlike in being with its maker

though it bears the imprint of the maker's will. See Oliver O'Donovan, *Begotten or Made?* (Oxford: Clarendon, 1984), for details of the fairly simple philosophical issues involved.

16. For a discussion of this new "definition," see Jonas, *Philosophical Essays*, 132–40.

17. Jacques Ellul, *The Technological System*, trans. J. Neugroschel (New York: Continuum, 1980).

18. Neil Everenden, *The Natural Alien* (Toronto: University of Toronto Press, 1985), 21.

19. Ellul, *Perspectives on Our Age*, 68–69.

20. Ibid., 69–70.

### 3. Phenomenalism

1. The allusion is to the magnificent opening words of Voegelin's *Order and History:* "God and man, world and society form a primordial community of being." Vol. 1, *Israel and Revelation* (Baton Rouge: Louisiana State University Press, 1956), 1. The term *phenomenalism* was developed in Eric Voegelin's "History of Political Ideas," to be published by Louisiana State University Press; the arguments and evidence are found in the chapters "Man In History and Nature" and "Last Orientation."

2. F. A. Hayek, *The Counter-Revolution Science: Studies on the Abuse of Reason* (Glencoe, Ill.: Free Press, 1955); Eric Voegelin, "The Origins of Scientism," *Social Research* 15 (1948): 462–94. This question is considered in detail in chap. 7 below.

3. The distinction sustained Pierre Duhem's masterful analysis in *Le système du monde*, 10 vols. (Paris: Hermann, 1913–59). The account presented here is chiefly taken from his *La théorie physique: Son object, sa structure*, (Paris: Rivière, 1914), trans. Philip P. Wiener as *The Aim and Structure of Physical Theory* (Princeton, N.J.: Princeton University Press, 1954). In this book, Duhem stated that the argument reflected as well his practical experience as a physicist (*Aim and Structure*, 3).

4. The hermeneutic question is distinct from what is currently called a "realist" account of scientific theories insofar as for the latter the phenomenalist assumptions are wholly unproblematic. The question here, however, is precisely to indicate what is problematic about the assumptions and not to consider "realism" at all.

5. Barry Cooper, "Reduction, Reminiscence and the Search for Truth," in Peter J. Opitz and Gregor Sebba, eds., *The Philosophy of Order: Essays on History, Consciousness and Politics for Eric Voegelin on his Eightieth Birthday*, (Stuttgart: Klett-Cotta, 1981), 316–31.

6. Duhem, *Aim and Structure*, 7–10.

7. Ibid., 19.

8. Ibid.

9. See Duhem, *Système du monde*, 2:50–179.

10. Duhem, *Aim and Structure*, 40.

11. Duhem, *Système du monde*, 4:182.

12. Edward Grant, "Late Medieval Thought, Copernicus, and the Scientific Revolution," *Journal of the History of Ideas* 23 (1962): 198–99, n. 4.

13. Heiko Oberman, "Reformation and Revolution: Copernicus' Discovery in an Era of Change," in Owen Gingerich, ed., *The Nature of Scientific Discovery: A Symposium Commemorating the 500th Anniversary of the Birth of Nicolaus Copernicus* (Washington, D.C.: Smithsonian Institution Press, 1975), 154–55.

14. Douglas Bush, *Science and English Poetry: A Historical Sketch, 1590–1950* (London: Oxford University Press, 1950), 54.

15. Duhem, *Aim and Structure*, 115.

16. Ibid., 275; Duhem, *Système du monde*, 6:728–29. Current philosophy of science is more likely to call Duhem's position an instrumentalist one.

17. "I have never concealed my faith," he said, "and that He in whom I hold it will keep me from ever being ashamed of it, I hope from the bottom of my heart." Duhem, *Aim and Structure*, 273–74.

18. Aron Gurwitsch, "Galilean Physics in Light of Husserl's Phenomenology," in Ernan McMullin, *Galileo: Man of Science* (New York: Basic Books, 1967), 401.

19. Aristotle *Posterior Analytics* 71b8–12 (book 1, chap. 2). See, for example, A. C. Crombie, *Robert Grosseteste and the Origins of Experimental Science* (Oxford: Oxford University Press, 1953).

20. Aristotle *Posterior Analytics* 78a22 (book 1, chap. 13). See also Melbourne G. Evans, "Causality and Explanation in the Logic of Aristotle," *Philosophy and Phenomenological Research* 19 (1958–59): 466–85.

21. See R. K. Sprague, "The Four Causes: Aristotle's Exposition and Ours," *Monist* 52 (1968): 298–300, or William A. Wallace, *Causality and Scientific Explanation*, vol. 1, *Medieval and Early Classical Science* (Ann Arbor: University of Michigan Press, 1972), chap. 1 for details.

22. See Jacob Klein, *Greek Mathematical Thought and the Origin of Algebra*, trans. Eva Brann (Cambridge, Mass.: MIT Press, 1968), and Klein, "The Concept of Number in Greek Mathematics and Philosophy," in *Lectures and Essays*, ed. Robert B. Williamson and Elliott Zuckerman (Annapolis: St. John's College Press, 1985), 43–52.

23. Aristotle *Meteorologica*, 390b17–20.

24. Ibid. 390a5–6.

25. See, for example, Leo Strauss, *Natural Right and History* (Chicago: University of Chicago Press, 1953), 122–23.

26. Friedrich Nietzsche, "How the 'True World' Finally Became a Fable," *Twilight of the Idols*, in *The Portable Nietzsche*, ed. and trans. Walter Kaufmann (New York: Viking, 1954), 486. See also Barry Cooper, "Technology and Nihilism," in Tom Darby et al., eds., *Nietzsche and the Rhetoric of Nihilism: Essays on Interpretation, Language and Politics* (Ottawa: Carleton University Press, 1989), 165–82.

27. Democritus (Diels-Kranz 9, 125), in G. S. Kirk and J. E. Raven, *The Presocratic Philosophers* (Cambridge: Cambridge University Press, 1969), 422, 424.

28. Hannah Arendt, *The Life of the Mind*, vol. 1, *Thinking* (New York: Harcourt Brace Jovanovich, 1978), 11.

29. Barry Cooper, "Ideology, Technology, and Truth," in Francis Canavan, ed., *The Ethical Dimensions of Political Life: Essays in Honor of John H. Hallowell* (Durham, N.C.: Duke University Press, 1983), 138–55.

30. For details, see Eric Voegelin, "Das Timurbild der Humanisten," in *Anamnesis* (German), 153–78; and his "Machiavelli's Prince: Background and Formation," *Review of Politics* 13 (1951): 153–65.

31. See Thomas Flanagan, "The Concept of *Fortuna* in Machiavelli" in A. Parel, ed., *The Political Calculus* (Toronto: University of Toronto Press, 1972), 127–56 and references. In general, see Hanna Fenichel Pitkin, *Fortune Is a Woman: Gender and Politics in the Thought of Niccolo Machiavelli* (Berkeley: University of California Press, 1984).

32. Werner L. Gundersheimer, *The Life and Works of Louis LeRoy* (Geneva: Droz, 1966), 7.

33. Still useful is Don Cameron Allen, *The Star-Crossed Renaissance* (Durham, N.C.: Duke University Press, 1941).

34. For an account of the qualifying details see Allen G. Debus, *Man and Nature in the Renaissance* (Cambridge: Cambridge University Press, 1978); Paul Oskar Kristeller, *Eight Philosophers of the Italian Renaissance* (Stanford, Calif.: Stanford University Press, 1964); in addition, the massive compendia by George Sarton (*A History of Science* [Cambridge, Mass.: Harvard University Press, 1953–59]) and Lynn Thorndike (*A History of Magic and Experiential Science* [New York: Columbia University Press, 1923–58]) should be consulted. Stephen A. McKnight, *Sacralizing the Secular: The Renaissance Origins of Modernity* (Baton Rouge: Louisiana State University Press, 1989), also contains a useful synthesis and summary.

35. Augustine, *De Civitate Dei* 21.1.

36. On this vexing matter, one should also consult Jonathan Swift's

"Bickerstaff Papers" in *Gulliver's Travels and Other Writings*, ed. Louis A. Landa (Boston: Houghton Mifflin 1960), 381–996.

37. Jacob Bronowski, "Copernicus as a Humanist," in Owen Gingerich, ed., *The Nature of Scientific Discovery*, 173. In antiquity Heraclides of Pontus and Aristarchus of Samos both argued for heliocentrism; in the fourteenth century Nicholas of Oresme proposed a heliocentric theory, as did Nicolas of Cusa in the fifteenth.

38. For computational details, see Otto Neugebauer, "On the Planetary Theory of Copernicus," in A. Beer, ed., *Vistas in Astronomy*, vol. 10 (New York: Pergamon, 1968), 58; Richard Berendzen, "Geocentric to Heliocentric to Galactocentric to Acentric: The Continuing Assault to the Egocentric," in A. Beer and K. A. Strand, eds., *Copernicus Yesterday and Today*, vol. *17 of Vistas in Astronomy* (New York: Pergamon, 1975), 75; Owen Gingerich " 'Crisis' versus Aesthetic in the Copernican Revolution," in Beer and Strand, eds., *Copernicus Yesterday and Today*, 87, 89; I. Bernard Cohen, *The Birth of a New Physics* (New York: Anchor, 1960), 58.

39. I. Bernard Cohen, *Revolution in Science* (Cambridge, Mass.: Belknap Press of Harvard University Press, 1985), 116.

40. Gingerich, " 'Crisis' versus Aesthetic," 89–90.

41. See also Duhem, *Sozein ta phainomena: Essai sur la notion de théorié physique de platon à galilée* (Paris: Hermann, 1908).

42. Edward Rosen, *Three Copernican Treatises* (New York: Octagon, 1971), 56; Edward Grant, "Late Medieval Thought, Copernicus and the Scientific Revolution," *Journal of the History of Ideas* 23 (1962): 212–13; Grant, "Hypotheses in Late Medieval and Early Modern Science," *Daedalus* 91 (1962): 601–2, 608–9; Dudley Shapere, "Copernicanism as a Scientific Revolution," in Beer and Strand, eds., *Copernicus Yesterday and Today*, 103–4.

43. *De Revolutionibus*, book 1, chap. 10.

44. See the discussion by Rosen in Gingerich, ed., *Nature of Scientific Discovery*, 388–89.

45. Benjamin Nelson, "The Early Modern Revolution in Science and Philosophy: Fictionalism, Probabilism, Fideism, and Catholic 'Prophetism,' " in Robert S. Cohen and Marx W. Wartofsky, eds., *Boston Studies in the Philosophy of Science*, vol. 3 (Dordrecht: Reidel, 1967), 1–40. See also Henry G. Van Leeuwen, *The Problem of Certainty in English Thought: 1630–1690* (The Hague: Martinus Nijhoff, 1963).

46. Nelson, "Early Modern Revolution," 4.

47. For details, see Gordon Leff, *Paris and Oxford Universities in the Thirteenth and Fourteenth Centuries* (New York: John Wiley and Sons, 1968), 222–40.

48. Duhem, *Système du monde*, 8:7–8. Edward Grant, "The Con-

demnation of 1277, God's Absolute Power, and Physical Thought in the Late Middle Ages," Essay 13 in his *Studies in Medieval Science and Natural Philosophy* (London: Variorum, 1981), has criticized Duhem's argument. Wallace, *Causality and Scientific Explanation*, 103ff., has provided a useful and philosophically more astute correction in detail.

49. See Leff, *Paris and Oxford*, 240–55; H. M. Carre, *Realists and Nominalists* (Oxford: Oxford University Press, 1946), 101–25.

50. For an account of the thinker who was the chief target of Tempier's condemnation, see Eric Voegelin, "Siger de Brabant," *Philosophy and Phenomenological Research* 4 (1943–44): 507–25.

51. Benjamin Nelson, "The Quest for Certitude and the Books of Scripture, Nature, and Conscience," in Gingerich, ed., *Nature of Scientific Discovery*, 358.

52. Edward W. Strong, *Procedures and Metaphysics: A Study of the Philosophy of Mathematical-Physical Science in the Sixteenth and Seventeenth Centuries* (Hildsheim: Olms, 1966), 8, 13. This is a photoreproduction of the original 1936 edition.

53. Alexandre Koyré, *Metaphysics and Measurement: Essays in Scientific Revolution* (1943; reprint, Cambridge, Mass.: Harvard University Press, 1968), esp. chaps. 1–2. See also Jacob Klein, "The World of Physics and the 'Natural' World," in Klein, *Lectures and Essays*, 1–34.

54. For a discussion of the question of Galileo's "Platonism" see Ernst Cassirer, "Mathematical Mysticism and Mathematical Science," E. W. Strong, "The Relationship between Metaphysics and Scientific Method in Galileo," and Thomas P. McTighe, "Galileo's 'Platonism': A Reconsideration," all of which are in McMullin, ed., *Galileo*, and all of which have extensive bibliographies.

55. Koyré, *Metaphysics and Measurement*, 38.

56. Jean Bodin, *Apologie de René Herpin pour la République de J. Bodin* (Paris: Samaritaine, 1581), 30v. This edition is bound with the *Six livres de la République* (Paris: Samaritaine, 1583). The actual copy used was a facsimile, published by Scientia Aalen, 1961.

57. The best short study of Bodin that focuses on his mystical contemplation of the hand of God in nature is Paul Lawrence Rose, *Bodin and the Great God of Nature: The Moral and Religious Universe of a Judaiser* (Geneva: Droz, 1980).

58. The Beatles, *Magical Mystery Tour*, Capital Records, 1969.

59. Eric Voegelin, *The New Science of Politics* (Chicago: University of Chicago Press, 1952), 122. Voegelin's understanding of the cognition of faith is taken from St. Thomas Aquinas *Summa theologica*, 2–2, q. 4, art. 1.

60. The story has recently been retold with great erudition by Co-

hen, *Revolution in Science*, parts 2 and 3.

61. The remark about free divine creation is from the preface to *De-Stella Nova* (1573) and Tycho's prognostications are found in the closing chapter on "the judicial astrology of the effects of the birth of this new moon." The edition consulted was a facsimile reprint by Culture et Civilisation, Brussels, 1969.

62. Parallax is the calculated angular amount of apparent displacement of a celestial object caused by changes in the point of terrestrial observation. Tycho traveled extensively to collect observational data and established that the parallax of the new heavenly body was less than that of the moon.

63. Thomas S. Kuhn, *The Structure of Scientific Revolutions*, 2d ed. (Chicago: University of Chicago Press, 1970).

64. For details see Frances A. Yates, *Giordano Bruno and the Hermetic Tradition* (London: Routledge and Kegan Paul, 1964), 440–47.

65. See Arthus Koestler, *The Sleepwalkers* (New York: Grosset and Dunlap, 1959), part 4.

66. Debus, *Man and Nature in the Renaissance*, 123.

67. Yates, *Giordano Bruno*, 403–7; see also Yates, *Theatre of the World* (Chicago: University of Chicago Press, 1969), chaps. 3 and 4; Yates, *The Rosicrucian Enlightenment* (London: Paladin, 1972), chap. 6.

68. The doctrine of Marxist ascesis did not appear until the publication of Lenin's *What Is to Be Done?* in 1902. The author's identification of himself with Rakhmetov in Chernyshevsky's novel of the same title indicates the need for a disciplined "party of steel" and how to forge it: raw beefsteak, black bread, prodigious reading, and no sex.

69. Aeschylus *Prometheus Bound* 28.

70. Ibid. 977–78.

71. Hans Jonas, *The Gnostic Religion*, 2d ed. (Boston: Beacon, 1963), 96.

72. Quoted in Ernst Cassirer, *Das Erkenntnisproblem der neueren Zeit*, 3d ed., vol. 1 (Berlin: Bruno Cassirer, 1922), 350ff.

73. The actions of men expressed a rehabilitated *curiositas*. No longer, as in antiquity and the Middle Ages, was it associated with idle care for superfluities but with the production of knowledge. Hans Blumenberg's treatment of the question in part 3 of *The Legitimacy of the Modern Age*, trans. Robert M. Wallace (Cambridge: MIT Press, 1983) is full of interesting detail but ignores the theoretical issue under discussion here. Nor is there consideration of it in his *Die Genesis der kopernikanischen Welt* (Frankfurt: Suhrkamp, 1975), which also contains a wealth of useful evidence.

74. See Carl Jung, *Collected Works*, vol. 12, trans. R. F. C. Hull,

*Psychology and Alchemy* (Princeton, N.J.: Bollingen, 1953), for details.

75. See D. P. Walker, *Spiritual and Demonic Magic from Ficino to Campanella* (London: Macmillan, 1958); Wayne Shumaker, *The Occult Sciences in the Renaissance* (Berkeley: University of California Press, 1972); Robert S. Westman, J. E. McGuire, *Hermeticism and the Scientific Revolution* (Los Angeles: Clark Memorial Library, 1977); Betty Jo Dobbs, *The Foundation of Newton's Alchemy* (Cambridge: Cambridge University Press, 1975).

76. Mircea Eliade, *The Forge and the Crucible: The Origins and Structures of Alchemy,* trans. Stephen Corrin (New York: Harper Torchbooks, 1971). See also Barry Cooper, "What Is Post-Modernity?" *Canadian Journal of Social and Political Thought* 9 (1985): 77–89.

77. For details, see D. W. Singer, *Giordano Bruno: His Life and Thought* (New York: Schuman, 1950); Arthur D. Imerti, introduction to Giordano Bruno's *The Expulsion of the Trimphant Beast* (New Brunswick, N.J.: Rutgers University Press, 1964); Hélène Vedrine, *La conception de la nature chez Giordano Bruno* (Paris: Vrin, 1967); A. M. Paterson, *The Infinite Worlds of Giordano Bruno* (Springfield, Ill.: Thomas, 1970); P. H. Michel, *The Cosmology of Giordano Bruno,* trans. R. E. W. Maddison (London: Methuen, 1973).

78. Giordano Bruno, *Cause, Principle and Unity,* trans. Jack Lindsay (Hedingham: Background Books, 1962), 145. The translation is slightly altered from *Le opere italiane di Giordano Bruno ristampate,* vol. 1, ed. P. de Lagarde (Goettingen: Horstman, 1888), 285.

79. Bruno, *Cause, Principle and Unity,* 138; *Opere,* 1:280.

80. Vedrine, *La conception de la nature chez Bruno,* 220. In *The Ash Wednesday Supper,* trans. and ed. Edward A. Gosselin and Lawrence S. Lerner, (Hamden, Conn.: Archon Books, 1977), 85, he compared Copernicus to a country bumpkin who reports news of a battle to a captain who was absent. It is not the reporter who understands "the proceedings, the reasons and the art by which the victory has been gained, but he who has experience and better judgment of the military art."

81. On the appropriateness of this epithet, see Cohen, *Revolution in Science,* 237–44.

82. Stillman Drake, "Copernicanism in Bruno, Kepler, and Galileo," in Beer and Strand, eds., *Copernicus Yesterday and Today,* 179.

83. Phenomenal evidence that might move complacent moderns in the direction of Bruno's meditation is presented in Alan Dressler, "The Large-Scale Streaming of Galaxies," *Scientific American* 257, no. 3 (September 1987): 46–54. The ikon presented on 54 is particularly powerful.

84. See Yates, *Giordano Bruno,* 176–78, 181–85.

85. For details see Paolo Rossi, *Philosophy, Technology and the Arts*

in the Early Modern Era, trans. Salvator Attanasio, ed. Benjamin Nelson (New York: Harper Torchbooks, 1970).

86. Blumenberg, *The Legitimacy of the Modern Age*, 382.

87. Klein, "The Copernican Revolution," in *Lectures and Essays*, 110–12.

88. Eric Voegelin, "The Eclipse of Reality," in M. Natanson, ed., *Phenomenology and Social Reality: Essays in Memory of Alfred Schutz* (The Hague: Nijhoff, 1970), 185–94.

**Part II**
**Introduction**

1. The following abbreviations are used in the text for Hannah Arendt's works: *HC: The Human Condition* (Chicago: University of Chicago Press, 1958); *OT: The Origins of Totalitarianism*, 3d. ed. (New York: Harcourt, Brace and World, 1966); *OT~1* refers to the first edition, 1951; *PF: Between Past and Future*, rev. ed. (New York: Harcourt Brace and World, 1968); *OV: On Violence* (New York: Harcourt, Brace and World, 1970); *CR: Crises of the Republic* (New York: Harcourt, Brace Jovanovich, 1972); *LM 1, LM 2: The Life of the Mind*, 2 vols. (New York: Harcourt Brace Jovanovich, 1978); *MDT: Men in Dark Times* (New York: Harcourt, Brace and World, 1968); *OR: On Revolution* (New York: Viking Press, 1963).

2. The best full-length study of Arendt is Leah Bradshaw, *Acting and Thinking: The Political Thought of Hannah Arendt* (Toronto: University of Toronto Press, 1989).

3. Karl Jaspers, *Man in the Modern Age*, trans. Eden Paul and Cedar Paul (Garden City, N.Y.: Anchor, 1951), 42.

4. Robert Burros, "Totalitarianism: The Revised Standard Version," *World Politics* 21 (1969): 277.

5. For details, see the splendid analysis by Donald R. Howard, *The Three Temptations: Medieval Man in Search of the World* (Princeton, N.J.: Princeton University Press, 1966), chap. 2.

6. *The City of God* 11.10; see also 14.11, where Augustine argued that, no matter how evil, no creature ever overcomes the goodness that comes from being a creature of God, and 22.24, where God's benevolence is described as being evident in human skill.

7. See Colossians 3:3; Romans 6:2, 8, and Galatians 2:19.

8. See Eric Voegelin, "Machiavelli's Prince: Background and Formation," *Review of Politics* 13 (1951): 142–68.

9. Howard, *Three Temptations*, 291.

10. Hannah Arendt, "Understanding and Politics," *Partisan Review* 20 (1953): 386.

11. See Eric Voegelin, *Order and History,* vol. 4, *The Ecumenic Age* (Baton Rouge: Louisiana State University Press, 1974), 59–113; Barry Cooper, *The Political Theory of Eric Voegelin* (Lewiston, N.Y.: Edwin Mellen, 1986), 125–60.

12. Hannah Arendt, "Discussion," in Carl J. Friedrich, ed., *Totalitarianism* (Cambridge, Mass.: Harvard University Press, 1954), 76.

13. Quoted in Robert Jay Lifton, *Death in Life: Survivors of Hiroshima* (New York: Random House, 1967), 79; see also Guenther Anders, "Commandments in the Atomic Age," in Carl Mitcham and Robert Mackey, eds., *Philosophy and Technology* (New York: Free Press, 1972), 130–35.

14. C. F. von Weizsaecker, *The World View of Physics,* trans. M. Greene (Chicago: University of Chicago Press, 1952), 199.

15. Hans-Georg Gadamer, *Reason in the Age of Science,* trans. Frederick G. Lawrence (Cambridge, Mass.: MIT Press, 1983), 3, 12.

16. Donald R. Howard, "Renaissance World-Alienation," in Robert S. Kinsman, ed., *The Darker Vision of the Renaissance: Beyond the Fields of Reason* (Berkeley: University of California Press, 1974), 75.

## 4. The Modern Human Condition

1. *Nicomachean Ethics* 1172b36.

2. See Heraclitus B86 Diels-Kranz; Gerhart B. Ladner, "Homo Viator: Medieval Ideas on Alienation and Order," *Speculum* 42 (1967): 233–59.

3. See Hannah Arendt, *Der Liebsbegriff bei Augustin* (Berlin: Springer, 1929). A synopsis is available in Elizabeth Young-Bruehl, *Hannah Arendt: For Love of the World* (New Haven: Yale University Press, 1982), 490–500. See also *HC*, 51–52, 76–77, 241–43; *OR*, 74–83.

4. Albert Borgmann, *Technology and the Character of Contemporary Life: A Philosophical Inquiry* (Chicago: University of Chicago Press, 1984), 223.

5. In addition to Arendt's *The Human Condition,* see also Wolfgang Mager, *Zur Entstehung des modernen Staatsbegriffs* (Weisbaden: Steiner, 1968).

6. Tocqueville, *Democracy in America,* book 2, chaps. 2, 14.

7. Arnold Gehlen, *Man in the Age of Technology,* trans. P. Lipscomb (New York: Columbia University Press, 1980), 97–98.

8. Canadians sometimes argue that Québec is a nation in the European sense. The argument has been politically useful in the bargaining process that constitutes Canadian political life, but the fraudulence of the claim has been public knowledge since the days of Lord Durham's *Report* (1839).

9. See also Jacques Ellul, *The Political Illusion*, trans. Konrad Kellen (New York: Knopf, 1967), 141; Jacques Ellul, *The Betrayal of the West*, trans. Matthew J. O'Connell (New York: Seabury, 1978), 192; Walter Ong, *The Presence of the Word* (New Haven, Conn.: Yale University Press, 1967), 205.

10. Hans-Georg Gadamer, *Reason in the Age of Science*, trans. Frederick J. Lawrence (Cambridge, Mass.: MIT Press, 1983), 73.

11. See Edgar Zilsel, "The Genesis of the Concept of Physical Law," *Philosophical Review* 51 (1942): 245–47.

12. Robert Eden, *Political Leadership and Nihilism: A Study of Weber and Nietzsche*, (Gainesville: University Presses of Florida, 1983), 229.

13. David Luban, "Explaining Dark Times: Hannah Arendt's Theory of Theory," *Social Research* 50 (1983): 229.

14. The fons et origo of the science of economic phenomena was, of course, Adam Smith. A recent and popular restatement of *The Wealth of Nations* (1776) is George Gilder, *Wealth and Poverty* (New York: Basic Books, 1980).

## 5. Modes of Active Life

1. The point, one need hardly add, is an anthropological not a theological one. Arendt, like Augustine, did not presume to pry into divine motivation but to describe the results of God's handiwork. One might as easily ask oneself (and not God), How can there be novelty?

2. Hannah Arendt, "Authority in the Twentieth Century," *Review of Politics* 18, no. 4 (October 1950): 417.

3. Arendt, "Understanding and Politics," *Partisan Review* 20 (1953): 389.

4. Such process language is to be distinguished from speculation on the process of reality insofar as the latter aims at the symbolization of a comprehensive experience, whereas the intramundane process language used by technological adepts is explicitly phenomenalist. The distinction is discussed at length in David J. Levy, *Political Order: Philosophical Anthropology, Modernity and the Language of Ideology* (Baton Rouge: Louisana State University Press, 1987).

5. Ronald Weber, "The View from Space," *Georgia Review* 33 (1979): 281. Tom Wolfe's account of "Spam in a can" is closer to the vernacular of the astronauts before they learned that public relations was part of going to the moon. See *The Right Stuff* (New York: Bantam, 1980).

6. Arendt, "History and Immortality," *Partisan Review* 24 (1957): 32.

### 6. The New Regime

1. Wayne Allen, "A Novel Form of Government: Hannah Arendt on Totalitarianism," *Political Science Reviewer* 16 (1986): 239.

2. Arendt, "A Reply," *Review of Politics* 15 (1953): 77.

3. The title *Origins of Totalitarianism* was not Arendt's first choice. She preferred the title under which the book appeared in its British edition, *The Burdern of Our Times. Origins* is not, one may add, a discussion of the internal operations of totalitarian regimes, though, of course, it relies on information about those operations.

4. "A Reply," 78.

5. See above, chap. 2, for discussion of questions posed in *The Technological Society,* xxxiii.

6. Arendt, "Social Sciences and the Concentration Camps," *Jewish Social Studies* 12 (1950): 64.

7. See, for example, the discussion in Carl J. Friedrich, ed., *Totalitarianism* (Cambridge, Mass.: Harvard University Press, 1954).

8. Arendt's account of the nation-state can be usefully contrasted to that of Michael Oakeshott, the only contemporary thinker who has written on the topic with comparable insight. See Oakeshott, *On Human Conduct* (Oxford: Oxford University Press, 1975).

9. Alexis de Tocqueville, *L'Ancient Régime et la Révolution,* book 2, chap. 1.

10. Arendt, "Ideology and Terror: A Novel Form of Government," *Review of Politics* 15 (1953): 323.

11. Arendt, "Imperialism, Nationalism, Chauvinism," *Review of Politics* 7 (1945): 444.

12. See James Bryce, *Studies in History and Jurisprudence,* vol. 1 (Oxford: Clarendon, 1901), 1–84.

13. See Richard Jenkyns, *The Victorians and Ancient Greece* (Oxford: Blackwell, 1980), chap. 13 and references.

14. Arendt, "Ideology and Terror," 303.

15. Arendt, "Discussion," in Carl J. Friederich, ed., *Totalitarianism* (Cambridge, Mass.: Harvard University Press, 1954), 133–34.

16. Arendt, "Social Sciences and the Concentration Camps," 55. In this regard, the differences between the Nazi extermination factories and the more primitive Soviet "labor" camps are nonexistent.

17. Arendt, "The Image of Hell," *Commentary* 2 (1946): 292–93.

### Conclusion

1. See Leah Bradshaw, *Acting and Thinking: The Political Thought of Hannah Arendt* (Toronto: University of Toronto Press, 1989), 72.

2. Eric Voegelin, "The Origins of Totalitarianism," *Review of Politics* 15 (1953): 73.

## Part III
## 7. Scientism

1. Edmund Husserl, *The Crisis of European Sciences and Transcendental Phenomenology,* trans. David Carr (Evanston, Ill.: Northwestern University Press, 1970), 6.

2. Blaise Pascal, *Pensées,* no. 228–29.

3. Thomas Hobbes, *Leviathan,* ed. M. Oakeshott (Oxford: Blackwell, n.d.), 63.

4. The edition consulted was *Mathematical Principles of Natural Philosophy,* trans. Robert Thorp, with an introduction by I. Bernard Cohen (London: Dawsons, 1969), along with I. Bernard Cohen, *Introduction to Newton's "Principia"* (Cambridge: Cambridge University Press, 1971).

5. J. Fiolle, *Science et scientisme* (Paris: Vrin, 1936); F. A. von Hayek, *The Counter-Revolution of Science* (Glencoe, Ill.: Free Press, 1955), an expanded version of a series of articles in *Economica* vols. 8–11 (1941–44); Eric Voegelin, "The Origins of Scientism," *Social Research* 15 (1948): 462–94.

6. A. N. Whitehead, *Science in the Modern World* (1925; reprint, New York: Mentor, 1948), 52–58. See also M. B. Foster, "Christian Theology and the Modern Science of Nature," *Mind* 45 (1936): 1–27.

7. Whitehead, *Science in the Modern World,* 53. The discussion is confined to space; it applies equally to time and thus to space-time.

8. Ibid., 56.

9. Hans-Georg Gadamer made essentially the same point: "And so philosophy entered into the bog of historicism, or got stranded in the shallows of epistemology, or goes back and forth in the backwaters of logic." *Reason in the Age of Science,* trans. Frederick G. Lawrence (Cambridge, Mass.: MIT Press, 1981), 6.

10. Eric Voegelin, *The New Science of Politics* (Chicago: University of Chicago Press, 1952), 5.

11. For details see Alexandre Koyré and I. Bernard Cohen, "The Case of the Missing Tanquam: Leibniz, Newton and Clarke," *Isis* 52 (1961): 555–66. Moreover, God put in an appearance in the first edition of the *Principia* (1687) at p. 415 that was removed from subsequent editions. There Descartes remarked, "God placed the Planets at different distances from the Sun, so that they would receive heat from the Sun according to the proportion of their densities." It was used as an author-

itative truth in Richard Bentley's *A Confutation of Atheism from the Origin and Frame of the World* (1693). For details, see Bernard Cohen, *Introduction to Newton's "Principia,"* 154–55, 216–18; Cohen, "Galileo, Newton and the Divine Order of the Solar System," in E. McMullin, ed., *Galileo, Man of Science* (New York: Basic Books, 1967), 207–31; Cohen, "Isaac Newton's *Principia*, the Scriptures and Divine Providence," in S. Morganbesser, P. Suppes, and Morton White, eds., *Essays in Honor of Ernest Nagel: Philosophy, Science and Method* (New York: St. Martin's, 1969), 523–48.

12. Thorp's annotation of his translation adverts to the controversy but only to proclaim Newton's essential soundness. (Thorp, trans. *Mathematical Principles*, 20–21).

13. Ernest Mach, *The Science of Mechanics: A Critical and Historical Account of Its Development*, trans. Thomas J. McCormack, introduction by Karl Menger, 6th ed. (LaSalle, Ill.: Open Court, 1960), 336–41.

14. Arendt, incidentally, discovered the same thing in a parable of Kafka: "He found the Archimedean point, but he used it against himself; it seems that he was permitted to find it only under his condition." *HC*, chap. 6.

15. Quoted in Marjorie Hope Nicolson, *Newton Demands the Muse: Newton's Opticks and the Eighteenth Century Poets* (Princeton, N.J.: Princeton University Press, 1946), 136.

16. Isaiah Berlin, *Personal Impressions* (Oxford: Oxford University Press, 1982), 144.

17. For details see Hayek, *Counter-Revolution of Science*.

18. The text used is in the *Oeuvres complètes de Voltaire*, nouvelle édition, vol. 22 (Paris: Garnier, 1879), 393ff. A more general historical summary is Margaret C. Jacob, *The Cultural Meaning of the Scientific Revolution* (Philadelphia: Temple University Press, 1988), chap. 4.

19. Voltaire's activism is found in his famous aphorisms directed at the church (*Ecrasez l'infâme*) or his recipe for liberating mankind by strangling the last king with the *tripes* of the last priest; his esotericism is found, for example, in the closing paragraphs of his *Lettres philosophiques*, 13, "Sur Mr Loke." The text used is the edition by Gustave Lanson (Paris: Didier, 1964), 1:175–76.

20. Book 3, chaps. 151–53. The text used was translated by Vernon J. Bourke (Notre Dame, Ind.: University of Notre Dame Press, 1975), 233–39.

21. Eric Voegelin, *From Enlightenment to Revolution*, ed. John H. Hallowell, (Durham, N.C.: Duke University Press, 1975), 25; see also his "Immortality: Experience and Symbol," *Harvard Theological Review* 60 (1967): 235–79.

22. Voltaire, "Elements," 403 (see n. 19 above).

23. Fortunately Pluto remained undiscovered until 1930. See Cohen, *Introduction to Newton's "Principia,"* 154–55, 192 n. 5.

24. See I. Bernard Cohen, *Revolution in Science* (Cambridge, Mass.: Belknap Press of Harvard University Press, 1985), 13; Frank Manuel, *A Portrait of Isaac Newton* (Cambridge, Mass.: Belknap Press of Harvard University Press, 1968); J. L. Heilbron, *Physics at the Royal Society during Newton's Presidency* (Los Angeles: Clark Library, University of California, 1983).

25. Voegelin, "Origins of Scientism," 489–94.

26. See Stephen Jay Gould, *Ontogeny and Phylogeny* (Cambridge, Mass.: Belknap Press of Harvard University Press, 1977), chaps. 2–3, for details.

### 8. Utopianism

1. Eric Voegelin, "More's Utopia," *Österreichische Zeitschrift für öffentliches Recht* n.s. 3 (1951): 458.

2. Ibid., 463.

3. Hans Jonas, *The Imperative of Responsibility: In Search of an Ethics for the Technological Age* (Chicago: University of Chicago Press, 1984), 90–93. Hans Lenk, "Notes on Extended Responsibility and Increased Technological Power," in Paul T. Durbin and Friedrich Rapp, eds., *Philosophy and Technology,* (Dordrecht: Reidel, 1983), 195–210, provides a Kantian critical analysis of Jonas's arguments.

4. Jonas, *Imperative*, 107.

5. Ibid., 142.

6. Wolfgang Harich, *Kommunismus und Wachstum* (Reinbeck: Rowolt, 1975).

7. Jacques Ellul, *The Technological Society,* trans. J. Wilkinson (New York: Vintage, 1964), 433–34.

8. Jonas, *Imperative*, 178.

9. Karl Marx and Friedrich Engels, "The German Ideology," in Robert C. Tucker, ed., *The Marx-Engels Reader,* 2d ed. (New York: Norton, 1978), 155. I have made some minor alterations in the translation Tucker used.

10. Ibid., 193.

11. Eric Voegelin, *From Enlightenment to Revolution,* ed. J. H. Hallowell (Durham, N.C.: Duke University Press, 1975), 242.

12. Hans-Georg Gadamer, *Reason in the Age of Science,* trans. Frederick G. Lawrence (Cambridge, Mass.: MIT Press, 1981), 148.

13. Mircea Eliade, *The Forge and the Crucible,* trans. Stephen Corrin (New York: Harper and Row, 1962), 47, 169.

14. Pierre Louis Moreau de Maupertuis, "Lettre sur le progrès des sciences" (1752), in *Oeuvres* (1768) (Hildsheim: Olms, 1965), 2:420.

15. *Leviathan,* chap. 16.

16. Oliver O'Donovan, *Begotten or Made?* (Oxford: Clarendon, 1984), chap. 4.

17. For details, see Jaroslav Pelikan, *The Christian Tradition: A History of the Development of Doctrine,* vol. 1, *The Emergence of the Catholic Tradition (100–600)* (Chicago: University of Chicago Press, 1971), 256ff.

18. Luke's attention to the birth of John the Baptist, 1:57ff., emphasized that all humans constitute a new beginning.

19. See George Grant, *Technology and Justice* (Toronto: Anansi, 1986), 103ff.

20. O'Donovan, *Begotten or Made?,* 59.

21. Hans Jonas, *Philosophical Essays: From Ancient Creed to Technological Man* (Englewood Cliffs, N.J.: Prentice-Hall, 1974), 152.

## 9. Vulgarity

1. See Jerry Weinberger, *Science, Faith and Politics: Francis Bacon and the Utopian Roots of the Modern Age* (Ithaca, N.Y.: Cornell University Press, 1985), esp. 17–41, 322–32. Weinberger's understanding of "utopia" differs somewhat from the one discussed in chapter 8.

2. *Odes* 3.1.1–4; *Iliad* 2.211–23; Shakespeare, *Troilus and Cressida,* act 1, sc. 3, line 73.

3. See Barry Cooper, "Culture and Anarchy: The Politics of Matthew Arnold," in John H. Hallowell, ed., *Prospects for Constitutional Democracy: Essays in Honor of R. Taylor Cole* (Durham, N.C.: Duke University Press, 1976), 21–35.

4. See Barry Cooper, "How to Watch TV News," *The Idler* (Toronto) 28 (May 1990): 17–22.

5. Quoted in Kevin Daly, " 'Your Marvellous Invention': The Early History of Recording," in Peter Gammond and Raymond Horrocks, eds., *The Music Goes Round and Round* (London: Quartet, 1980), 10.

6. Quotations are taken, without further reference from his *Works* (London: Chapman and Hall, 1904), 5:471–92.

7. Langdon Winner, *Autonomous Technology: Technics-out-of-Control as a Theme in Political Thought* (Cambridge, Mass.: MIT Press, 1977), 262.

8. Ibid., 227.

9. Norbert Wiener, *The Human Use of Human Beings: Cybernetics*

and Society (New York: Doubleday, 1956), 46. 10. William Leiss, *The Domination of Nature* (Boston: Beacon, 1972); Leiss, *The Limits to Satisfaction*, rev. ed. (Toronto: University of Toronto Press, 1979); see also Leiss, Stephen Kline, and Sut Jhally, *Social Communication in Advertising* (Toronto: Methuen, 1986).

11. P. L. Kapitza, "Recollections of Lord Rutherford," in his *Experiment, Theory, Practice: Articles and Addresses* (Dordrecht: Reidel, 1980), 270.

12. Besides, they have been set out at great length in Barry Cooper, *The End of History: An Essay in Modern Hegelianism* (Toronto: University of Toronto Press, 1984).

13. All these terms, and others that may appear even more unusual, have been explicated at length in Cooper, *End of History*. What is presented here is a kind of summary of certain arguments of Hegel and their misuse, nothing more.

14. Saul Friedlaender, "Themes of Decline and End in Nineteenth-Century Western Imagination," in Friedlaender, Gerald Holton, Leo Marx, and Eugene Skolnikoff, eds., *Visions of Apocalypse: End or Rebirth?* (New York: Holmes and Meier, 1985), 76.

15. Edgar Allen Poe, "MS. Found in a Bottle" in *The Complete Tales and Poems* (New York: Modern Library, 1938), 125.

16. Reprinted in *Oeuvres* (Paris: Gallimard, 1970), 1:971–87.

17. A generation earlier Gladstone observed, "Bismarck has made Germany great and the Germans small." A generation later Karl Jaspers made essentially the same point. *Man in the Modern Age*, trans. Eden Paul and Cedar Paul (1931; reprint, Garden City, N.Y.: Doubleday, 1951), 226.

18. See Q. D. Leavis, *Fiction and the Reading Public* (1932; reprint, Harmondsworth: Penguin, 1979).

19. C. P. Snow, *The Two Cultures and the Scientific Revolution* (Cambridge: Cambridge University Press, 1959).

20. F. R. Leavis, *Two Cultures? The Significance of C. P. Snow* (New York: Random House, 1963).

21. J. Edward Chamberlin, "Images of Degeneration: Turnings and Transformations," in Chamberlin and Sander L. Gilman, eds., *Degeneration: The Dark Side of Progress* (New York: Columbia University Press, 1985), 264.

22. Allan Bloom, *The Closing of the American Mind* (New York: Simon and Schuster, 1987).

23. *Merchant of Venice*, act 5, sc. 1, lines 58–65, 79–88. The phrase "Platonic speech" is from Allan Bloom, "On Christian and Jew, *TheMerchant of Venice*," in Bloom, with Harry Jaffa, *Shakespeare's Politics*

(New York: Basic Books, 1964), 30; see also Bloom's "Interpretive Essay" added to his translation of *Republic* (New York: Basic Books, 1968), 358.

24. Bloom, *Closing of the American Mind*, 68–81.

25. Again Jaspers had made the same point a generation ago in *Man in the Modern Age*, 48, 59, 112. See also Walter J. Ong, *The Barbarian Within* (New York: Macmillan, 1962), 263, 283; and Sherry Turkle, *The Second Self: Computers and the Human Spirit* (New York: Simon and Schuster, 1984), chaps. 2, 8, 9; Harvey Brooks, "Technology-Related Catastrophes: Myth and Reality," in Friedlaender, et al., eds. *Visions of Apocalypse*, 132–33.

26. Walter J. Ong, *Rhetoric, Romance and Technology: Studies in the Interaction of Expression and Culture* (Ithaca, N.Y.: Cornell University Press, 1971), 264.

27. Ibid., 277–78.

28. Ibid., 294.

29. *Lyrical Ballads*, ed. R. L. Brett and A. R. Jones (London: Methuen, 1963), 251, 253–54.

30. T. C. Keefer, *The Philosophy of Railroads* [1850], ed. H. V. Nelles (Toronto: University of Toronto Press, 1972), 10–11.

31. Michael Rostovtzeff, *The Social and Economic History of the Roman Empire*, 2d ed. (Oxford: Clarendon, 1957), 1:541.

32. George Steiner, *In Bluebeard's Castle: Some Notes towards the Re-definition of Culture* (London: Faber and Faber, 1971), 85–86.

33. The following more detailed remarks rely chiefly on Robert Pattison's *The Triumph of Vulgarity: Rock Music in the Mirror of Romanticism* (New York: Oxford University Press, 1987). This book, published the same year as Bloom's, analyzes what Bloom describes with aphoristic pungency. At times they use nearly the same words.

34. Ibid., vii.

35. See Nancy L. Rosenblum, *Another Liberalism: Romanticism and the Reconstruction of Liberal Thought* (Cambridge, Mass.: Harvard University Press, 1987).

### Conclusion: Paying for It

1. Leo Strauss, *The City and Man* (Chicago: Rand McNally, 1964), 1–12.

2. Barry Cooper, *The End of History* (Toronto: University of Toronto Press, 1984).

3. Maurice Merleau-Ponty, *Signes* (Paris: Gallimard, 1967), 366–84; see also Barry Cooper, *Merleau-Ponty and Marxism* (Toronto: University of Toronto Press, 1979), 147–50.

4. Strauss, *City and Man*, 5.

5. Stanley Rosen, *Nihilism: A Philosophical Essay* (New Haven: Yale University Press, 1969).

6. Rosen, "Nihilism," in J. M. Edie, ed., *New Essays in Phenomenology: Studies in the Philosophy of Experience* (Chicago: Quadrangle Books, 1969), 158.

7. Eric Voegelin, *Die politischen Religionen* (Stockholm: Bermann-Fisher, 1939), 55.

8. Immanuel Kant, "Idea for a Universal History with Cosmopolitan Intent," in Carl Friedrich, ed., *The Philosophical of Kant* (New York: Modern Library, 1949).

9. Maurice Blanchot, "The Limits of Experience: Nihilism," in David B. Allison, ed., *The New Nietzsche* (New York: Delta, 1977), 122.

10. *Zarathustra*, part 4, sec. 13:3.

11. George Grant, *Time as History* (Toronto: CBC, 1969), 33.

12. Strauss, *On Tyranny* (Ithaca, N.Y.: Cornell University Press, 1963), 223; Rosen, *Hermeneutics as Politics* (New York: Oxford University Press, 1987), 139.

13. Laurence Lampert, *Nietzsche's Teaching: An Interpretation of "Thus Spoke Zarathustra"* (New Haven: Yale University Press, 1986), 25. Consider also Bloom's portrait of the last man in a Walkman in *The Closing of the American Mind* (New York: Simon and Schuster, 1987), 74–75, discussed in the previous chapter.

14. *Zarathustra*, part 1, sec. 15.

15. Michel Foucault's announcement of this implication caused a great scandal among the intellectual herd. See *The Order of Things: An Archeology of the Human Sciences* (London: Tavistock, 1970), 387, concluding sentence. See also Barry Cooper, *Michel Foucault: An Introduction to His Thought* (New York: Mellen, 1981), chap. 6.

16. *Will to Power*, sec. 1054; *Beyond Good and Evil*, sec. 225.

17. Strauss, *What is Political Philosophy? And Other Studies* (Glencoe, Ill.: Free Press, 1959), 55.

18. Erazim Kohak, *The Embers and the Stars: A Philosophical Inquiry into the Moral Sense of Nature* (Chicago: University of Chicago Press, 1984), 82–83.

19. Donald Phillip Verene, "Technique and the Directions of the Human Spirit: Laughter and Desire," in David Lovekin and Verene, eds., *Essays in Humanity and Technology* (Dixon, Ill.: Sauk Valley College, 1978), 89.

20. Ibid., 110.

21. George Grant, *Technology and Empire* (Toronto: Anansi, 1969), 132.

22. Anaximander frag. 9 Diels-Kranz.

# Index